最受关注的

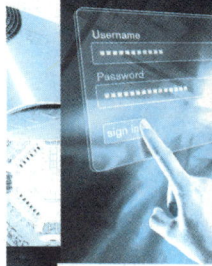

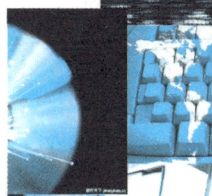

科技创意

SCIENCE AND TECHNOLOGY

英文资讯

主　编：金　利

副主编：谭若辰　杨云云　高楠楠

编　委：肖严艳　贾玉双　黄江露　范芙蓉　蒋志华

　　　　李素素　何　静　李岩岩　陈　娜　肖　琦

　　　　白　敏　马晓龙　李逸民　彭凌燕　史丽月

大连理工大学出版社
DALIAN UNIVERSITY OF TECHNOLOGY PRESS

图书在版编目（CIP）数据

最受关注的科技创意英文资讯：汉英对照 / 金利主编 . — 大连：大连理工大学出版社，2014.8
ISBN 978-7-5611-9333-4

Ⅰ . ①最… Ⅱ . ①金… Ⅲ . ①英语 – 汉语 – 对照读物 ②科学知识 – 普及读物 Ⅳ . ① H319.4：Z

中国版本图书馆 CIP 数据核字 (2014) 第 162186 号

大连理工大学出版社出版
地址：大连市软件园路 80 号　　　　邮政编码：116023
发行：0411-84708842　邮购：0411-84703636　传真：0411-84701466
E-mail:dutp@dutp.cn　　　　URL: http://www.dutp.cn
大连金华光彩色印刷有限公司印刷　　　　大连理工大学出版社发行

幅面尺寸：168mm×235mm	印张：14.75	字数：348 千字
印数：1~5000		
2014 年 8 月第 1 版		2014 年 8 月第 1 次印刷

责任编辑：马嘉聪　　　　　　　　　　　　　责任校对：刘东娜
装帧设计：对岸书影

ISBN 978-7-5611-9333-4　　　　　　　　　　定价：28.80 元

众所周知，想要提高英语阅读能力，增加阅读量是不二法宝。英美人写出的地道文章当然是最佳选择。因此，许多人倾向于选择英美报刊上的文章来提高阅读水平，这些文章的语言虽然地道，但多数英语学习者却遇到了这样的问题：

1. 大多数英语新闻太过枯燥，读不下去；

2. 盲目读了很多文章，可还是抓不住细节和作者意图，阅读水平无法真正得以提升；

3. 虽然进行了大量阅读练习，可由于缺乏技巧，做题的正确率不高。

要想提高阅读水平，选对阅读材料至关重要。如果所选的文章太简单，起不到提高英语水平的作用；如果所选的内容太难，理解起来会很吃力，甚至还有可能打击学习积极性；如果所选的内容很无趣，读起来会感觉味如嚼蜡。那么，什么样的文章才能满足既新鲜有趣，难度又很适中的特点呢？

随着科学技术的发展，科技和创新等方面的话题正在被越来越多的人关注，因此，我们从英美主流报刊上选取了42篇有关科技创意的英文资讯文章。通过阅读这些文章，不但可以提高英语水平，还能开阔眼界。

我们编写这本书的主要意图是帮助读者提高阅读水平。因此，本书根据每篇文章提出问题，再以这些题目为例，为读者提供实用的阅读技巧，以帮助读者明确解题思路。

本书具有以下特点：

最吸引人的科技资讯

我们为读者精选最有吸引力的文章，这些文章不涉及高深而又艰难晦涩的科学技术，而是定位于新鲜有趣的科技创意资讯。从新奇创意，再到科技如何使我们过上更好的生活——这些文章语言地道，难度适中。阅读这些文章，不但能提高阅读水平，还能了解到丰富的科技知识。

实用阅读技巧助力提高

由于缺乏阅读技巧，很多读者虽然做了大量练习，却仍然没有得到预想的效果。因此，我们在每篇文章后面都设有3道选择题，读者可通过这些题目检测自己对文章的掌握情况；除了对问题进行讲解，我们还为读者讲述实用的阅读技巧，以帮助读者进一步提升阅读水平。

总结新事物的英文说法

为了使读者更深入地了解英美文化，我们在"炫·知识"版块为读者提供与文章相关的背景知识。不但总结习语和典故，还会讲解文中出现的时下流行事物的说法，比如我们都很熟悉的"推送"，在英文中就可以用push来表示。

想要提高英语阅读能力确实不是一件简单的事，需要进行大量的练习。我们精心选择了这些难度适中、语言地道、内容丰富的文章，作为大家的学习资料。我们希望本书能使原本枯燥的学习过程变得更轻松、更有趣一些，帮助大家找到阅读的乐趣。

编者
2014年 7月

Contents · 目 录

Chapter 01 热点话题 Hot Point

Chapter 2 尖端科技 Edge Technology

Chapter 3 科技风向 Trends

Chapter 4 通信与互联网 Communication&Internet

3

Chapter 5 环境保护 Environmental Protection

Chapter 6　医学与健康　Medical&Health

Chapter 01
热点话题 Hot Point

Passage 01

Just Press "Print"
——只需按下"打印"键
——Mar. 31st, 2012, Economist

Reading Guide

基因复制技术的出现如今使宠物也可以定制了，无论是皮毛的颜色，还是体型的大小，甚至是宠物的性格，都可以由主人来决定。新兴技术带动了宠物印刷机的诞生，日后我们再也不必为训练宠物而烦恼，更不必为了寻找心目中的那个"它"而发愁了。基因复制技术让个性定制上升到了一个全新的高度。

One of the most interesting technological trends in the past few years has been the rise of additive manufacturing. This technique, which uses three-dimensional printing to make objects ranging from violins to pilotless aircraft, allows the construction of individual objects at the **whim** of the designer. Now, a small Californian company, the Gene Duplication Corporation, based in San Melito, proposes to push the technology to its limits. It will announce plans to use 3D printing to make bespoke pets.

GeneDupe, as the firm is known colloquially, has previously focused on the genetic engineering of animals. However, Paolo Fril, the company's boss, is keen to expand into manufacturing them from scratch. PrintaPet does just that.

The idea of printing organs such as kidneys for transplant has been around for several years. It

在过去几年里，最有趣的技术动向之一就是添加剂制造业的兴起。大到无人驾驶飞机，小到小提琴，都可以采用这种三维立体印刷技术制作出来，这使设计师可以将他们的奇思妙想制作成产品。如今，一家总部设在加利福尼亚圣米立多的专门研究基因复制的小型公司提议最大限度地推广这项技术。他们宣布将使用3D印刷技术来制造定制的宠物。

通俗地说，基因复制公司GeneDupe以前主要致力于研究动物基因工程。然而，公司老板保罗·福瑞尔强烈地希望从头做起，将公司业务扩展到动物制造上。这正是通过宠物打印制造技术（PrintaPet）来实践的。

打印器官的理念出现许多年了，例如用于移植的肾脏器官。这项技术通过

---

whim [hwim] n. 奇想

works by growing separate cultures of individual cell types, and then spraying them out, layer by layer, **in combination with a binding agent** called **hydrogel,** to build up the correct shape.

Printing an organ in this way is fairly easy. A kidney, for instance, has only eight cell types. An entire **mammalian** body, though, has 220 cell types. Laying these down in the correct order is a much more complex problem. To solve it, GeneDupe's researchers used nanotomography, a precise form of CT scanning X that has a resolution of 500 nanometers (billionths of a meter), to analyze the position and nature of every single cell in a variety of animals, particularly breeds of dog. This knowledge not only permits existing breeds to be re-created, but allows entirely new combinations of form, color and behavior to be invented, at the customer's command.

GeneDupe's universal pet printer is loaded with each of the 220 cell types (grown from stem cells in the company's **histology** laboratory), and is programmed with a three-dimensional map of the creature which is to create. That is devised by the firm's scientists, based on what the nanotomographic analysis has told them about the results of arranging cells in different ways in an animal's body.

The cells themselves are stored **in suspension,** in glass **reservoirs,** and each reservoir is connected to a computer-controlled spray gun. The hydrogels (several sorts are needed) are stored separately.

培养互相独立的个体细胞类型，然后将它们一层一层地喷出，与一种叫做水凝胶的粘合剂结合起来，就制成了恰当的形状。

通过这种方式打印一个器官相当简单。比如拿肾脏来说，一个肾脏只有八种细胞类型。而一个哺乳类动物的整体也只有220种细胞类型。因此如何以正确的顺序罗列这些细胞类型才是更复杂的问题。为解决这个问题，基因复制公司的研究人员使用了纳米断层摄影技术来分析各种动物的每一个单独细胞的位置和特性，尤其是不同品种的狗。这种纳米断层摄影技术是一种精密形式的X射线计算机断层扫描，其分辨率高达500纳米（十万分之一米）。这项技术不仅可以重新创造现有的品种，也能全部创造全新的形态、毛色和行为方式的组合。

GeneDupe公司宠物打印机装载着这220种细胞类型中的每一种（在公司的组织学研究室里利用干细胞生成），并且可以把需要创造的生物的三维染色体图谱程序化。公司的科学家基于纳米断层摄影技术分析揭示的不同动物身体里排列细胞的不同方式而设计的。

细胞本身是在玻璃储液器中悬浮储存的，每一个储液器都与由电脑控制的喷枪连接。水凝胶（需要很多种）则是分开存放的。其中一种被称为成骨质水凝胶特别重要，它通过凝结来提供动物最

---

in combination with 与……结合
binding agent 粘合剂
hydrogel ['haidrəudʒəl] n. 水凝胶
mammalian [mæ'meiliən] n. 哺乳类

histology [hi'stɔlədʒi] n. 组织学
in suspension 悬浮中
reservoir ['rezəvwɑ:] n. 蓄水容器

One, known as osteogel, is particularly important, as this solidifies to provide the animal's initial skeleton. Once the new creature is up and running (both literally and metaphorically), the various hydrogels are gradually replaced by natural secretions. In the case of osteogel, that secretion is bone.

The biggest difficulty Dr. Fril has encountered is with nerve cells. Unlike most other types of cells, which are small, the protuberances from a nerve cell, known as axons and dendrites, may stretch from the animal's **spinal cord** to the tips of its toes. To deal with this problem, the pet printer leaves a hole in each layer of cells at every point through which a nerve cell is supposed to pass. The holes are then filled with nerve-growth factor before the next layer is printed, so that when the main body of the nerve cell is sprayed into place it rapidly grows axonal and dendritic protuberances to the right destinations.

Knowing how to print nerve cells, is, in fact, the key to the whole thing. Size apart, a healthy heart, kidney or liver is pretty much the same in a retriever or a Rottweiler. Coat color, an important consideration for many owners, is easily dealt with by picking the right pattern of melanocyte cells in the skin. But an animal's temperament is a very different matter.

Controlling temperament means laying down the right mixture of nerve cells in the brain, since different types of cells have different effects on personality. Having worked out how to do this, GeneDupe is able to offer pets that have had their behavioral characteristics fine-

初的骨架。一旦新的生物站立起来，并向前跑动（既是字面意思也是比喻意思），各种各样的水凝胶就会逐渐被自然的分泌物取代，而取代成骨质的分泌物就是骨骼。

福瑞尔博士遇到的最困难的问题是神经细胞问题。与大部分其他种类的细胞不同，神经细胞很小，而被称为轴突和树突的神经细胞的突起可能会从动物的脊髓延伸到脚趾尖。为了解决这个问题，宠物打印机在每层的细胞中，那些神经细胞可能会通过的点上都留下了一个小孔。在下一层细胞打印出来之前，就在这些孔里填满神经生长因子。所以当神经细胞的主体被喷射就位时，轴突和树突就会在正确的位置上迅速生长。

了解过如何打印神经细胞之后，实际就了解了整个打印过程的关键。无论是制作寻回犬还是罗特维尔犬，除了体型不同之外，制作健康的心脏、肾脏或者肝脏的过程都是一样的。而皮毛的颜色这一许多宠物主人着重考虑的因素，只要通过从皮肤里的黑素细胞中提取合适的样式就很容易解决了。然而，动物的性情就要另当别论了。

由于不同种类的细胞对性格有着不同的影响，所以控制性情意味着在大脑中正确地将神经细胞混合起来。GeneDupe公司已经掌握了如何操作这个过程，因此能够提供行为特征经过精心调整的宠物。不管你是想要一只温顺的罗特维尔犬，或是一只好斗的寻回犬，你都能拥有一只按照

spinal cord 脊髓

tuned. If you want a **docile** Rottweiler, or even an aggressive retriever, you can have one made to your exact specifications. Dr. Fril, though, thinks that the most popular modification will be his tweaking of canine scent-marking behavior so that local lampposts are no longer the preferred sites of relief and communication. Instead, GeneDupe's pooches are pre-wired to recognize the company's proprietary DoggieLoos, which have a distinctive odor that is perceptible to canids, but not humans.

There are still a few technical difficulties to overcome, of course, but Dr. Fril plans to start taking orders soon. And he is already looking forward to the firm's next product, custom-printed boyfriends and girlfriends for those who cannot find the right partner by conventional means—a surprisingly large proportion of the population. If all goes well, it will be available by St. Valentine's Day. If not, customers will probably have to wait until April 1st of next year.

你给出的精确参数制造的宠物。然而，福瑞尔博士认为最受欢迎的改变将是他对犬类留味行为的轻微调整。这样，当地的路灯就不再是狗狗们方便和交流的首选地点了。与此相反，GeneDupe公司的杂种犬被预制为可以识别名为DoggieLoos的狗狗厕所——这种公司的专利产品有着能被犬科动物感知、但无法被人类识别的特殊气味。

当然，现在仍有一些技术方面的难题尚未克服，但是福瑞尔博士计划马上开始接受预订。而且他期待看到公司的下一个产品——为那些无法通过传统方式找到合适伴侣的人们打印的定制男友和女友，而这类人在全部人口中占有惊人的比例。如果一切进展顺利，这项业务会在情人节之前面世。如果不能的话，那么顾客可能就要等到明年愚人节了。

炫 · 知识

1. pilotless aircraft 无人驾驶飞机

无人驾驶飞机简称"无人机"，是利用无线电遥控设备和自备的程序控制装置操纵的飞机。这种飞机通常不载人。

2. push sth. to limits 最大限度地推进……

要表示"最大限度地推进……"的含义，push sth. to limits这一表达十分生动。其中limit是"极限"的意思。此外，push oneself to limits则可以表示"挑战自我"。

3. from scratch 从头做起

单词scratch有"起跑线"的含义，因此from scratch就有了"从头开始"、"白手起家"的含义。

docile ['dəusail] a. 温顺的

4. CT scanning X 射线计算机断层成像

CT是computed tomography的缩写，意思是"计算机断层扫描"。其工作程序是首先根据人体不同组织对X线的吸收与透过率的不同，应用灵敏度极高的仪器进行测量，再将所获数据输入计算机中进行处理，摄下人体被检查部位的断面或立体图像，从而发现体内的细小病变。

5. three-dimensional 三维的

three-dimensional就是我们常说的3D，也就是"三维的"的意思。三个维度包括三个坐标，即长、宽、高。而今天常说的3D主要是基于电脑及互联网技术的立体成像技术。

阅读技能练习场

Exercises:

1 Where is Gene Duplication Corporation based?

A. California.

B. Melito.

C. Mexico.

D. Not mentioned.

2 How many cell types are there in an entire mammalian body?

A. 8.

B. 220.

C. 500.

D. It's uncountable.

3 According to the passage, what will replace the osteogel when the animal is alive?

A. Bone.

B. Hydrogels.

C. Skin.

D. We cannot infer.

Answers: 1.A 2.B 3.A

Reading Skills

1. 根据关键词回到文中定位 ★★★★★

通常问题的答案都在文章里，只要仔细阅读就能找到准确的答案。在遇到这类问题的时候，可以通过关键词回到原文定位，这样很快就能选出答案。

> **Q1解析：** 问题考查这家公司的总部位于何地。根据关键词Gene Duplication Corporation和based，可以在第一自然段找到答案：a small Californian company, the Gene Duplication Corporation, based in San Melito, proposes to push the technology to its limits. 所以答案是：A。
>
> **Q3解析：** 这道题的关键词自然就是osteogel，由于这是一个新词，所以很容易在文章第六段发现它的"踪迹"，仔细阅读这一段之后，不难发现取代这种水溶胶的是动物的骨骼。因此选A。

2. 对数字要敏感 ★★★★★

很多出题者都会针对数字提问，而我们在原文中通常会发现许多数字，这时只有仔细阅读问题，才能找到正确的答案。

> **Q2解析：** 根据：An entire mammalian body, though, has 220 cell types.这句话不难得知，哺乳动物体内共有220种不同的细胞类型。因此正确答案是B。

Passage 02

The World Is Not Enough for Google Bosses
——地球对谷歌老板们来说已不够大
——Apr. 22, 2012, Independen

Reading Guide

谷歌在统治网络世界之后，开始着眼于浩淼的太空，在那里它也会有一番作为吗？地球资源日益枯竭，其他星球上的资源也许能给人类带来帮助。太空之旅会带来我们需要的吗？他们如何进入太空并得到他们想要的呢？

Not content with the domination of cyberspace, Google's billionaire founders have set their sights on outer space—and the mining of natural resources from asteroids.

Having created one of the titans of cyberspace, which helps to run the lives of billions, Larry Page and Eric Schmidt may well regard themselves as masters of planet Earth. Google's mega-rich founders have built a global empire worth over $120bn by channeling unimaginable volumes of information to our cherished laptops, smartphones and tablets.

But it seems that, for Page and Schmidt, the world is no longer enough. The pair are now staking a claim for galactic domination by backing a plan to mine asteroids. Google's chief executive and executive chairman are named as key players in Planetary Resources Inc., which appears set to

谷歌身价上亿的创始者们不满足于仅在网络空间占据主导地位，他们已经把视线投向了外太空——想要开采小行星上的自然资源。

由于创造了网络空间巨头谷歌公司，且谷歌影响着数十亿人的生活，拉里·佩奇和艾瑞克·施密特或许会将自己看作这个星球的主宰者。谷歌的百万富翁创始者们将难以想象的信息传输到我们珍视的笔记本、智能手机和平板电脑上，打造了一个价值超过1200亿美元的全球帝国。

但是似乎对于佩奇和施密特来说，世界已经不够他们施展拳脚。他们两个支持一项开采小行星的计划，声称他们有权对银河进行统治。谷歌的CEO和执行总裁被任命为行星资源股份有限公司的关键人物，该公司似乎将要无所畏惧

---

asteroid ['æstərɔid] n. 小行星
titan ['taitən] n. 巨人

galactic [gə'læktik] a. 银河的

go boldly where no **magnate** has gone before.

The exact nature of the business will be revealed, but it appears Page and Schmidt are aiming high. "The company will overlay two critical sectors——space exploration and natural resources——to add trillions of dollars to the global GDP," Planetary Resources said in a press release. "This innovative start-up will create a new industry and a new definition of 'natural resources'."

Others investing in the new business include Avatar director James Cameron; Ross Perot Jr., son of the former presidential candidate; and billionaire Microsoft alumnus Charles Simonyi, who has already made two trips to the International Space Station. The announcement comes just as scientists are embracing the idea of mining "near-Earth asteroids".

A study by NASA concluded that, for a cost of $1.6bn, robotic spacecraft could capture a 500-ton asteroid seven meters in **diameter** and bring it into orbit around the Moon to be explored and mined. The spacecraft would have a flight time of 6 to 10 years, and humans would be able to carry out the task by around 2025.

President Barack Obama has already talked of sending a manned mission to an asteroid by the same year, while NASA is working on an unmanned mission, called Osiris-Rex, that would launch in 2016 and land on an asteroid, bringing a small **chunk** of it back to Earth by 2023.

地挑战一些新领域，而这些领域是更大的公司都没有涉足过的。

这项业务的真实本质将要公诸于世，但是看上去佩奇和施密特似乎把目标定得很高。"公司这次行动将包含两个关键方面——太空探索和自然资源开采——希望以此给世界GDP带来上万亿美元的增长，"行星资源公司在一场新闻发布会上说道，"这个充满创新的开始将创造一个全新的产业，甚至重新为'自然资源'下定义"。

其他投资这项新产业的还有：电影《阿凡达》的导演詹姆斯·卡梅隆，前总统候选人之子小罗斯·佩罗，以及曾两次前往国际空间站的亿万富翁、前微软成员查尔斯·西蒙尼。而且这一消息的公布恰逢科学家们认同开采"近地小行星"的想法。

美国太空总署的一项研究称，无人航天器可以捕捉一颗重五百吨，直径七米的小行星，并把它带到环月轨道以便探索和开采，这需要花费十六亿美元。航天器的飞行寿命是六到十年，大约到2025年人类或许才能实施这个任务。

在同一年，巴拉克·奥巴马总统也已经谈及向一颗小行星发射载人航天器。与此同时，美国太空总署正致力于研究名为欧西里斯-雷克斯的无人航天器，它将于2016年被发射到一颗小行星上，到2023年的时候，它将把小行星的一小部分带回地球。

magnate ['mægneit] n. 大资本家
diameter [dai'æmitə] n. 直径

chunk [tʃʌŋk] n. 大块

9

The costs would be as eye-watering as a Martian atmosphere, but the potential rewards are vast. Large amounts of water, oxygen and metals could be extracted to help further space exploration by allowing humans to build space stations and fuel spacecraft. The resources could also be brought back to Earth to **bolster** diminishing reserves. And with the likes of the Google bosses on board, the project would appear to have plenty of financial support. Schmidt was awarded a compensation package worth $62m last year for shifting from CEO to executive chairman.

Planetary Resources was co-founded by Eric Anderson, a former NASA Mars-mission manager, and Peter Diamandis, the commercial space entrepreneur behind the X-Prize competition, which offered $6m to a group that launched a reusable manned spacecraft.

The venture will be the latest **foray** into the far-flung for Cameron, who last month dived in a mini-submarine to the deepest spot in the Mariana Trench. It also has echoes of his 2009 science fiction **blockbuster** *Avatar*, which concerned mining on alien planets.

Planetary Resources will be the second billionaire-backed private space company to be announced within the past six months. Microsoft co-founder Paul Allen unveiled his new firm, Stratolaunch Systems, which plans to build the world's largest aircraft and use it as an air-based launch pad to send people into orbit.

但这一切花费是极其昂贵的，仿佛火星大气一样贵重，而潜在的利润却非常可观。在小行星上可以提取大量的淡水、氧气和金属，这些资源可以用于建造太空站和太空燃料储备站，以此为帮助人类进一步探索太空。也可以将这些资源带回地球，用来补充日益减少的资源储备。由于有像谷歌老板们这样的人物参与其中，这个项目似乎就具备了足够的财政支持。去年，由于施密特从公司CEO转职为执行总裁，他获得了价值6200万美元的资金补偿。

行星资源公司由埃里克·安德森和彼得·戴曼迪斯共同创办，他们分别是前美国太空总署的火星任务主管和X-Prize大赛的幕后的太空商业企业家。曾有参赛小组发射了一个可重复使用的载人航天器，因此X-Prize大赛提供了六百万美元的奖金。

这次风投将是卡梅隆对广阔世界最近的一次"袭击"。上个月，他乘一艘小型潜水艇潜入了马里亚纳海沟的最深处。而这次探索正好与他2009年的科幻大片《阿凡达》的情节呼应，这部电影讲述了开采外星球的故事。

行星资源公司将成为过去半年中所公开的第二家背后有亿万富翁支持的私人太空公司。而微软的联合创始人保罗·艾伦也为他的新公司Stratolaunch Systems揭幕，该公司计划建造世界最大的飞行器，并计划将其用作将人送入太空轨道的空基发射台。

---

bolster ['bəulstə] v. 支持
foray ['fɔrei] n. 攻击

blockbuster ['blɔk,bʌstə] n. 大片

炫 · 知识

1. cyberspace 网络空间

网络空间也可以音译为赛博空间，是哲学和计算机领域中的一个抽象概念，它是指计算机网络里的虚拟现实。赛博空间一词是由控制论(cybernetics)和空间(space)两个词合成而来，是由居住在加拿大的科幻小说作家威廉·吉布森在短篇小说《融化的铬合金》(Burning Chrome)中首创，并在后来的小说《神经漫游者》中普及使用的。

2. NASA 美国太空总署

美国太空总署也称国家航空航天局，是美国联邦政府的一个行政机构，负责美国的民用太空计划与航空科学及太空科学的研究。其全称是National Aeronautics and Space Administration。

3. eye-watering 贵得离谱的

eye-watering这个词很有意思，表示"贵得离谱的"。它的字面意思是"眼睛里流出泪水的"，也许是因为太贵才导致这种结果。

4. Avatar《阿凡达》

对于电影《阿凡达》，我们都十分了解。其实电影名称avatar这个单词本身的意思是"化身"，而这与电影情节契合。

阅读技能练习场

Exercises:

1 What do we know about the Planetary Resources, Inc.?

    A. It's a firm co-founded by Page and Schmidt.

    B. It is the first billionaire-backed private space company.

    C. Space exploration and natural resources are the two major sections of the company.

    D. Only Page and Schmidt invested in it.

2 Why do you think that Google takes an interest in asteroids?

    A. To add trillions of dollars to the global GDP.

    B. The space exploration and natural resources attract the company most.

    C. Because the world is no longer big enough.

D. They're rich in water, oxygen and metals.

3 Which of the following is incorrect according to the passage?

A. No billionaire has ever been to the International Space Station.

B. The cost of the action on asteroids is huge.

C. James Cameron has invested in Planetary Resources.

D. Stratolaunch Systems plans to build the world's largest aircraft.

Answers: 1.C 2.B 3.A

Reading Skills

1. 留意关键词 ★★★★★

在做题的时候，可以把与题目相关的词语用笔标记出来，而且在浏览文章时可以多注意一下关键词出现的地方，细读这个部分的内容，搜集相关信息，以便接下来回答问题。

Q1解析：A项：Page是谷歌创始人之一，而Schmidt是谷歌执行董事长，他们不是Planetary Resources创始人(可以多注意下此词出现的地方)；B项相对应的原文为Planetary Resources will be the second billionaire-backed private space company… 文章第五段介绍了其他的投资者，故D项错误。因此选C。

2. 把握小细节 ★★★★★

细节的把握对解题来说十分重要，很多科技类的文章大部分题目都是针对细节的考查，对于这类题目，可以把题目中的内容与文章对照阅读。不多留心的话，很可能做出错误的选择。

Q2解析：由The pair are now staking a claim for galactic domination by backing a plan to mine asteroids.和The company will overlay two critical sectors—space exploration and natural resources…这两句话，可得知B项正确。

Q3解析：根据…billionaire Microsoft alumnus Charles Simonyi, who has already made two trips to the International Space Station.可知A项错误。

Passage 03

The Strange Rise of the Artisanal Internet
——奇特的手工互联网的兴起
——Apr., 1st, 2012, The Washington Post

Reading Guide

在互联网热潮兴起的今日，有一群人却另辟蹊径。他们试图打造一个纯手工生产的互联网世界。他们穿着工装裤在种着花草的办公室里走来走去，他们将手工打造的电子产品称作"庄稼"。在这个忙碌而冷漠的电子世界里，他们要将过去的传统发扬光大。

Across America, in tech hubs from Silicon Valley to Silicon Alley, a curious new movement is taking shape: the Artisanal Internet. Young entrepreneurs dressed in denim overalls, plaid lumberjack shirts, rugged work boots and black-rimmed, non-prescription **hipster** glasses are attempting to return the tech sector to an earlier, less corporate era.

Unlike their Internet entrepreneur **peers** in tech hubs across the country, however, they are not rushing out to buy the latest high-tech **gadgets** or **hanging out** for hours in Apple retail stores in their free time. If anything, their purpose is more foolish. They refer to their fellow employees as "artisans," their products as "crops," their offices as "farms" and they are hard at work at creating new technology products hand-crafted from

遍布美国各地，从硅谷到硅巷的高科技中心，有种神秘的新兴运动正在逐步成形：那就是手工互联网。穿着牛仔工装裤、伐木工格子短衬衫、粗糙的工装靴子，戴着不寻常的时髦黑框眼镜的年轻企业家们正在尝试，他们想使高科技产业回到那个更早的、企业更少的时期。

但是，与美国其他高科技中心的互联网企业家同行们不同，他们并不急于购买时下最流行的高科技产品，或是把空闲时间都用于在苹果零售店闲逛上。他们如果那么做，那这样的目的就真是太愚蠢了。他们将自己的员工和同事称为"手工艺者"，把他们的产品称为"庄稼"，还称他们的办公室为"农场"。他们辛苦地工作，用一种会让人

---

hipster ['hipstə] n. 时髦的人
peer [piə] n. 同行

gadget ['gædʒit] n. 小玩意儿
hang out 闲逛

natural materials in a way that is **reminiscent** of America's great past.

If there's one individual who best **epitomizes** this nascent trend of the Artisanal Internet, it's A. Preel Ful, an earnest twenty something from Brooklyn with a wispy goatee who dresses for work each day in denim overalls and a T-shirt bearing the image of an 8-bit video game. Generally recognized as the creator of this movement, Mr. Ful refers to his Internet start-up—the Brooklyn Server Farm—as the first-ever farm-to-table company, and indeed, the entire layout of his office in Williamsburg resembles nothing so much as a miniature urban farm where tech products are raised in small batches before being harvested and brought to market. As if to underscore this point, Mr. Ful gestures to the back of the office with a knowing glance where the "server farm" resides and racks of wires are being "sun-ripened on the vine" along exposed brick walls lit by artisanal light bulbs.

This trend toward the Artisanal Internet is best thought of as a cross between the urban farming movement embraced by hipsters and the DIY "Maker Movement" that is starting to sweep through the tech hobbyist landscape. Now that new tools such as 3D printers are entering the mainstream, the Artisanal Internet has started to **resonate** with designers and craftsmen. Rather than buy bright, shiny tech gadgets manufactured in massive factories outside of the U.S., they prefer to buy their products from local craftsmen

们想起美国伟大的历史的方式，将天然的原料通过手工加工，制造出新的科技产品。

如果要找一个最能诠释手工互联网初期趋势的个体的话，那就是A．普瑞来·富尔了。他是一名来自布鲁克林、留着稀疏的山羊胡子、做事认真诚恳的20来岁的年轻人。他每天穿着牛仔工装裤，以及印有8位电子游戏里面的图案的T恤来上班。通常被认为是这场运动的创始人的富尔先生把他开创的互联网——布鲁克林服务器农场——称为是迄今为止的第一家"从农场到餐桌"的公司。的确，他位于威廉斯堡的办公室的整体布局活像一个小型的城市农场。在这里，科技产品在大批量收获和上市之前都要从小批量起步。好像是要强调这一点，富尔先生会心照不宣地警向办公室后面，那里放着"服务器农场"，而货架上的电线就像"晒熟了的藤"，沿着暴露在外的砖墙，被手工制作的灯泡照亮。

最好把这种手工互联网的趋势看作一种跨界合作，是时尚人士崇尚的城市农业运动与心怀席卷全国的愿景的高科技爱好者发起的自己动手"制造者行动"之间最好的合作。如今，例如三维打印机等新式工具正在进军主流市场，手工互联网则开始让设计者和技术工人产生共鸣。比起购买国外大型工厂制造的鲜艳闪亮的科技小玩意儿，他们更愿意购买自己的科技产品，这些产品是当地的手工艺者利用全天然的材料，从头

---

reminiscent [ˌremiˈnisənt] a. 使人想起的
epitomize [iˈpitəmaiz] v. 概括

resonate [ˈrezəneit] v. 共鸣

who design and create their tech products from scratch using all-natural materials. They are even manufacturing small batches of tablets made from materials such as reclaimed wood, which gives their products a distinctive look compared to the shiny black and white tablets of today.

While there are only pockets of the Artisanal Internet that have formed so far, the movement is accelerating in places like Austin, Brooklyn and, of course, Portland. Young tech workers are re-designing their urban studio lofts to resemble rural barns, trading in their J. Crew Ludlow Suits for denim overalls, and toting growlers to work rather than water bottles. If you listen carefully in the background of your office, it might just be possible to hear the slow rumble of a tractor over the din of noisy taxicab horns honking outside.

Indeed, there is something wonderfully **retro** about the Artisanal Internet. In an era of vintage Hipstamatic filters, an **obsession** with 8-bit video games, and antique-looking tablet covers, the return to the crafts era of American manufacturing in the tech sector is perhaps to be expected. While lounging around during breaks, eating their artisanal cheeses and charcuterie, is it foolish to think that people would not also want their artisanal tech products as well?

开始设计并创作的。他们甚至利用诸如可再生木料等原料制造了一小批平板电脑，这使它们拥有与当今那些闪亮黑色和白色的平板电脑不同的独特外观。

尽管到现在为止，只有很少的手工互联网已经初具规模。但是这场运动在奥斯汀、布鲁克林，当然还有波特兰这样的城市正在加速发展。年轻的科技工作者将他们位于城市中的跃层工作室重新设计成像是乡下谷仓的样子，他们把 J. Crew 的勒德洛套装换成背带牛仔裤，提着装啤酒的酒壶而不是水瓶来工作。如果你仔细倾听办公室的背景音，就有可能听到外面拖拉机缓慢驶过的隆隆声盖过了出租车喇叭的嘈杂声。

确实，手工互联网有一些非常奇妙的复古特性。在古老的胶片相机滤镜效果盛行的时代，在沉迷8位电子游戏、以及古式造型的平板电脑外壳盛行的时代，也许人们更希望看到美国制造业的手工艺时代在高科技领域的回归。在休息之余，漫步闲逛的时候，吃着手工制作的奶酪和熟食时，如果还要说人们不想要手工的科技产品，岂不是很愚蠢的想法吗？

炫 · 知识

1. Silicon Alley 硅巷

Silicon Alley的说法来源于Silicon Valley(硅谷)，是对美国曼哈顿互联网和新兴媒体公司的聚集地区的一种称呼。

retro ['retrəu] n. 复古   obsession [əb'seʃən] n. 沉迷

15

2. take shape 粗具规模

shape有"形状，具体化"的含义，因此take shape就表示"粗具规模"，这种说法既简洁又到位，听起来十分地道。

3. farm-to-table 从农场到餐桌

farm-to-table是指"从农场到餐桌"运动，指的是在当地生产食物，然后将食物运送给当地的消费者。这样可以保证食物新鲜。

4. tablet 平板电脑

tablet作为名词时，其"药片"的意思为人们所熟知。但在科技领域表示"平板电脑"。而pad也可表示"平板电脑"，这个词因苹果公司生产的大受好评的iPad而为更多人所知，其原意为"垫子；便签纸"，比喻其外型及功能。

阅读技能练习场

Exercises:

1. According to the first two paragraphs, which is the typical character of the Artisanal Internet entrepreneurs?

   A. They take the latest high-tech gadgets.

   B. They hang out for hours in Apple retail stores.

   C. They work hard on the farm with their employees.

   D. They often dress in labor suits such as denim overalls.

2. What does the word "crops" refer to in Paragraph 2?

   A. New technology products.

   B. Sun-ripened raisins on the vine.

   C. The Artisanal Internet.

   D. The J. Crew Ludlow Suits.

3. According to the whole passage, which description is correct?

   A. Mr. A. Preel Ful is the creator of farm-to-table movement.

   B. The entire layout of the office in Brooklyn resembles nothing so much as a miniature urban farm.

   C. People who advocate the DIY "Maker Movement" prefer to buy their products from local craftsmen rather than the tech gadgets manufactured outside of the U.S..

D. The return to the crafts era of American manufacturing in the tech sector is highly expected.

Reading Skills

1. 小心偷换概念 ★★★★★

如果出题人针对文章的某些细节出题，就很有可能会改变其中一些很小的细节。而注意这些细节是得分的关键。

> **Q1解析**：本题考查手工互联网工作者的特点，在文章的前两段不难找到答案。根据原文可知A、B都与事实相反，C项虽然乍一看很像正确答案，但其实互联网工作者们并不是真的在田间工作的。所以本题选D。

2. 注意指代词前后的句子 ★★★★★

对于考查某个词或句子的意思的题目，一定要考虑这个词或句子与周边的句子的关系。因为这些临近的句子可能就是对这个词的解释说明。

> **Q2解析**：因为关键词是crops，所以要迅速回到文中找到相应句子：They refer to their fellow employees as "artisans," their products as "crops," their offices as "farms"，由此可知，这些人把他们的产品称作"庄稼"。因此选A。

3. 注意表示程度的词 ★★★★★

有时候一个表示程度的词被换掉，整个句子的意思就不一样了。因此不要被出题人迷惑了。

> **Q3解析**：这道题的A、B选项都存在明显的错误，很容易排除。D选项看似正确，但是原文中的表达是：the return to the crafts era of American manufacturing in the tech sector is perhaps to be expected. 而在选项中，perhaps to be expected却被换成了程度更深的highly expected，所以D也是错误答案，本题选C。

Passage 04

The Neuroscience of Creativity: Why Daydreaming Matters

——为什么白日梦对创意十分重要

——Mar. 23rd, 2012, Matthew E. May

Reading Guide

走神和白日梦是两个看起来不太讨喜的词汇，然而它们却是创造力的"祖先"。科学和实践证明，创造力并不是源于有目的的思考，而是来自那些不经意的突发奇想。正是这些奇思妙想使许多的创意走进了我们的生活。

Most people know that 3M's Arthur Fry was not trying to invent the thing he invented in 1974 ——the Post-it Note——he was daydreaming in church.

As neuroscientists now know, and was conclusively shown in 2009, it's when our minds wander that our brains do their best work—it's when we're not trying to think creatively that we're often most creative. That's when a still mysterious process in the right hemisphere of the brain behind the right ear makes connections between seemingly unrelated things, and those connections then bubble up as sudden insights, as if **out of nowhere**.

Jonah Lehrer, through our discussion of his just released new book *Imagine: How Creativity Works*, helped us **sort out** and **make sense out of** the latest discoveries, and what the results might

1974年，3M公司的亚瑟·弗莱发明了即时贴，很多人都知道，其实亚瑟·弗莱并没有试图去发明它，而是在教堂做白日梦的时候无意中想到的。

正如神经学家今天所了解、且最终于2009年所展示的那样，当我们的意识游走时，就是大脑发挥到极致地工作之时——当我们并没有想要创造什么的时候，通常就是我们最有创意的时候。在右耳后方的大脑右半球中存在一个神秘程序，这个程序将原本貌似不相干的事情联系在一起。然后这些联系会突然涌现成深刻的见解，仿佛凭空而来一样

通过我们对乔纳·莱勒刚发行的新书《想象力：创造力如何工作》的讨论，可以帮助我们甄选并了解最近的发现，而结果可能会像任何人所希望的那

out of nowhere 突然冒出的   make sense out of 了解
sort out 挑选出

imply for anyone wishing to better tap into their natural creativity.

"It's not an accident that Arthur Fry was daydreaming when he came up with the idea for a sticky bookmark," advises Jonah. "A more disciplined thought process wouldn't have made the connection between the annoying little pieces of paper he used to bookmark his choir music and a weak **adhesive** another 3M engineer had developed. The **errant** daydream is what made Post-it Notes possible."

Jonah believes that the kind of thinking that enables these unexpected connections is the essence of creativity, and people who daydream seem to be better at it. The trick, though, is daydreaming and letting your mind wander, yet remaining aware enough to recognize a sudden insight when it comes. He makes the point that if you don't notice an idea, it's not useful daydreaming: "The reason why Fry is such a good inventor—he has more than twenty patents to his name, **in addition to** Post-it Notes—isn't simply that he's a prolific mind-wanderer. It's that he's able to pay attention to his daydreams and to detect those moments when his daydreams generate insights."

What that means is that not all daydreaming is created equal. Sitting around the house all day in one long protracted daydream won't produce any insights, unless there was a certain density of attention paid to a specific problem that preceded it. It's dedicated daydreaming—purposeful mind-wandering that yields productive creativity.

样，更好地发掘他们天生的创造力。

"弗莱在空想的时候想出书签即时贴的创意并非偶然，"乔纳这样忠告大家。"如果他的思维过程更加训练有素，那么他就不会把他自己夹在唱诗班乐谱中的小纸片书签与另一名3M公司工程师设计的黏合剂联系起来。漫无目的的空想让即时贴的出现成为可能。"

乔纳相信那种能将这些意外关联起来的思想就是创造力的本质，而那些空想的人在这方面更有潜力。不过诡计都是空想的形式，能让你的思维活跃起来，同时也能认识到突发奇想的见解到来。他证明了这一点：如果你没有注意到一个想法，那么你的空想就是没有用的："除了即时贴以外，以弗莱的名字命名的专利还有二十个以上，但是为什么说弗莱是一名优秀的发明者？这不仅是因为他是一名多产的思考者，还因为他能注意到他那些空想产生的见解，并即时察觉它们。"

这就意味着，并不是所有空想都是同等的。如果整天坐在家里，拖拖拉拉地做一个长久的白日梦，这样不会产生任何见解，除非特殊的命运让你在此之前就有几次注意到这个特定的问题。专注的空想——也就是说有目的的神游，才能产生有用的创造力。

---

adhesive [əd'hi:siv] n. 黏合剂
errant ['erənt] a. 周游不定的

in addition to 此外

"When our minds are **at ease**," says Jonah, "we're more likely to direct the spotlight of attention inward, toward that stream of remote associations emanating from the right hemisphere. In contrast, when we are diligently focused, our attention tends to be directed outward, toward the details of the problems we're trying to solve. While this pattern of attention is necessary when solving problems analytically, it actually prevents us from detecting the connections that lead to insights."

Naturally, I'm curious about the role of daydreaming in Jonah's own creative process.

"I think about this great Albert Einstein line," he tells me. "The one about 'creativity is the residue of time wasted.' In my own creative process, I now feel much more comfortable knowing that when I've hit a wall, spent a day tinkering with the same stupid paragraph—that it's time to take a walk and accept the fact that the most productive thing I can do will look really unproductive to everyone else. I now take longer, more languid showers and don't feel guilty when I take long walks in the middle of the day."

"Answers to my toughest problems come to me while I'm walking, when I'm not thinking about them. I know when I'm stuck that I'm not going to solve them by just playing with words on my computer screen—I need to get away."

"I think about Jonathan Schooler, who has pioneered the study of daydreaming and mind wandering. He's shown that people who daydream score higher on creativity tests. He

"当我们的意识放松时，我们就更有可能会将内在的注意力直接放在那些右脑发出的远程关联上，"乔纳说，"相反，当我们认真关注某事时，我们的注意力就会直接关注外在，关注那些我们试图解决的问题的细节。而这种关注的模式在通过分析来解决问题的时候是必要的，这实际上阻止了我们察觉到那些带来见解的关联。"

自然而然的，我很好奇空想在乔纳自己创作的过程中起到什么作用。

"我想起了伟大的爱因斯坦的句子，"他这样告诉我。"一个有关'创造就是浪费你剩下的时间'。现在在我创造的过程中，当我碰壁的时候，花一整天的时间胡乱修改同一个愚蠢的段落时——我知道这时我应该去散散步了，而且我会接受这个事实：此刻我能做的最有创意的事情在别人看来也非常没有创意。而这些想法使我感到宽慰。如今我花费更长的时间慵懒地沐浴，而且当我有一天花了很长一段时间来散步的话，我也不会有罪恶感。"

"当我散步的时候，那些我认为是最难的问题的答案就会浮现，那时我并没有思考这些问题。我知道当我感觉思维卡住了的时候，我并不会通过在电脑上玩文字游戏来解决这些问题——我需要走出去。"

"我想到了乔纳森·斯库勒，他是研究空想和神游的先驱。他的研究表明，那些善于空想的人在创造力测试上得分较高。他每天都在圣巴巴拉北部，

at ease 自由自在

takes a dedicated daydreaming walk every day on this beautiful bluff along the Pacific, just north of Santa Barbara. He talks about how he always knows when he **desperately** needs a daydreaming walk."

"It's the problems that really seem impossible, where there's no feeling of knowing, no sense of a solution, no sense of progress—those really hard problems that are most likely going to be solved by long walks, showers, **meditation**, games of ping-pong... those kinds of things."

What *Imagine* and the literature about the neuroscience of creativity say is, when we need moments of insight, when we need to find **far-reaching** connections between seemingly unrelated ideas, when we've really hit the wall... that's when we need to relax, to stop thinking about work, because the answer will only arrive when we stop looking for it.

The next time someone catches you daydreaming on the job and asks you why you're not working, tell them that in fact you're doing your best, most creative work.

太平洋海域的一段风景秀美的断崖边专注地一边空想一边散步。他谈到了每当自己非常需要这样一边空想一边散步的时候，他是如何知道的。

"那些没有认知的感觉、没有意义的解决方法，以及没有意义的进展，都是些看起来似乎不可能解决的问题——虽然这些问题都很难解决，但是最有可能通过长时间的散步、冲凉、冥想、打乒乓球等方式来解决。"

《想象》一书和与创意有关的神经科学文献都表达这样的思想：当我们需要深刻见解的时刻，当我们需要发现那些看起来似乎毫无联系的想法之间存在的深刻联系，当我们真的遇到阻碍时……就是我们需要放松、停止考虑工作的时候了，因为只有当我们停止寻找的时候，答案才会出现。

下次如果有人发现你在工作时空想，并问你为什么不在工作的时候，你就告诉他们，事实上你正在做着最棒的、最富有创造性的工作。

炫 · 知识

1. 3M

3M公司的全称是Minnesota Mining and Manufacturing，即明尼苏达矿务及制造业公司。该公司创建于1902年，总部设在美国明尼苏达州的圣保罗市，是世界著名的产品多元化跨国企业。

2. Post-it Note 即时贴

即时贴的发明十分偶然。公司原本是想要研究一种黏性很强的胶水，但最后却得到了黏性较弱的胶水。于是，这就变成了一个可以赚取几十亿美元的商机。

desperately ['despərətli] ad. 极度地
meditation [ˌmedi'teiʃən] n. 冥想

far-reaching ['fɑː'riːtʃiŋ] a. 深远的

3. tap into 发掘

tap有"轻敲"的含义，而短语tap into则表示"发掘，深入"。

4. hit a wall 碰壁

hit a wall的字面意思是"碰到一堵墙"，而这与我们在中文里常说的"碰壁"是同样的意思，就是指遇到了某些困难。

阅读技能练习场

Exercises:

1 Did Fry invent the Post-it Note on purpose?

A. Yes, he worked hard to create it.

B. No, he didn't.

C. We cannot know from the passage.

D. It depends.

2 How many patents did Fry have?

A. Only the Post-it Note.

B. More than twenty patents.

C. Hundreds of patents.

D. The author didn't mention.

3 According to the passage, when we get stuck while we are thinking about a solution, what should we do?

A. Concentrate on the problem.

B. Ask for help.

C. Relax and stop thinking about it.

D. Search on the Internet.

Answers: 1.B 2.B 3.C

Reading Skills

1. 排除干扰项 ★★★★★

在做阅读题目的时候，通常我们可以通过排除干扰项的方法来节约做题时间。如果能迅速排除掉不可能正确的答案，选择正确的几率也就大大地提高了。

> **Q1解析：** 根据问题，我们首先可以排除答案D选项。即时贴的发明是作者举的第一个例子，根据文章第一段，很容易得知亚瑟·弗莱是无意中发明的。因此选项B是正确的。

2. 用巧妙办法找到关键词的出处 ★ ★ ★ ★ ★

许多人面对细节题总是感觉无从下手，但其实这类题目只要在文中找到出处，答案通常是显而易见的。对于有些题目，如果其关键词是数字或者大写字母，或者词型比较特殊的单词，通常在原文中会比较明显。

> **Q2解析：** 这道题考查亚瑟·弗莱获得的专利数。我们知道即时贴是他的专利，而这个单词Post-it Notes的形态比较容易区分。因此在文中很容易找到he has more than twenty patents to his name, in addition to Post-it Notes这个句子。所以答案是B。

3. 根据文章主题思想推断 ★ ★ ★ ★ ★

在判断一个选项正确与否的时候，我们可以在阅读文章后，根据文章的主旨来进行推断。因为那些明显与主旨不符的选项，通常是错误的。

> **Q3解析：** 根据文章，首先我们可以排除选项A，因为与全文的观点不符。而B和D选项在文中均未提及，所以答案是C。

Passage 05

Should Your Dog Be Watching TV?

——你的狗狗也能看电视?

——Apr. 25th, 2012, New York Times

Reading Guide

因为工作，没有时间陪伴狗狗，长时间会影响狗狗的身心健康。这种情况下，那就给它们看专门为狗狗设计的电视节目吧！这个节目能够缓解宠物狗独自在家无人陪伴的焦虑，也能让它自娱自乐。但是，专家认为：再好的电视节目也还是不能代替主人的陪伴。有时间就多陪你的宠物做做运动吧！

Plenty of things will grab a dog's attention: **squirrels**, tennis balls, funny smells, other dogs. But a TV channel?

Absolutely, say the makers of DogTV, the first cable network to deliver 24-hour programming for dogs. The idea, they say, that **flipping** on the channel while you go out for the day will keep your pet stimulated, entertained and relaxed. Call it "Sesame Street" for those who will never learn their ABCs.

The shows on DogTV are actually three-to six-minute segments featuring grassy fields, bouncing balls and humans rubbing dog tummies. There are also segments featuring noiseless vacuum cleaners and muted doorbells to help make dogs more comfortable around such common household **agitations**.

很多事情都会吸引狗的注意：松鼠，网球，奇特的气味，或是其它的狗。但电视节目也可以吸引它们吗？

绝对可以，狗狗电视的节目制作人这样说。狗狗电视是第一个通过有线网络为宠物狗提供24小时节目的电视频道。他们表示，当你白天要外出时，让你的宠物在电视机前换频道的这个想法会使它感到刺激、娱乐和放松。对那些没有学习过基础知识的观众来说，我们称这个节目为"芝麻街"。

狗狗电视上的节目实际上是3－6分钟的片段，主题是芦地、弹力球和抚摸狗肚子的主人。也有以无声的吸尘器和静音的门铃作为主题的影像片段，以此来帮助宠物狗在这种热闹的家庭环境中感觉更加舒适。

---

squirrel ['skwirəl] n. 松鼠
flip [flip] v. 快速翻转

agitation [,ædʒi'teiʃən] n. 鼓动

Executives at the network say their programming is scientifically designed to appeal to dogs. "We have three years of research on how dogs react to different **stimuli**," said Bonnie Vieira, a spokeswoman for DogTV.

"For instance," she explained, "For dogs who suffer from separation anxiety, DogTV is a tool that might help ease them, so maybe they're not getting into trouble, and they're happier, more relaxed when you get home."

But can dogs actually watch, and benefit from television? Like most questions regarding canine consciousness, the answer depends on whom you ask.

"I think a lot of this is to make us feel better but fails to make the pet happier," said Dr. Ann E. Hohenhaus, a staff **veterinarian** for the Animal Medical Center in Manhattan. "Your pet needs adequate exercise and an interesting environment. You cannot just turn on the TV and hope your dog is going to get better."

Still, if the dog is paying attention to the screen, odds are that it likes what it sees. "If the dog didn't enjoy it, he would find something else to do, like nibbling on the end of a sofa," Dr. Hohenhaus said. In that way, dog-oriented shows "could be a component" in a program designed to alleviate separation anxiety.

In a test of DogTV at the Escondido Humane Society in California, the pets were housed in a "behavior evaluation ward"—essentially a holding pen for new residents—found that exposure to the channel at least temporarily helped reduce barking and antsy behavior.

Whether your dog actually pays attention to the TV may have more to do with the screen than what's on it, said Stanley Coren, a professor of

网络公司的高管表示他们的节目是经过科学地设计来吸引狗狗的。"在狗对不同的刺激会如何反应上，我们进行了3年的研究。"狗狗电视的女发言人邦尼·维埃拉说。

"例如，"她解释道，"针对那些患有分离焦虑症的狗，狗狗电视是一个可以帮助它们放松下来的工具，这样也许它们就不会陷入困境中。当你回到家的时候，它们就会很开心，很放松。"

但是，宠物狗真的能看电视，并从中获益吗？就像大多数关于犬类意识的问题那样，答案取决于你问的对象是谁。

"我认为多数情况下这样做只是让我们感到很好，而不能让宠物感到快乐，"曼哈顿动物医疗中心的一位兽医工作者，安·E·霍恩豪斯医生说，"你的宠物需要充足的运动和一个有趣的环境。你不能只是打开电视机，从而期望你的狗狗会变得更健康。"

然而，如果狗正将注意力集中在电视屏幕上，有可能它喜欢正在看的节目。"如果狗狗不喜欢这个节目，它就会去找别的事情做，比如咬沙发角，"霍恩豪斯医生说。那样的话，以狗为定位的电视节目很可能是为缓解分离焦虑症而设计的节目中的"一个组成部分"。

在加利福尼亚的埃斯孔迪多动物保护协会的一次狗狗电视测试中，将宠物放在一间"行为评估监视房间"内——实际上是要对新入驻的宠物进行跟踪记录——我们发现节目的播放至少可以暂时帮助狗减少大叫和焦虑不安的行为。

你的狗是否真的会将注意力集中在电视上更多地取决于电视屏幕而不是电视内容，一位名为史丹利·科

---

stimuli ['stimjuli] n. 刺激　　veterinarian [ˌvetəriˈneəriən] n. 兽医

psychology at the University of British Columbia. He should know of what he speaks: in 2007, he created a series of DVDs for canines called "The Dog Companion".

"Dogs have terrific motion sensitivity," Dr. Coren said, meaning that the optical illusion that makes still images on a TV which appear fluid won't fool them as easily as it does humans. "For many dogs, that's a turn-off. It doesn't look real to them."

To increase the chances that your dog will pay attention, place the high-definition TV at the pet's eye level, Dr. Coren advised. "Some people wrote to me and said, 'This DVD didn't work, because my dog paid no attention to it,'" he said. "Well, a lot of people just plugged the image into their wall-mounted TV sets, and the truth of the matter is, your dog is not going to look up there."

But, like people, some dogs just aren't that into TV, said Teoti Anderson, a former president of the Association of Pet Dog Trainers. "Two of my dogs do pay attention to the TV depending on what's on," she said. "One of them couldn't care less."

If your dog does show interest, it probably can learn from what it sees on a television, Ms. Anderson said. Exposing a pet to muted versions of everyday irritants like **vacuum cleaners** and doorbells, for example, is a time-tested method for reducing the animal's fear of them. But an important aspect of the technique is amping up the volume as the dog grows comfortable— so, depending on how quickly a dog learns, the owner may want to hover nearby to turn up the DogTV volume.

But—of course—dog owners shouldn't mistake TV time for quality time, animal behaviorists

伦的不列颠哥伦比亚大学的心理学教授表示。他应该熟知他所说的：2007年，他曾创作了一系列关于犬类、被称为"狗伴侣"的DVD光碟。

科伦博士说"狗类有非常高的动作灵敏度"，意思是说狗狗们不会像人类一样被电视上出现的看似流畅的画面所愚弄。"对于很多狗来说，那是很扫兴的事情。对它们来说，一点都不真实。"

为了使你的宠物狗更可能集中注意力，科伦博士建议，将一个高清电视放置在宠物视线的水平角度。"有的人写信给我说道，'你的DVD光盘没有起作用，我的狗一点都不看。'"他说到，"但许多人只是将影像输入到他们的壁挂式电视机内，而事情的真相是，你的狗狗并不打算抬头观看。"

但是，像人一样，有一些狗并不是那么喜欢看电视，宠物狗培训师协会前主席特奥蒂·安德森说。"我的两只狗的确会看电视，但取决于电视里演的是什么，"她说，"我的另一只狗就特别不喜欢看。"

如果你的狗感兴趣，它很有可能从它所看的电视节目中学到东西，安德森夫人说。比如，将你的宠物放置在日常刺激事物都安静的环境下，比如吸尘器、门铃，可以减少动物对它们的恐惧感，这是一个经过时间检验过的方法。但是这种方法中很重要的一点就是当狗感觉很舒适的时候，要调大音量——所以根据狗狗自己领悟的速度，主人可能也需要在旁边徘徊，以调大狗狗电视的音量。

但是——当然狗的主人不应该误将电视时间当成黄金时间，动物行为

vacuum cleaner 真空吸尘器

cautioned. "It definitely isn't a **substitute** for playing time with your dog," Ms. Anderson said. "Exercise can solve a lot of behavioral problems."

DogTV has been available through cable providers in San Diego since February and can also be accessed online. Its purveyors aim to put it on cable systems nationwide by the end of the year.

学家提醒道。"这毫无疑问不能替代你陪伴宠物狗进行娱乐的时间，"安德森夫人说，"运动能解决很多行为上的问题。"

在圣地亚哥从二月份开始，狗狗电视台已经可以通过有线电视提供商进行收看了，也可以在线观看。供应商打算在今年年底之前将该节目放入全国有线电视系统。

炫 · 知识

1. DogTV 狗狗电视频道

2012年2月在美国加利福尼亚州第二大城市圣迭戈开通的，专为独自在家的狗狗所打造的一个电视频道。如今该电视频道已经可以在网络上收看了，频道负责人正计划把该频道推广至美国全境。

2. appeal to 对……产生吸引力

appeal to还有"申诉；呼吁"之意，但在文中表示吸引狗的注意力。

3. separation anxiety 分离焦虑症

也称dissociative anxiety，是指婴幼儿因与亲人分离而引起的焦虑、不安、或不愉快的情绪反应，又称离别焦虑。

4. high-definition TV 高清电视

High-Definition TV可以缩写为HDTV。它是DTV(Digital TV，即数字电视)的一种格式。高清电视已经在美国、澳大利亚和日本等国家进入了普及阶段，在国内也有些城市进行了试运行。如今，在网络上经常能看到各种视频的高清版。

阅读技能练习场

Exercises:

1 According to the passage, which saying about DogTV is NOT correct?
A. It is the first cable network for dogs.
B. It delivers 24-hour programming.

substitute ['sʌbstitjuːt] n. 替代品

C. There are only some segments about grassy fields, bouncing balls and humans rubbing dog tummies.

D. It can help dogs reduce barking and antsy behavior.

2 What's Dr. Hohenhaus' opinion about DogTV?

A. It's a tool to ease the dogs who suffer from separation anxiety.

B. He is a staff veterinarian for the Animal Medical Center in Manhattan.

C. Dogs have terrific motion sensitivity. People can't fool them easily.

D. Dogs can't get better without adequate exercise and an interesting environment.

3 What's the main purpose of this passage?

A. It's to advise that dogs should watch TV.

B. It's to show DogTV can actually work in some way, but the owners should play with their pets.

C. It's to tell pet owners that they can leave the dogs alone at home in the daytime.

D. It's to advertise the DogTV in a scientific way.

Answers: 1.C 2.D 3.B

Reading Skills

1. 注重文章细节 ★★★★★

议论文中一般会出现不同观点，或是一种观点的不同方面。因此在总览全文主旨的基础上，要注重理解文章细节。

Q1解析：首先要注意题干，选择"不正确一项"；其次，把握文章细节，可以知道狗狗电视频道不仅有涉及青草地、弹力球等的画面，还有一些静音的吸尘器和门铃的影像。因此选C。

Q2解析：第七段中提到，宠物需要充足的锻炼和有趣的环境。主人不能只是打开电视机以希望狗狗可以变得更快乐。因此选D。

2. 根据文章主旨推理判断 ★★★★★

很多题目都在考查读者对文章主旨的把握。因此，读懂文章整体内容，才能真正了解作者意图。

Q3解析：根据文章结构以及内容，可以发现作者借由狗狗电视频道来引出不同人对狗狗电视频道的不同观点。科学实验证明狗狗电视可以在一定程度上减少宠物不安情绪，但却不能从根本上解决狗狗的分离焦虑的问题。因此选B。

Passage 06

Space Elevator Could Be Built within 40 Years
——游客有望在四十年内搭"电梯"去太空
——Feb. 22nd, 2012, Daily Mail

Reading Guide

人类探索太空的脚步一直没有停止。置身浩淼的太空中，回望我们蔚蓝色的星球，那种感觉一定十分美妙。让我们一起来感受科学家为此付出的努力吧。

Japanese engineers are drawing up plans to put tourists into space within 40 years using a massive elevator that travels more than 22,000 miles into orbit.

If created, up to 30 passengers at a time would spend a week travelling a quarter of a way to the moon at speeds of 120mph.

At the end they would reach a space station where they could get an astronaut's view of the earth with little or no training **beforehand**.

There are also plans that could allow scientists to travel beyond this first station using carbon **fibre** ribbon that is anchored to our planet from a satellite in space.

日木工程师正在计划在未来40年内，使用一部巨大的电梯把游客送到太空，这一电梯将运行22000多英里进入轨道。

如果成功的话，这一电梯一次将搭载多达30名的乘客，可以以每小时120英里的速度，花费一周时间，就能到达距离月球四分之三处的轨道。

最终，乘客将到达一个空间站，在那里他们将可以像宇航员一样观赏地球，而之前只用接受少量的培训或者不用培训。

也有让科学家通过使用碳纤维带从第一个太空站航行到宇宙更深处的计划。碳纤维带的一端来自太空中的卫星，另一端抛到地球。

beforehand [bi'fɔ:hænd] ad. 事先　　fibre ['faibə] n. 纤维

The construction, which **echoes** the vision of British science fiction author Arthur C Clarke, is estimated to cost £6 billion.

Satomi Katsuyama, the project's creator, said: "Humans have long adored high towers. But rather than building it from the earth, we will construct it from the space."

Dr. Obayashi is confident her plan will work, although she admits that the locations of the construction and who would pay for it are still unknown.

Previous suggestions have included using a platform in the ocean off Ecuador as a station on the earth because this is near the equator and closer to the orbit.

Dr. Obayashi is just days away from completing work on Japan's tallest structure, the Tokyo Sky Tree, which will stand 2,080 feet tall.

The tower will serve as a digital broadcasting **antenna** as well as a sightseeing attraction that allows uninterrupted views of the Japanese capital and beyond.

"We were inspired by construction of Sky Tree," which will open for business in May, she said. "Our experts on construction, climate, wind patterns, design, say it's possible."

When Obayashi is not drawing up plans to conquer space she works on a number of projects from building corporate headquarters, bridges and power plants to **renovating** ancient temples.

Among her **portfolio** are the Dubai Metro in United Arab Emirates, Universal Studios Osaka,

这个工程，与英国科幻小说家阿瑟·C·克拉克的想法不谋而合，预计花费60亿英镑。

这项工程的创始者，Satomi Katsuyama，说："长期以来，人类崇拜高塔。但我们并不是在地球上建造高塔，而是从太空建造。"

Obayashi博士对自己的计划非常有信心，但是她承认工程的地点和资金来源仍是未知数。

之前有建议说在厄瓜多尔附近的大洋搭建一个平台，作为在地球上的站点，因为这个位置靠近赤道并且距轨道较近。

Obayashi博士还有几天时间就将完成日本最高的建筑——东京晴空塔，这个建筑高达2080英尺。

除了作为一个观光景点，让人们一览无余地欣赏东京及更远处的景观外，它还可以作为一个数字传播的天线。

她说，"我们从晴空塔的建造中得到了灵感，"它将在五月投入使用。"我们在建筑、气候、风向和设计方面的专家说这项计划是可能实现的。"

当Obayashi不忙于征服宇宙的计划时，她致力于几项工程：从建筑公司总部、桥梁、电站到修复古寺。

她的文件包里有：迪拜地铁——阿拉伯联合酋长国，大阪环球录音

---

echo ['ekəu] v. 类似
antenna [æn'tenə] n. 天线

renovate ['renəuveit] v. 翻新，修复
portfolio [,pɔ:t'fəuliəu] n. 公文包

Japan, and Stadium Australia, which was used for the Sydney Olympics.

If realized, the space elevators could become another of the **outlandish** predictions by Clarke, who died in 2008, to become reality.

In 1945, Clarke made perhaps his most famous and accurate prediction.

He wrote an article in *Wireless World* predicting that, one day, it would be possible to use satellites in fixed "geostationary" orbits, 23,000 miles above the earth, as **in effect** giant radio masts, allowing radio, telephony and television signals to be relayed from any point on the planet to another.

Although this was a dozen years before the first satellite would be launched, Clarke had come up with the idea for worldwide satellite broadcasts.

One short story made him famous.

The Sentinel—a tale of a mysterious alien race which had accelerated human evolution—was noticed by the film director Stanley Kubrick, who met Clarke in Trader Vic's bar in New York to discuss how it could be turned into "the perfect science fiction movie".

From the roof of Kubrick's Manhattan apartment, the pair spotted a mysterious object tracking across the sky. The UFO was, they decided, a good **omen** and they signed the deal. (The UFO turned out to be a secret Pentagon spy satellite). The result was **spectacular**.

And *2001: A Space Odyssey*, released in

室——日本及曾在悉尼奥运会时使用的澳大利亚体育馆。

如果这项计划实现了，太空电梯将会成为克拉克（于2008年去世）又一个成为现实的奇特预言。

在1945年，克拉克做出了可能是他最著名、最准确的预言。

他为《无线世界》写了一篇文章，他预测总有一天，使用与地球相距23000英里以外相对位置不变的轨道上的卫星，就像使用巨大的天线杆一样，可使无线电、电话和电视信号在地球任何位置之间进行转播。

尽管这个预言比发射第一颗卫星早了十二年，但是克拉克也提出了在全世界使用卫星通讯的想法。

一个短小的故事让他闻名世界。

《哨兵》是一个神秘的外星人竞赛加速了人类进化的故事——这个故事得到了电影导演斯坦利·库布里克的注意，他在纽约的Trader Vic酒吧与克拉克见面，讨论如何使这个故事成为"最完美的科幻电影"。

在库布里克的曼哈顿公寓的屋顶上，他们两人看见了一个神秘物体在天空飞过。他们认为这个UFO是个好兆头，并签下了协议。（这个UFO后来被证实是五角大楼的秘密侦探卫星。）这一切的结果很壮观。

1968年上映的电影——《2001太

outlandish [aut'lændiʃ] a. 古怪的，奇异的
in effect 事实上

omen ['əumən] n. 预兆
spectacular [spek'tækjulə] a. 壮观的

1968, has been hailed by its fans as the best science fiction movie ever made.

空漫游》，被其粉丝追捧为有史以来最棒的科幻电影。

炫 · 知识

1. the Tokyo Sky Tree 东京晴空塔

东京晴空塔(Tokyo Sky Tree)，又译为东京天空树，位于东京都墨田区，主要用于发射数字电视信号，是目前世界第一高塔。

2. Dubai 迪拜

迪拜市是阿联酋第二大城市，位于阿拉伯半岛中部、阿拉伯湾南岸，是海湾地区中心，被誉为海湾的明珠。

3. Odyssey 长途的冒险旅行

奥德赛也是一本书的名字，《奥德赛》是一部著名的古希腊史诗，相传为荷马所作。主要取材于希腊英雄奥德修斯在特洛伊战争后的一段奇异经历，并穿插许多神话和传说。

阅读技能练习场

Exercises:

1 What do we know about the space elevator, according to the passage?

A. It is designed by scientists from different countries.

B. The destination of the space elevator is the moon.

C. It travels more than 22,000 miles into orbit.

D. If it is built, people could view the earth on the moon.

2 Which of the following statements is correct about the Tokyo Sky Tree?

A. It'll be 2,080 feet tall.

B. It will serve as a digital broadcasting antenna only.

C. We can only see the view within Tokyo on the tower.

D. It has already come into use.

3 Which of the following has nothing to do with Arthur C Clarke?

A. The prediction about the space elevator.

B. The author of *The Sentinel*.

C. The film—*2001: A Space Odyssey*.

D. The launch of the first satellite.

Answers:
1.C　2.A　3.D

Reading Skills

1. 注意模棱两可的选项 ★★★★★

许多选项具有模糊性，这些模棱两可的句子看起来似乎正确，但当我们仔细阅读文章之后，就会发现选项的表述中存在问题。因此做题时一定要从原文出发，根据文中的线索进行选择。

> **Q1解析**：A项错在设计者文中已明确说明来自日本。B项错在目的地并非月球。D项与B选项一样，人们搭乘太空电梯并不能到达月球。

2. 利用选项中的已知信息 ★★★★★

利用选项所提供的信息，就可以知道原文中哪些内容对于解答问题来说是重要的，这样就可以快速筛选出重要的信息，并忽略不必要的内容。

> **Q2解析**：关于东京晴空塔的描述，正确答案是A。这一点在文中有明确提到。B项only一词表达不准确，原文还提到了可以作为一个观光景点。C项不仅可以观赏整个东京，还包括"beyond"。D项东京晴空塔并未启用，对比"which will open for business in May"可得知。

> **Q3解析**：D项不当之处为原文表达为Although this was a dozen years before the first satellite would be launched, Clarke had come up with the idea for worldwide satellite broadcasts.

Passage 07

Wearable Devices Track People Via Wireless Network

——穿戴式设备通过无线网络追查踪迹

——May. 1st, 2012, USA Today

Reading Guide

　　父母们总会在上班时担心顽皮的孩子在幼儿园是否听话；成年子女也会担心患有老年痴呆症的家人在家是否安好；而医生们会担心刚出院的病人的康复状况。如今，移动通讯技术能够帮您远程监控到您所关心的人。该设备在跟踪人物坐标、评估物体移动、实时发送综合数据上有极大优势。

　　Mobile technology is opening new channels for remotely monitoring family members and others who need to be tracked.

　　Several companies, including medical device manufacturer Boston Scientific, have struck deals with major wireless carriers to support a new generation of products of incorporate sensors, accelerometers, GPS and technologies that use cell towers to help triangulate positions and locate people.

　　ABI Research, a research firm, estimates the market for GPS personal tracking devices will grow 40% or more annually and exceed $1 billion by 2017.

　　Family members use them to track toddlers or parents with Alzheimer's. And doctors and military medics have adopted the technology

　　移动通讯技术将开放用来远程监控家庭成员和其他需要被跟踪的人们的新渠道。

　　包括医疗设备制造商波士顿科学国际有限公司在内的一些公司已经取得了与主要无线运营商的合约，合约支持集成传感器、加速度计、全球定位系统和利用信号发射塔来帮助三角定位和定位人物坐标的技术。

　　市场调研公司**ABI Research**预计GPS个人追踪设备的市场将每年增长40%或是更多，到2017年将会超过10亿美元。

　　家庭成员使用它们来跟踪学步的儿童或患有老年痴呆症的父母。医生和军队的医务人员也会采用这项技术

to remotely track the health conditions—**EKG** readings, body temperature, heart rate, and stress or **dehydration** levels—of recently released patients or soldiers on dangerous assignments.

Wireless carriers, looking for ways to make money beyond transmitting data along their networks for smartphones and tablets, are fueling the boom. "We think this is the single-biggest growth opportunity—that every device is connected," says Glenn Lurie, head of AT&T's emerging device team.

But for consumers, the tracking services aren't cheap, requiring an **upfront** cost for devices and a subscription plan, ranging from $10 to $40 a month.

Limited emergency medical alert systems have been around for years, relying on the telephone landline. But the new devices **are** vastly **superior in** locating people, assessing motion and sending comprehensive data in real time to doctors, parents and other caregivers, companies say. "GPS alone would only work when you're outside and you have a good view of the sky," says Daniel Graff-Radford, vice president of sales for Omnilink, a tracking-device maker. "You need sensors. You need cell towers and the software to locate cell towers and satellites."

Some examples:

•Comfort Zone is a web-based service for remotely monitoring a person with Alzheimer's. The alert device, which is made by Omnilink and sold by the Alzheimer's Association, is about the size of a Tic Tac and can be installed in a car or

远程追踪近期刚出院的病人或执行危险任务的士兵的健康状况——他们的心电图读数、体温、心率、压力或脱水等级。

那些正在寻求通过网络为智能手机和平板电脑传输数据以外的赚钱方式的无线运营商们热情高涨。"我们认为这绝对是一个最大的增长机会——让每个设备都连接到网络上。"美国电话电报公司新兴设备团队的领导格伦·劳瑞说。

但是对于消费者来说，跟踪服务并不便宜，要求设备前期投入费和跟踪服务的订制费，每个月要花费10—40美元。

诸多公司表示，虽然依赖于电话座机的有限紧急医疗报警系统已经存在了很多年，但是新的设备在追踪人物位置、评估物体移动及向医生、父母和其他护理人员实时发送综合数据方面有极大的优势。"全球定位系统只有当你在户外并能看到晴朗的天空的情况下才能运行，"跟踪设备制造商Omnilink公司的销售副总裁丹尼尔·格拉夫·雷德福说。"你需要传感器、信号发射塔及用来定位信号发射塔和卫星的软件。"

一些实例：

•"舒适地带"是一项用来远程监控老年痴呆症患者的网络服务。这个报警装置由Omnilink公司研制，由老年痴呆症协会出售，体积大约是一颗Tic Tac薄荷硬糖那么大，可以

EKG 心动电流图(=Electrocardiograph)
dehydration [ˌdi:haiˈdreiʃ ən] n. 脱水

upfront [ˈʌpfrʌnt] a. 预付的
be superior in 在……方面表现优越

worn around the neck. Aetrex, a shoemaker, also inserts the device into special shoes.

• AmberWatch GPS uses the same technology but is marketed by the AmberWatch Foundation. School-age children can clip it to a backpack. "If someone leaves a (preset) zone, the loved one gets a text on their phones," says Graff-Radford of Omnilink.

• BioHarness sensors by Zephyr Technology are worn as a patch or strap by U.S. Special Forces troops, pro athletes and hospital patients. Information about their health condition is sent to cloud servers, and doctors download it to their computers or phones. "It has to be wearable and fashionable," says Brian Russell, CEO of Zephyr. "Even 70-year-olds don't want to look silly."

• Exmobaby, a line of infant pajamas with sensors that send vital signs (heart rate, temp) and information about the baby's "emotional state" to parents' mobile devices, will be on sale later this year, says David Bychkov, CEO of Exmovere, which makes the product.

• Boston Scientific is updating its 6-year old Latitude **implanted** heart monitor, which was once dependent on landlines, so that doctors can receive information on their mobile devices throughout the day. "People are abandoning landlines," says Kenneth Stein, chief medical officer of Boston Scientific's Cardiac Rhythm

安装在车内或是戴在脖子上。制鞋商Aetrex公司也将在专用鞋中嵌入该装置。

· 报警手表的全球定位系统也使用相同的技术，但由AmberWatch基金会推向市场。学龄儿童能够将它夹在双肩书包上。"如果这个人离开了某（预先设定的）区域，关心他的人就会在手机上收到一条短信，"格拉夫·雷德福说。

· 西风科技公司研制的生物马具传感器以补丁或是皮带的方式供美国特种部队、职业运动员和医院的病人使用。他们的健康状况信息被发送到云服务器上，医生将其下载到自己的电脑或手机中。"它必须兼顾可穿戴性和时尚性，"西风的首席执行官布赖恩·罗素说，"即便是70岁的人也不想看起来像个傻瓜。"

· Exmobaby，一款带有传感器的婴儿睡衣，能够把婴儿的生命体征（心率、体温）和"情绪状态"发送到父母的移动设备上。它将在今年年底上市，该产品的制造商Exmovere公司的CEO大卫·毕契科夫说。

· 波士顿科学国际有限公司正在更新已经使用了6年的曾一度依靠电话座机的植入式心脏监视器"纬度"，以便医生们能全天在他们的移动设备上接收到信息。"人们正逐渐放弃使用座机，"该公司心脏节律管理项目的首席医疗官肯尼思·斯坦说。"对

---

implant [im'plɑːnt] v. 嵌入

Management Program. "It's also to make it **portable** for patients who are moving around."

于那些正在到处走动的患者来说，这也使其变得可携带了。"

炫 · 知识

1. AT&T 美国电话电报公司

全称American Telephone & Telegraph, Inc.，世界500强公司。在悠久的历史中，AT&T因为垄断曾成为世界上最大的电话及有线电视运营商。

2. Tic Tac

一种薄荷硬糖，是费列罗公司1969年推出的糖果品牌。当你晃动塑料盒的时候，糖果就会相互碰撞，发出嘀嗒的声音，Tic Tac糖果由此得名。

3. cloud server 云服务器

云服务器是一种基于Web的服务，提供可调整云主机配置的弹性云技术，整合了计算、存储与网络资源的Iaas服务。云是互联网的一种比喻说法。

阅读技能练习场

Exercises:

1 What can the doctors do with the technology?

A. Track their toddlers' growing condition.

B. Follow their parents with Alzheimer.

C. Make a research on their patients.

D. Remotely track the health conditions of their patients.

2 Which of the following statements about Daniel Graff-Radford is not true?

A. He believes GPS could only work when users are outside.

B. He works with a tracking-device maker.

C. He is the vice president of marketing for Omnilink.

D. He thought sensor, cell tower and the software to locate towers and satellites were necessary.

portable ['pɔːtəbl] a. 可携带的

3 What can we infer from the passage?

A. Comfort Zone: the alert device which is made and sold by Omilink can be installed in a car or worn around the neck.

B. AmerWatch GPS: if the child leaves a zone which his parents preset, his parents will get a text on their cell phones.

C. BioHarness sensors: it is wearable for U.S. Special Forces troops, pro athletes and hospital patients, but its appearance is outdated.

D. Boston Scientific can receive vital signs and information about the baby's emotional state.

Answers: 1.D 2.C 3.B

Reading Skills

1. 留意文章与选项的细微差别 ★★★★★

干扰项往往与文章所述有所偏差，需要通过分析与对比才能得出正确答案。

> **Q1解析**：信息集中在文章第四段。选项A和B的对象并非doctors，而是family members。而选项D针对的客体是病人和士兵，主体是医生，因此选D。
>
> **Q2解析**：关于Daniel Graff-Radford的描述集中在文中的第七段。在第七段中可以发现Daniel是销售(sales)VP，而不是市场(marketing)VP，因此选C。

2. 仔细阅读，避免张冠李戴 ★★★★★

有些选项所述客体与原文一字不差，但其主体却是张冠李戴。没有仔细辨认的同学就会误选。因此，在做题时，要仔细阅读，认真分析。

> **Q3解析**：最后的五段，每个段落都是一个实例，通过仔细阅读，认真分析，选B。选项A中made and sold by Omilink的说法不准确，应是sold by the Alzheimer's Association；选项C与文中It has to be wearable and fashionable的说法相悖；选项D将Exmoboby和Boston Scientific混淆。

Chapter 02
尖端科技 Edge Technology

Passage 08

The Flying Car: Are We There Yet?

——会飞的汽车：我们实现了吗？

——Apr. 3rd, 2012, The Washington Post

Reading Guide

上下班高峰期，拥堵的交通状况是不是令你气愤又无奈？你是否也幻想过如果自己的车子能飞起来该会多么爽快？PAL-V公司和Terrafugia公司已经领先一步，研制出会飞的汽车，并试飞成功。但是，这种"陆空两栖"的交通工具普及的可能性会有多大呢？

You're sitting in bumper-to-bumper traffic, the radio is on the fritz and it's a sweltering 100 degrees outside. As you **mumble** a list of ear-blistering obscenities to yourself, you imagine how wonderful it would be if your car could just **lift off** and fly away.

Ah, yes, the flying car.

We've all wanted one, and it appears two companies have come one step closer to grasping one of engineering's many Holy Grails.

The two companies are Netherlands-based PAL-V and Massachusetts-based Terrafugia. On Sunday, PAL-V released a video on YouTube showing what the company says is the successful **maiden flight** of its "flying car", the PAL-V One.

路上车水马龙，你正坐在车里，收音机出了故障，外面的天气酷热难耐，有100度。当你对自己小声嘀咕着一串只有自己能听到的脏话时，你想象一下，如果你的汽车能腾空而起飞走的话，该多好啊！

啊，是的，会飞的汽车。

我们都想要一台这样的汽车。似乎已经有两家公司距离完成这项几乎不可能完成的工程又近了一步。

这两家公司分别是总部位于荷兰的PAL-V公司和总部位于马萨诸塞州的Terrafugia公司。星期日，PAL-V公司在YouTube上发布了一个视频，展示了该公司所说的其"飞行汽车"PAL-V一号的处女飞成功。

---

mumble ['mʌmbl] v. 小声嘀咕
lift off 起飞，升空

maiden flight 首次飞行

Meanwhile, on Monday, Terrafugia announced that its prototype, the Transition, had completed its first flight and would be presented at the New York International Auto Show later this week. The company aims to sell the car next year, having originally set a target date of 2011. One hundred people have already placed a down payment of $10,000 on the car, which costs $279,000—the price of a home (or two) in some parts of the United States.

While others have been innovating in the flying-car arena, Terrafugia and PAL-V are "the two that have led the pack," says Mark Levine, president and co-founder of the International Flying Car Association. The association has existed informally for more than two years, according to Levine, but formally being registered to become a nonprofit this month as news about flying cars has attracted more attention—going from what Levine calls "crazy or hokey" designs that "didn't make commercial sense" to commercially viable flying cars that will be sold in the market.

The PAL-V One

The PAL-V One may look like a helicopter, but it's not. It's a gyrocopter. It achieves lift by an auto-rotated rotor and moves forward thanks to a push propeller at the rear. It also runs on the same gasoline as a regular automobile.

"Our next step is bringing commercial product into the market that is envisioned for delivery in 2014. Then we will start making small quantities compared to the big automobile companies."

与此同时，Terrafugia公司也于星期一宣布了它的飞行汽车原型Transition已经完成了首次试飞，并将在本周的纽约国际车展上展出。公司预计会在明年开始销售这款车，原定以2011年为目标日期。已有100人为该款汽车预付了1万美元作为定金，而该车型价格高达27.9万美元，相当于美国某些地区一套房子（或是两套）的价格了。

正当其他公司在飞行汽车领域不断进行创新的时候，Terrafugia和PAL-V两家公司"已经走在了该领域的前沿，"国际飞行汽车协会主席兼创始人之一的马克·莱文说。据莱文说，这个协会已经存在2年多了，虽然是非正式的，但是这个月已经正式注册，成为一个非盈利组织，尽管关于飞行汽车的新闻已经吸引了更多的注意——从莱文所谓的"疯狂的或是做作的"并"没有什么商业意识"的设计到可能具有商业价值、将在市场上销售的飞行汽车。

PAL-V一号

PAL-V一号看起来像一架直升飞机，但却并非如此。它是一台旋翼机。它实现了通过一个自动旋转的旋翼升空，并通过后部的推动式螺旋桨向前推进。像普通汽车那样，它也依靠同样的汽油运行。

"我们下一步就是要将商业化的产品推向市场，预计将在2014年交货。随后，我们将开始生产制造与大型汽车公司相比的小批量的飞行汽车。"

As for whether China was on the company's radar, Dingemanse said, "It's more the other way around. We are on the radar of China."

But China will have to wait for PAL-V. Dingemanse says he firmly believes in doing first production and marketing near his engineers, who are based in Europe, before expanding to more-distant markets. "China will, in the near future, become one of the countries that will be interesting for us."

Dingemanse has also visited India, another country plagued by traffic congestion, and says he will be returning there soon.

The Transition

While the PAL-V approaches its flying-car technology primarily from the perspective of bringing drivers into the air, Terrafugia's Transition is geared more toward giving pilots more options on the ground. "You do have to be at least a sport pilot to operate this aircraft," said Terrafugia CEO/CTO Carl Dietrich during a phone call Tuesday.

The Federal Aviation Administration (FAA), however, released a statement Tuesday evening saying:

"The manufacturer has not yet applied for an FAA airworthiness certificate, so the FAA has not yet determined what level of pilot certificate and training would be required to operate the Terrafugia Transition as an aircraft."

So, it appears there are some details that have yet to be worked out regarding what it will take to be considered as a qualified pilot.

至于中国是否在该公司的销售范围内，Dingemanse表示，"还有更多其它的方法。我们公司已经引起中国的注意与重视了。"

不过，中国只能等待PAL-V。Dingemanse说他坚信在扩展更远的市场之前，应该创造出第一个产品，并在欧洲地区销售，这里也是工程师们居住的地方。"在不久的将来，中国将会成为我们感兴趣的国家之一。"

Dingemanse也访问了印度，另一个饱受交通拥堵之苦的国家，他说他不久还会回来的。

Transition飞行汽车
PAL-V公司从把汽车驾驶者带到空中的角度来研发它的飞行汽车技术，而Terrafugia公司的Transition飞行汽车的制造更倾向于在路面上给飞行员更多的选择。"的确，你必须至少是一名运动飞行员，才能操作这部飞行器，"在周二的一次通话中，Terrafugia的首席执行官兼首席技术官卡尔·迪特里希说。

但是，联邦航空管理局(简称FAA)在周二晚上发表了一项声明，表示：

"生产商还没有申请联邦航空管理局的适空证书，所以联邦航空管理局还没有最终决定飞行员执照等级和驾驶作为飞机的Terrafugia公司的Transition飞行汽车所需的培训。"

所以，似乎有一些细节尚有待解决，那就是关于如何才能被认定为是一名合格的飞行员。

plague [pleig] v. 使受苦

42

The company, which was started in 2004, flew a proof-of-concept aircraft back in 2009 and is now flying a production prototype, which is going through its final tests this year, according to Dietrich. In June 2011, the National Highway Transportation and Safety Administration granted Terrafugia's **petition** for a temporary exemption from certain Federal Motor Vehicle Safety Standard **provisions**, including tire and rim requirements and "occupant crash protection".

That's not to say the company isn't concerned about safety.

"We are bringing automotive safety technology to general aviation," said Dietrich. "We've got things like safety cage, crumple zones. … We see that as a critical thing in order to lower the barriers to entry."

"If we want to fundamentally expand the market, which we do, we need to go out there and start addressing these concerns," he continued.

The Transition, which runs on super **unleaded** automotive gasoline, also comes with a built-in parachute—a safety mechanism to further ensure gradual descent in the event of an emergency. The vehicle also provides what Dietrich calls a "psychological safety net", allowing pilots to satisfy their desire for mission completion by landing and driving to their destination in **inclement** weather.

But Dietrich acknowledges that the technology is far from what people imagine when they are sitting in traffic.

该公司创立于2004年，在2009年试飞了一款概念型飞机，现在正在试飞产品原型，并将于今年完成最后的测试，据迪特里希透露。2011年6月，国家高速公路运输和安全管理局同意了Terrafugia公司的申请，暂时不受某些特定的联邦机动车安全标准规定的限制，包括轮胎和（安装轮胎的）辋圈要求，及"乘客的碰撞保护"规定。

这并不是说该公司没有考虑到安全因素。

"我们将汽车安全技术载入专用飞机上，"迪特里希说。"我们有诸如安全笼、倒坍区这样的东西。……为了降低屏障以供进入，我们将其视为最关键的东西。"

"如果我们想要从根本上拓展市场，这也是我们现在正在做的，我们就需要走出去，并开始解决这些问题，"他继续说。

Transition飞行汽车会耗费优质的无铅车用汽油，还备有内置的降落伞——以确保在紧急状况下能够平稳降落的安全装置。这台汽车也提供迪特里希所说的"心理安全网络"，能够使飞行员完成在恶劣的天气状况下着陆或飞抵目的地的任务。

但是迪特里希承认，这项技术还远不如人们在交通拥堵的等待中想象的那么完善。

---

petition [pi'tiʃən] n. 申请
provision [prəu'viʒən] n. 条款，规定

unleaded [ˌʌn'ledid] a. 无铅的
inclement [in'klemənt] a. 恶劣的

"I think everybody has had that frustration and shares that dream a little bit—any sort of vehicle that you would build that would lift out of traffic," he said.

他说，"我想每个人都曾有过那样的沮丧，也多少分享了这样一个梦想——你所创造的任意一款可以从车水马龙中解脱出来的交通工具。"

炫 · 知识

1. bumper-to-bumper 一辆接一辆的

bumper本意指"(汽车上的)保险杠"，bumper-to-bumper直译就是"保险杠挨着保险杠"，形象地描绘出车一辆接着一辆的场面。

2. on the fritz 出故障

短语on the fritz是"出故障"的意思，主要表示机器出故障。关于这个说法的来历，有人认为fritz很像电机出故障时那种滋滋作响的声音；也有人认为Fritz是一部动画片里的人物，这个叫做Fritz的孩子总是调皮捣蛋，给人制造麻烦，所以用on the fritz表示"出故障"。

3. Holy Grail 圣杯

在基督教中，关于圣杯的传说由来已久，据说寻找圣杯是骑士的最高目标。后来Holy Grail演变成一种崇高的理想，常常被用来代表众人追求的最高目标，也暗示希望渺茫。文中引用Holy Grail来说明制造飞行汽车是一件很难但又吸引工程师不断探索的事情。

4. New York International Auto Show 纽约国际车展

该车展始于1990年，在每年的3月底或4月初举行。许多参展商都会在车展上展出本公司的新产品或传达新的汽车理念。

5. Federal Aviation Administration 美国联邦航空管理局

简称FAA，负责民用航空管理的机构，其职责是负责民用航空安全，开发和经营空中交通管制、导航系统的民用和军用飞机等。

阅读技能练习场

Exercises:

1 Which saying is not correct about the International Flying Car Association?

A. It is an informally association.

B. Its president and co-founder is Mark Levine.

C. It has established for more than two years.

D. It has become a nonprofit association this month.

2 How much did the customers need to pay for the new car in advance?

    A. $10,000.

    B. $2,790.

    C. The price of a house.

    D. The price of a house in England.

3 What does "But China will have to wait for PAL-V" mean?

    A. China has already ordered the PAL-V and waited for its volume production.

    B. China will produce its own PAL-V later.

    C. The first production of PAL-V won't happen in China and we will consider Chinese market in the future.

    D. Dingemanse will market his production in China first.

Reading Skills

Answers: 1.A 2.A 3.C

1. 读懂原文的"时态潜台词"。 ★★★★★

有时选项会对文章进行断章取义，文章中所用的过去时态或者现在完成时态，选项会直接用现在时态来进行叙述，但是一定要看上下文所做的信息补充，看过去的状态是否也适用于现在时。

> **Q1解析**：在文中第六段，用现在完成时表示其状态，has existed informally for more than two years...but formally registered to become a nonprofit this month，因此informally不是现在的状态，选A。

2. 从文中找答案关键点 ★★★★★

有些题的答案就在原文中。回归原文，细致分析，结合上下文，答案自现。

> **Q2解析**：根据第五段 "One hundred people have already placed a down payment of $10,000 on the car, which costs $279,000"，答案选A。
>
> **Q3解析**：根据第十段内容可知，Dingemanse打算先在欧洲市场上销售自己的汽车飞机，之后再扩大市场，抵达中国。而中国也会成为PAL-V感兴趣的市场。根据文中 "China will, in the near future, become one of the countries that will be interesting for us."，因此选C。

Passage 09

Unblinking Eyes in the Sky
——无人驾驶飞机：不眨眼的空中监视器
——Mar. 3rd, 2012, Economist

Reading Guide

如今，无人驾驶飞机已不仅仅局限为一种武器用在军事领域了，它的使用领域在逐渐拓宽，除了侦察，它还能够监控交通状况、检查电缆与管道、勘察森林和作物、航拍、巡逻林区是否有火情等。然而，其应用仍存在一定的危险性——如何察觉并避让同一空域中的其他飞机。

When environmental activists start using **drones** to **track down** Japanese whaling vessels, as they did in December, it is a sure sign that UAVs (unmanned aerial vehicles) are no longer the sole prerogative of the armed forces. Police around the world **are keen to** use small pilotless aircraft to help them nab fleeing criminals and monitor crime scenes from above. With price tags of a little more (and, in some cases, a good deal less) than the $40,000 of a patrol car, a new generation of micro-UAVs is being recruited to replace police helicopters costing $1.7m and up.

Aside from helping enforce the law, any civilian activity that could be improved by having an aerial view—monitoring traffic, checking electricity cables and pipelines, surveying forestry and crops, taking aerial photographs,

当环保主义者在12月份开始使用无人驾驶飞机追踪日本的捕鲸船时，就明确示意我们UAVs（无人驾驶的飞行器）不再是只有武装部队才能享用的特权了。全球各地的警方都热衷于使用小型的无人机来协助他们追捕在逃的罪犯，在空中监视犯罪现场。因为无人机的价格只比一台千万美元的警用巡逻车高一点点（有时候要低得多），他们正在购买新一代微型无人机取代价值170万美元甚至更多的警用直升飞机。

除了协助执法外，任何市政活动，都可以通过一个俯视角度的鸟瞰得到改善——监控交通状况，检查电缆与管道，勘察森林和作物，航拍，巡逻林区是否有火情——都将得益于

---

drone [drəun] n. 无人驾驶飞机
track down 追踪，跟踪

be keen to 渴望
aside from 除……之外

patrolling wooded areas for fire—would benefit from the use of UAVs. The limiting factor is not technological, but regulatory. In America the Federal Aviation Administration (FAA) currently allows the recreational use of drones, but not commercial use: earlier this year estate agents in Los Angeles were banned from using drones to take aerial photos of properties they were selling, for example.

Change is coming, however. The European Commission has held a series of hearings on the subject, the most recent on February 9th, to determine a regulatory framework to enable the wider use of UAVs by civilians. In America, a bill passed by the Senate on February 6th and now awaiting presidential approval requires the FAA to **draw up** new rules so that the skies can be safely opened to drone flights from October 2015.

That will be easier said than done. How, for example, should a UAV respond if it loses its communications link with the operator on the ground? Should it automatically return to some pre-assigned location, or head for the nearest open space? Should it have a parachute arrangement—like an increasing number of private planes—to lower it gently to the ground in an emergency, or put itself immediately into a **stall**?

Another question is how UAVs should detect, sense and avoid other aircraft operating in the same airspace. So far the FAA has issued around 300 temporary permits for testing drones in airspace where commercial air traffic and private aircraft operate. But because none of the pilotless

无人机的使用。而其限制因素不在技术上，而是如何管理、调度上。在美国，联邦航空管理局（简称**FAA**）目前允许娱乐用途的无人飞机升空，但不允许用作商业活动：比如说，今年早些时候，洛杉矶的房地产经纪人就被禁止使用无人机来航拍他们要出售的房产。

然而，变化正在发生。欧盟委员会已经针对此项议题展开了一系列的听证会，最近的一次在2月9日，确定了一个管理框架，以确保普通人可以更广泛地使用无人驾驶飞机。在美国，2月6日，一项议案已经在参议院被通过，正等待总统批准。该议案要求美国联邦航空管理局起草新的规定，以便从2015年10月起，安全的航空秩序可以为无人机的飞行敞开大门。

说着容易，做着难。比如，如果无人机失去了与地面调度员的通讯联系，它该做出什么反应？应该主动返回某个预先指定的位置呢？还是应该朝最近的空地飞呢？无人机应该安装降落伞装置——像日益增加的私人飞机那样——使它能够在紧急情况下平稳下降并着陆？还是让它立即冲向某个货摊？

另一个问题就是无人驾驶飞机要如何发现、检测并避开同一空域正在飞行的其他飞机。到目前为止，美国联邦航空管理局已经为无人机在商用航空交通和私人飞机所在空域的测试颁发了300多个临时许可证。但是，由

draw up 起草，拟定

stall [stɔːl] n. 货摊

47

aircraft intended for civilian use can yet comply with the FAA's "sense and avoid" rules, a ground observer or chase aircraft is required to keep the drone in sight at all times to act as its eyes.

The FAA's rationale is that drones piloted remotely by operators on the ground cannot see other aircraft in the sky in the way airborne pilots can. Its preferred approach is for UAVs to be fitted with equipment to avoid mid-air collisions and near misses. One solution to the sense-and-avoid problem is to use an array of **lightweight** acoustic probes coupled to a signal processor. By filtering out wind noise, this set-up can listen for and locate other aircraft in the sky—and then transmit avoidance instructions to the drone's operator on the ground, or enable it to take evasive action itself. One such system, developed by SARA, a contract-research firm based in Cypress, California, weighs little more than eight ounces (225 grams).

But given the small size of many drones, and the environments in which they will be used, requiring them all to have elaborate sense-and-avoid systems may be overkill. The majority of pilotless planes that civilian agencies have their eyes on are a little bigger than model aircraft and weigh much the same. One that is fancied by America's 18,000 police forces is a pilotless helicopter called the Qube. This four-rotor craft, made by AeroVironment of Monrovia, California, weighs in at 5.5lb (2.5 kg) and fits easily in the boot of a car. It can be assembled in minutes to provide an immediate eye in the sky capable of

于计划民用的无人驾驶飞机没有一架能够遵守联邦航空管理局的"察觉和避让"条款，因此要求地面观察员或是伴随飞行的飞机充当无人机眼睛的角色，使无人机时刻在其视线范围之内。

联邦航空管理局的理由是远程飞行的无人驾驶飞机是由地面上的操作者操控的，无人机不能像空中的飞机驾驶员那样看到其他飞机。无人机首选的方法就是配备相应的设备，以避免空中的撞机事故和近距离飞行。对于察觉和避让问题，其解决方法就是将一系列比较轻的声波探测器与信号处理器相连接。经过过滤风噪声，这套设备就能够察觉并定位空中的其他飞机了——然后向地面无人机的操作者传送避让指令，或是让无人机本身采取避让行为。这样一个系统，重量不足八盎司(约225克)。由SARA公司研制。该公司的本部设立在加州的塞朴拉斯市，是一家契约研发公司。

但是由于无人机大都体型较小，而这些无人机的使用环境要求它们都要具备复杂的察觉和避让系统，这似乎有点过分了。大部分民间机构看中的无人驾驶飞机都要比现代飞机稍大一点，而重量几乎相等。一架受到美国18000人的警察部队所喜爱的无人驾驶直升机叫做"Qube"。这架拥有四个螺旋桨的飞机是由加州蒙罗维亚的AeroVironment公司制造的，其重量为5.51磅(2.5千克)，可以轻松放进汽车后备箱里。它可以在几分钟内组装完毕，立刻升空监察，每次可在空

---

lightweight ['laitweit] a. 重量轻的

staying aloft for 40 minutes at a time (after which its battery needs recharging).

The Qube and similarly sized drones have about the same kinetic energy as a large bird. In other words, the threat they pose to other planes in the sky and property on the ground **is akin to** a bird strike. That is not to be taken lightly, but is something society has learned to live with. Moreover, such drones are expected to fly well below 400 feet (120 metres), and probably (like the rules governing model aircraft) no closer than 3 miles (5 km) from an airport. That is not exactly Class A airspace used by commercial air traffic, making life-threatening mid-air collisions unlikely.

中停留40分钟（直到电池需要充电为止）。

"Qube"和类似大小的无人机拥有与一只大鸟相同的动能。换句话说，它们对空中的其他飞机和对地面上的房屋的威胁就像鸟类与飞机相撞。这种情况不能掉以轻心，但也需要整个社会学着去接受。此外，人们期望这样的无人机在400英尺（120米）以下平稳飞行，（就像管理模型飞机的规定一样）可能距离飞机场要至少3英里（5公里）。这并不完全是用于空中商业运输的甲级空域，也就不大可能造成威胁生命的空中撞击事件了。

炫·知识

1. European Commission 欧盟委员会

简称欧委会，是欧盟的常设执行机构，也是欧盟惟一有权起草法令的机构。

2. chase aircraft 伴随飞机

这里指能够确保无人机安全飞行的伴随飞机。另外，Chase Aircraft也可指Chase Aircraft Company，是美国的飞机生产制造商。

3. acoustic probe 声波探测器

一种安全救生系统，可以使搜救工作比以往更迅速、更精确，也更安全。

阅读技能练习场

Exercises:

① What does the "nab" mean in the first paragraph?

　A. Supervise.

　B. Follow.

　C. Catch.

　D. Question.

be akin to 类似

2 Why did the author say "That will be easier said than done" in the fourth paragraph?

A. The UAVs need more tests.

B. The European Commission didn't agree a wider use of UAVs.

C. The president didn't approve of the new rules by FAA.

D. UAVs can't detect, sense or avoid other aircrafts operating in the same airspace by themselves.

3 What does "boot" mean in the last but one paragraph?

A. A kind of shoes.

B. Truck.

C. Guide.

D. Back seat.

Reading Skills

1. 锻炼猜词能力，掌握熟词僻义 ★★★★★

阅读中遇到生词，或是熟词放在短语中就不知其意，这是很正常的现象。但是遇到问题不要慌张，从上下文中可以确定其词性、大体词义范围等；对于熟词僻义平时也要不断积累，这样有助于更快地理解文章内容。

> Q1解析：根据上下文猜词义。supervise表"监督"，follow表"跟随"，catch表"抓捕"，question表"询问"，根据题意，选C。

> Q3解析：这道题考查的是单词的熟词僻义。boot一词常见意思是"靴子"，但还有另一个含义是指"汽车后部的行李箱"，这样in the boot of a car就不难理解了，选B。

2. 通过上下文理解句子 ★★★★★

对句子的理解，一定要回到原文中。想要的答案也许就在句子周围，但有时也需要通读全文，对文章大意了解之后，才能对某个句子的含义进行准确的理解。

> Q2解析：首先找到文中这句话的位置。通过上下文可知，想要真正在生活中使用无人机不像想象的那么简单，还有许多问题有待解决。最重要的就是无人机是通过地面的调度人员进行操控，如何在飞行时观察到，并避免与其他飞机相撞成为无人机是否能投入使用的核心问题。因此选D。

Passage 10

Swiss Scientists Demonstrate Mind-controlled Robot
——瑞士科学家展示由意志控制的机器人
——Apr. 24, 2012, The Associated Press

Reading Guide

最近，一个瑞士科学家团队研制出了一种部分瘫痪的人可以通过意志独自控制的机器人。这种机器人对那些手脚麻痹、行动不便，但意志清晰的患者来说，简直是一件意外的礼物。

但是控制这样的机器人也是受很多条件制约的。如何能让患者真正轻松地控制机器人，是科学家们接下来将要面临的挑战。

Swiss scientists have demonstrated how a partially **paralyzed** person can control a robot by thought alone, a step they hope will one day allow immobile people to interact with their surroundings through so-called avatars.

Similar experiments have taken place in the United States and Germany, but they involved either able-bodied patients or invasive brain implants.

On Tuesday, a team at Switzerland's Federal Institute of Technology in Lausanne used only a simple head cap to record the brain signals of Mark-Andre Duc, who was at a hospital in the southern Swiss town of Sion 100 kilometers (62 miles) away.

Duc's thoughts—or rather, the electrical

瑞士科学家们展示了如何让一个部分瘫痪的病人仅凭意志就能控制机器人，他们希望这一进展终有一天能通过这个所谓的"阿凡达"，让不能活动的人与他们的四周有所互动。

在美国和德国也进行过类似的实验，但是他们的试验参与对象要么是体格健全的患者，要么是大脑有植入物的患者。

星期二，在洛桑，瑞士联邦科技研究所的一个团队仅仅使用了一个简单的帽子就记录了马克·安德鲁·德的大脑信号。马克·安德鲁·德在距离锡安山100公里(62英里)远的瑞士南部小镇的一所医院里接受治疗。

德的思想——更确切地说，是当

---

paralyzed ['pærəlaizd] a. 麻痹的，瘫痪的

signals emitted by his brain when he imagined lifting his paralyzed fingers—were decoded almost instantly by a laptop at the hospital. The resulting instructions—left or right—were then transmitted to a foot-tall robot **scooting around** the Lausanne lab.

Duc lost control of his legs and fingers in a fall and is now considered partially quadriplegic. He said controlling the robot wasn't hard on a good day.

"But when I'm in pain it becomes more difficult," he told the Associated Press through a video link screen on a second laptop attached to the robot.

Background noise caused by pain or even a wandering mind has emerged as a major challenge in the research of so-called brain-computer **interfaces** since they first began to be tested on humans more than a decade ago, said Jose Millan, who led the Swiss team.

While the human brain is perfectly capable of performing several tasks at once, a paralyzed person would have to focus the entire time they are directing the device.

"Sooner or later your attention will drop and this will degrade the signal," Millan said.

To **get around** this problem, his team decided to program the computer that decodes the signal so that it works in a similar way to the brain's subconscious. Once a command such as "walk forward" has been sent, the computer will **execute** it until it receives a command to stop or the robot encounters an obstacle.

The robot itself is an advance on a previous project that let patients control an electric wheelchair. By using a robot complete with a

他想象着举起他麻痹的手指时经由大脑发出的脑电波信号——被医院里的一台笔记本电脑几乎同时破译。而随之产生的结果指令——相差无几——就被传送给了一个在洛桑实验室里跑来跑去的一英尺高的机器人那里。

一次摔倒后，德失去了对腿和手指的控制力，现在他被认为是局部的四肢瘫痪者。他说身体状况好的时候，控制机器人不是什么难事。

"但是当我感到疼痛时，控制机器人就变得困难了，"他通过附属于机器人的另外一台笔记本电脑上连接画面的视频告诉美联社。

带领这个瑞士团队的乔斯·米兰说，自从十多年以前，他们第一次开始将所谓的脑-机接口在人体上进行试验开始，疼痛或者甚至是思维游离所导致的背景噪音已经成为所谓的人脑-机脑接口研究中的一个主要挑战。

虽然人类大脑完全有能力同时完成好几个任务，但是一个瘫痪的人在指挥装置的时候必须得集中所有注意力。

"迟早你的注意力会下降，这会使信号降低，"米兰说。

为了解决这个问题，他的团队决定对计算机进行编程来破译这个信号，这样它就能以类似于人脑的潜意识的方式进行工作了。一旦一个指令如"向前走"被发出，电脑就要执行指令，直到收到停止指令或是机器人遇到障碍为止。

对比以前让患者控制电轮椅的项目来说，机器人本身已经是一种进步了。利用装有照相机和屏幕的机器

---

scoot around 漫游
interface ['intəfeis] n. 接口

get around 克服
execute ['eksikju:t] v. 执行

camera and screen, users can extend their virtual presence to places that are **arduous** to reach with a wheelchair, such as an art gallery or a wedding abroad.

Rajesh Rao, an associate professor at the University of Washington, Seattle, who has tested similar systems with able-bodied subjects, said the Lausanne team's research appeared to mark an advance in the field.

"Especially if the system can be used by the paraplegic person outside the laboratory," he said in an email.

Millan said that although the device has already been tested at patients' homes, it isn't as easy to use as some commercially available gadgets that employ brain signals to control simple toys, such Mattel's popular MindFlex headset.

"But this will come true in a matter of years," Millan said.

人，使用者能够扩展他们实际所能到的范围，而这些都是轮椅很难到达的地方，比如说一个美术馆或是一场国外的婚礼现场。

西雅图华盛顿大学的拉杰什·饶副教授曾经用类似的系统在体格健全的受试者身上做过实验，他说洛桑团队的研究似乎标志着这一领域的一次进步。

"尤其是如果这一系统能够被实验室以外的下身瘫痪的病人所使用，"他在邮件中谈到。

米兰说尽管这一设备已经在患者家中进行了试验，但是它并不像一些市面上销售的利用大脑信号来控制简单玩具的小工具那样容易操作，比如马特尔公司生产的广受欢迎的MindFlex耳机。

"但是这将会在未来几年实现，"米兰说。

炫 · 知识

1. so-called avatars 所谓的"阿凡达"

电影《阿凡达》中，男主角双腿瘫痪，是通过意志来控制身高约10英尺(约3米)的克隆蓝色类人生物Na'vi族人。这里借用电影《阿凡达》中的情节作比喻，表示可以通过意志来控制机器人。

2. left or right 相差无几

这里left or right与上文instantly相呼应，可以理解为"几乎同时，相差无几"，说明在电脑即时解码的同时，分析结果也会传送到机器人体内。

3. subject 受试者

这个单词释义很多，"主题；对象；主语"等都很常用，而作为"受试者，测试者"常见于实验、论文中。

---

arduous ['ɑːdjuəs] a. 辛劳的，费力的

阅读技能练习场

Exercises:

1 Which country hasn't had the similar experiments?

A. The United States.

B. Germany.

C. England.

D. Switzerland.

2 What's wrong with Duc's body?

A. His thoughts could be emitted to a laptop.

B. He lost control of his part of body in a fall.

C. He lost control of his legs and fingers in a test.

D. He couldn't control the robot when he's in pain.

3 What could make it more difficult for Duc to control the robot?

A. When he is eating.

B. When he is sleeping.

C. When he feels happy.

D. When he is painful.

Reading Skills

Answers: 1. C   2. B   3. D

1. 读懂题干，利用排除法 ★★★★★

有时选项的描述均正确，但却与题干无关，很容易被误选。因此，首先要理解题干，针对题干对选项进行筛选。

> Q1解析：本题较为简单，可从原文第二段与第三段找到答案，使用排除法。选C。

> Q2解析：读懂题干。选项A与D与题干都没有关系。因此在B与C中选，根据第五段第一句话，可以排除C。

2. 根据上下文，准确找出指代物 ★★★★★

为了不重复描述，已经描述过的事情、动作等一般用it，they等代替。但在记叙文或议论文中，句型结构复杂，因此根据上下文找准所代词指代的具体事物是准确理解文章的关键。

> Q3解析：通过阅读文章，不难发现，第六段引号中的话，正是Duc自己描述的，"但是当我疼痛时，就会更困难，"并且根据上一段controlling the robot wasn't hard on a good way可以推断，it表示的就是controlling the robot这件事。因此，选D。

Passage 11

Breakthrough Announced in Aging Genes Study
——衰老基因研究宣告有新的突破
——Apr. 20th, 2012, Independent

Reading Guide

科学家发现四种人体基因能够决定人类衰老的速度和健康水平。而这些衰老基因是否起作用还要取决于环境因素和生活方式。科学家发现环境中的外界因素导致的DNA化学变化是衰老的重要因素，即后生因素。

Four "Father Time" genes that help determine how fast we age have been uncovered by scientists.

The **aging genes** are switched on or off by environmental and lifestyle factors such as diet, and may be programmed from an early age.

Knowing how the genes are altered could **pave the way to** new generations of anti-ageing drugs, researchers believe.

Scientists already knew that "epigenetic" changes—chemical alterations to DNA made by external factors in the environment—are important to ageing.

The new research goes some way towards solving the **riddle** of how and when these effects

科学家已经发现了四种可以决定我们衰老速度的"时间老人"基因。

这些衰老基因是否起作用要取决于环境因素和生活方式因素，如饮食，而且这些基因可能会在年龄很小的时候就开始起作用。

研究者相信，了解基因是如何变异的可以为研究新一代的抗衰老药做好准备。

科学家已经掌握了"表观的"变异——由环境中的外界因素而造成的DNA的化学变化——是衰老的重要因素。

某种程度上，新的研究是为了解开这些效应是如何产生、何时发生的

aging gene 衰老基因
pave the way to 为……铺平道路，为……做铺垫

riddle ['ridl] n. 谜语

occur.

Dr. Jordana Bell, from King's College London, one of the study authors, said: "We found that epigenetic changes associate with age-related traits that have previously been used to define biological age.

"We identified many age-related epigenetic changes, but four seemed to impact the rate of healthy ageing and potential **longevity** and we can use these findings as potential markers of aging.

"These results can help understand the biological mechanisms underlying healthy ageing and age-related disease, and future work will explore how environmental effects can affect these epigenetic changes."

The scientists, whose work is reported in the online journal *Public Library of Science Genetics*, first looked for epigenetic changes in the DNA of 172 twins aged 32 to 80.

Twins are often used in such studies because identical pairs share exactly the same genes, making it possible to tease apart genetic and environmental effects.

It one identical twin displays very different characteristics from the other, it means the cause cannot be genetic.

Analysing the changes in relation to **chronological** age, the researchers identified 490 age-related epigenetic changes.

Matching these to specific age-related traits

这个谜团。

来自伦敦国王学院的乔达娜·贝尔博士，该项研究的作者之一，说："我们发现表观变异与年龄相关的特征有关，而这些特征之前是用来定义生理年龄的。"

"我们发现了许多与年龄相关的表观变异，但是其中四种因素似乎影响着健康老化的速度与潜在寿命，我们可以利用这些研究结果作为人体衰老的潜在标志。"

"这些成果能够帮助我们理解健康衰老和与年龄相关的疾病的生物机制，并且未来的工作就是探索环境效应是如何影响这些表观变异的。"

科学家们的著作被刊登在网络杂志《公共科学图书馆遗传学》上。他们首先研究了年龄在32岁到80岁之间的172名双胞胎的DNA上的表观变异。

双胞胎经常被用在这类研究中，这是因为每一对同卵双胞胎恰好拥有相同的基因，这就使区分基因影响与环境影响成为可能。

如果同卵双胞胎其中之一表现出与其双胞胎兄弟（姐妹）相差很大的特征，这就说明不可能是遗传基因因素引起的。

经过分析与年龄大小有关的变异，研究者认定了490种与年龄相关的表观变异。

把这些表现差异与具体的年龄相

---

longevity [lɔn'dʒevəti] n. 寿命；长寿　　　　chronological [,krɔnə'lɔdʒikəl] a. 按时间顺序的

highlighted four genes displaying changes linked to **cholesterol** levels, lung function and maternal lifespan.

Further research showed that many of the epigenetic DNA alterations were also present in a group of 44 younger twins aged 22 to 61.

This suggests that while many age-related genetic changes caused by environmental factors occur throughout a person's life, some might be triggered early on.

Professor Tim Spector, director of the Department of Twin Research at King's College, said: "This study is the first glimpse of the potential that large twin studies have to find the key genes involved in aging, how they can be modified by lifestyle and start to develop **anti-aging** therapies.

"The future will be very exciting for age research."

Gene **experts** at the Wellcome Trust Sanger Institute in Hinxton, Cambridgeshire, played a key role in the study.

Sanger scientist Dr. Panos Deloukas pointed out that the research was still at an early stage.

"Our study interrogated only a fraction of sites in the genome (genetic code) that carry such epigenetic changes; these initial findings support the need for a more comprehensive scan of epigenetic variation," he said.

关的特征相匹配,就凸显出了与胆固醇水平、肺功能和产妇寿命有联系的四种基因。

进一步的研究表明许多表观遗传的DNA变异在年龄在22岁到61岁之间的22组年轻一点的双胞胎中也出现了。

这说明,尽管由环境因素所引起的许多与年龄相关的基因变异会自始至终影响一个人的一生,但一些基因变异有可能是在早期就发生了。

国王学院双胞胎研究部的主任,蒂姆·斯佩克特教授,表示:"这项研究使用了大量的双胞胎,第一次为找到与衰老相关的决定性基因提供了可能性,研究了它们是如何被生活方式所改变的,并开始开发抗衰老的治疗方法。"

"未来对年龄的研究将会非常令人兴奋。"

在剑桥郡的辛克斯顿镇,威康信托基金会桑格研究所的基因专家们在这项研究中起到了决定性的作用。

桑格的科学家帕诺斯·迪鲁卡斯博士指出这项研究仍处于初级阶段。

"我们的研究仅仅是对在基因组(遗传密码)上带有同样表观变异的一小部分人进行了询问调查;这些初步的研究表明我们需要对表观变异进行更全面的研究,"他说。

---

cholesterol [kə'lestərɔl] n. 胆固醇
anti-aging [ˌænti'eidʒiŋ] a. 抗衰老的

expert ['ekspə:t] n. 专家

炫·知识

1. "epigenetic" changes 表观变异

正如文中所解释的那样，是一种由环境中的外界因素所引起的DNA的化学变化。而表观遗传学(epigenetics)则是指基于非基因序列改变所致基因表达水平变化。

2. King's College London 伦敦国王学院

伦敦国王学院简称为KCL或King's，是全英赫赫有名而且世界知名的国际顶尖大学，其医学、法律更是享誉海内外。

3. identical pairs 同卵双胞胎

在文中指代identical twins。与其相对fraternal twins为"异卵双胞胎"。两者区别在于是否由同一受精卵分裂而成。医学上认为同卵双胞胎是真正的双胞胎，因为其性别相同，身体许多基因及特征也相似，这也正是科学家用同卵双胞胎做实验的原因。

阅读技能练习场

Exercises:

1. What does "switched on or off" mean in the second paragraph?

    A. Turn on or off.

    B. Work or not.

    C. Open or close.

    D. Right or wrong.

2. How many age-related epigenetic changes may impact the rate of aging and longevity?

    A. 4.

    B. 5.

    C. 6.

    D. 7.

3. What can the scientists infer from the further research?

    A. Many genetic changes are caused by the environment.

B. Many of the epigenetic DNA alterations are present in the group of 44 twins.

C. Many age-related genetic changes occur throughout one's life.

D. Four genes are linked to cholesterol levels, lung function and lifespan.

Answers:
1.B 2.A 3.C

Reading Skills

1. 根据上下文，充分理解句意 ★★★★★

在特殊环境下，单词或者词组可以指代特定的事物。正确判断其意义就要根据上下文，全面思考。

> **Q1解析：** 根据第二段第一句话的意思，理解为衰老基因是否起作用，取决于周围环境和生活方式等因素。因此选B。
>
> **Q3解析：** 首先要在原文中找到further research。因此通过第14和15段可以找出further research的研究结果，选C。

2. 注意文章中出现的数字 ★★★★★

议论文中对论点的描述会分几个方面，并对其一一进行说明。加强对数字的敏感度，可以更快地梳理文章结构。

> **Q2解析：** 加强对数字的敏感度。根据第七段内容，可以知道答案为A。

Passage 12

The Smarter Cars Keep Older Drivers on the Roads Longer

——智能汽车延长老年司机的驾驶寿命

——Apr. 23rd, 2012, Independent

Reading Guide

老年人能否安全开车上路？近日，科学家专门为65岁以上的老人设计了一款汽车，它能实时监控老年驾驶者的健康状态及驾驶状态，提高了老年人开车上路的安全性。该款汽车将在六月美国老龄化、流动性与生活质量的论坛上公开亮相。新车测试将会持续一年之久。

Scientists have built an "emotionally intelligent" electric car that aims to keep people over 65 on the roads for longer.

Fitted with **a range of** devices from eye-tracking **goggles** to biometric technology that monitors heart rates and **cardiovascular** health, the modified Peugeot iOn will monitor drivers' concentration, stress levels and driving habits. It is hoped that the findings will pave the way for new technology that will **instill** confidence in drivers over 65 and keep them safe on the road for longer.

Scientists at Newcastle University created the so-called "Drivelab" as part of a wider research project that comes amid concern for the safety

科学家已经制造出一款具有"情商"的电动汽车，旨在延长年逾65的老年人的驾驶寿命。

装置了从眼球追踪护目镜到生物识别技术等一系列能够监控驾驶者的心率和心血管健康状况的设备，这款改进后的标致iOn将会监控驾驶者的注意力、紧张程度和驾驶习惯。人们希望测试结果会为新技术的发展铺平道路，这种新技术将会增添65岁以上驾驶员的信心，从而延长他们的驾驶寿命。

纽卡斯尔大学的科学家们创设了所谓的"驾驶实验室"，作为进行更广泛研究的项目的一部分，该项目

---

a range of 一系列
goggle ['gɔgl] n. 护目镜
cardiovascular [ˌkɑːdiəu'væskjulə] a. 心脑血管的
instill [in'stil] v. 逐渐灌输

of elderly drivers. Statistics from the Department of Transport suggest they are one of the highest-risk groups for injury or death on Britain's roads. There are now up to six million licence-holders over 70, compared with fewer than a million 35 years ago.

Phil Blythe, who is leading the project, said, "We have to accept that, as we get older, our reactions slow down and this often results in people avoiding any potentially challenging driving condition and losing confidence in their driving skills."

"The result is that people stop driving before they really need to. We are looking at ways of keeping people driving safely for longer, which in turn **boosts** independence and keeps us socially connected."

The findings may eventually lead to a range of new technologies to help elderly motorists. They include sensors that assist with parking blind spots, "forward-facing radars" that warn drivers how close they are to other vehicles, as well as "heads up" dashboard displays projected on to the windscreen.

The group will also research new satellite navigation technology that is more suitable for over-65s. Instead of the traditional direction-led audio navigation, this could include directions given through visual cues such as an upcoming post box, pub or petrol station.

The research is part of a project funded by the Research Councils U.K. Digital Economy

关注的是老年驾驶者的安全问题。来自运输部的统计数据表明，他们是英国道路事故伤亡的高危人群之一。目前，年龄超过70岁的驾照持有人数高达600万，而35年前这一数字还不足100万。

领导该项目的菲尔·布莱斯表示："我们不得不接受这一事实，随着我们变老，我们的反应也会慢下来，而这常常会导致人们避开任何具有潜在挑战的驾驶环境，并对自己的驾驶技术失去信心。"

"结果便是人们会在真正不能驾驶之前就放弃开车了。我们正在研究的就是能延长人们安全驾驶时间的方法，这也恰恰能够增强我们的独立能力，保持我们与社会的联系。"

研究结果可能最终会催生出一系列有助于老年驾驶员的新技术。它们包括传感器——能够帮助人们盲点停车，"车头前置雷达"——提示驾驶者与其他车辆之间的距离，还有投射在挡风玻璃上的"警觉"仪表显示盘。

该团队还将研发新的更适合65岁以上人群使用的卫星导航技术。与传统引导方向的声音导航不同，新技术还包括通过视觉线索给出方向，比如即将到达的邮筒、酒吧或加油站。

该项研究是英国研究理事会总会的数字经济计划所资助的项目的一

---

boost [buːst] v. 提高

Programme. The car will be unveiled at a **seminar** on ageing, mobility and quality of life in the U.S. in June. Trials will continue over the next year.

部分。新款汽车将在六月举行的关于"美国老龄化、流动性与生活质量"的论坛上公开亮相。新车测试将会持续一年的时间。

炫 · 知识

1. Peugeot 标致

标致是世界十大汽车公司之一，法国最大的汽车集团公司，雄狮形象是该品牌的标识。1896年，别儒在蒙贝利亚尔创建了标致汽车公司。1976年该公司与雪铁龙汽车公司组成标致集团，成为欧洲第三大汽车公司。

2. blind spot 盲点

在医学上，视网膜上无感光细胞的部位称为盲点。汽车后视镜的盲点在45度左右的地方。当你跟在别人的车后面时，最好不要长时间呆在前车的盲区，以免对方看不见你而突然转向。

3. satellite navigation technology 卫星导航技术

用导航卫星对地面、海洋、空中和空间用户进行定位导航的技术。文中所述的新型卫星导航不仅可以对位置进行定位、导航，还可以对附近的邮箱、酒吧、加油站等进行定位。

阅读技能练习场

Exercises:

1 What can't the Peugeot iOn do for older drivers?

    A. Monitor the drivers' concentration.

    B. Monitor the drivers' stress levels.

    C. Monitor the drivers' diet.

    D. Monitor the drivers' driving habits.

2 Why did the project develop smarter cars for older drivers?

    A. The older people are the highest-risk group for injury or death on roads.

seminar ['seminɑː] n. 研讨会

B. The older drivers on roads are dangerous to others.

C. When people get older, their reactions slow down.

D. To keep older drivers safe on the roads longer.

3 Where and when will we see this kind of car on public?

A. In the lab of Newcastle University next year.

B. At a seminar in the U.S. in June.

C. On the Britain's roads 35 years later.

D. At a post box, pub or petrol station now.

Reading Skills

1. 仔细阅读文章，巧用排除法 ★★★★★

阅读文章时，不能凭主观想象作答，这样很容易出错。我们应该通过仔细阅读文章来发现选项中的陷阱，并避免犯错。

> **Q1解析：** 根据第二段第一句话：Fitted with a range of devices from eye-tracking goggles to biometric technology that monitors heart rates and cardiovascular health, the modified Peugeot iOn will monitor drivers' concentration, stress levels and driving habits. 因此可知选C。

> **Q3解析：** 仔细阅读文章不难发现，在前面描述的针对老年人的智能汽车都是基于数据、原理等的实验过程，并没有成品。而最后一段倒数第二句话告诉我们智能汽车将最终展出，选B。此题较简单。

2. 理清事情的前因后果 ★★★★★

当题干对事情的原因设问时，选项中往往会给出几个干扰项来分散答题者的注意力。这时，要通过文章理清事情的前因后果，自然就能轻松排除干扰选项。

> **Q2解析：** 理清事物的因果关系。题干问的是Why，即原因，选项A是对数据结果的陈述，选项B在文中没有提到，选项C是原因的理论支持，而选项D是开展该项目的直接原因。

Passage 13

Bell Labs and Innovation：The Organization of Genius
——贝尔实验室与创新：天才的摇篮
——Apr. 21st, 2012, Economist

Reading Guide

1947年12月，第一个晶体管在贝尔实验室诞生。从贝尔实验室创办开始到现在，它不断给全世界带来科技的创新和技术的突破。在当今世界，它依然能给人们带来惊喜吗？它在哪方面又有了新的创意和发展呢？

—*The Idea Factory: Bell Labs and the Great Age of American Innovation.*

"My first stop on any time-travel **expedition**", Bill Gates once said, "would be Bell Labs in December 1947." That was the time and place of the invention of the **transistor**, which powered the technology revolution that built today's connected world. The handful of scientists who gathered in downtown Manhattan to witness the first demonstration of this transformational technology understood that it was special. The transistor was, one observer noted, "a basically new thing in the world" (other Bell Labs discoveries would earn the same astonished praise). The breakthrough was so big that William Shockley, the boss of the two scientists who made it, spent the next weeks

——创意工厂：贝尔实验室和美国创新的伟大年代。

比尔·盖茨曾经说过，"如果可以进行时间旅行探索，那么我首选的第一站无论哪次都会是1947年12月的贝尔实验室。"晶体管这种新事物就是那个时候在那里发明的，正是它促成了技术革命，才使今日的互联网世界能够得以构建。当时曾聚集在曼哈顿市中心的为数不多的几位科学家亲眼目睹了这种转换技术的首次展示，所以他们理解这项技术的特别之处。一位观察员解释道，晶体管的本质是"世界上的一种全新事物"（贝尔实验室的其他发明也得到了同样令人震惊的赞誉）。这次巨大的突破让实验室

---

expedition [ˌekspiˈdiʃən] n. 探险

transistor [trænˈsistə] n. 晶体管

in torment until he designed a better version. In doing so he broke a **sacred** Bell Labs rule— "absolutely never to compete with underlings"— for which he was never forgiven.

The men of Bell Labs (the scientists were **overwhelmingly** male) are brought to life by Jon Gertner in "The Idea Factory", his wonderful history of the most influential corporate-research lab the world has seen. A writer for the *New York Times* Magazine, Mr. Gertner does a super job of making complex science **intelligible** to the lay reader. He frequently evokes a sense of awe at how this army of scientists (Bell Labs employed about 15,000 people at its 1960s peak) made a reality of what even for them was often unthinkable. The first transistor was a quarter of the size of an American penny; now a computer-processor chip, the size of a postage stamp, contains 2 billion transistors. Intel makes 10 billion transistors every second. Who could have imagined it?

Bell Labs, the research arm of AT&T, was created in the second decade of the 20th century. Its original job was to work out how to make telephone calls from New York to San Francisco, but it was also meant to **deflect** criticism of the

老板，制造了晶体管的两名科学家之一的威廉姆·肖克利在接下来的几周里备受煎熬地进行研究，直到设计出更好的版本。这样做使他违背了贝尔实验室的一项神圣规则——"绝对不要与下属竞争"——也正是因为这一点，他一直没有得到原谅。

贝尔实验室的男士们（绝大多数科学家都是男性）因乔恩·格特尼的"创意工厂"获得新生，这是这家世界上最有影响的企业研究实验室的伟大历史。作为《纽约时报》的作者，格特尼先生将一些复杂的科学知识转化成了通俗易懂的、可以被大众接受的知识，他在这方面做得非常出色。他经常激起人们对这支科学家大军(在20世纪60年代，贝尔实验室的顶峰时期雇员达到了大约一万五千人)的敬畏，因为他们将那些甚至是他们自己都不可想象的事情变成了现实。第一个晶体管是一美分硬币的四分之一大小；现在，邮票大小的电脑处理器芯片中包含着20亿个晶体管。英特尔每秒钟制造100亿个晶体管。谁曾幻想过这些呢？

贝尔实验室作为AT&T的科研武装力量，创建于二十世纪的20年代。它最初的工作是解决纽约与旧金山之间通电话的问题，但也有意通过成为美国电话通信的研究动力，来转移他

---

sacred ['seikrid] a. 神圣的
overwhelmingly [,əuvə'welmiŋli] ad. 压倒地

intelligible [in'telidʒəbl] a. 可理解的
deflect [di'flekt] v. 偏离

firm's **monopoly** by becoming America's engine of telephonic research. Bell Labs grew to do everything, from basic science with little obvious practical application to the detailed work of turning an idea into a marketable innovation. Its later buildings in New Jersey were designed with long corridors to ensure unplanned interactions between people, some of whom were notably **eccentric**—Claude Shannon, the father of information theory, rode down these hallways on a unicycle—but all were strikingly bright, and several won Nobel prizes. The best bosses, such as John Pierce, were not so good at managing people but were masters at managing ideas.

Now owned by Alcatel-Lucent, what remains of Bell Labs is a shadow of its former self, and not just because its longtime mission of achieving "universal connectivity" has been surpassed. AT&T's monopoly has gone, and companies care more about short-term profits than costly blue-sky research on the scale Bell Labs once had, even at Apple, IBM or Google. Besides, thanks to Silicon Valley, with its angels and **venture** capitalists, hot start-ups and billionaire **entrepreneurs**, a new, disaggregated model of research and innovation is in vogue. But after a few hours of time-travel into "The Idea Factory", this does not feel entirely like progress.

人对公司垄断的批评之声。随着贝尔实验室的发展，它开始踏入更多领域，从那些几乎没有明显实际用途的基础科学，到将创意转变成可以到市场上出售的创新产品的详细工作都有涉及。贝尔实验室后来位于新泽西的大楼都设计有长长的走廊，保证人们之间可以自然地与他人交流互动，这些科学家中的一些人极其古怪——比如信息理论之父克劳德·香农，他曾沿着走廊骑独轮车——但这些人都极其聪明，有几位还获得了诺贝尔奖。最棒的老板们虽然对管理员工不太在行，但却是管理创新理念的大师，比如约翰·皮尔斯。

现在由阿尔卡特·朗讯公司经营的贝尔实验室仅是它前身的影子，这不仅是因为它长期以来实现"全球联通"的目标已被超越。AT&T的垄断已经不复存在，各家公司也更在乎短期的获利，而不是贝尔实验室曾经从事的那种大规模的昂贵且不切实际的研究，即使是苹果、IBM或者谷歌也如此。另外，幸亏还有硅谷以及那里的天使投资支持者和风险投资家，热门新兴企业和亿万富翁企业家，一种全新的、分散的研究与创新模式正在蔚然成风。但经过"创意工场"几小时的时间旅行之后，就会感觉这并不完全是进步。

monopoly [mə'nɔpəli] n. 垄断
eccentric [ik'sentrik] a. 古怪的

venture ['ventʃə] n. 风险
entrepreneur [,ɔntrəprə'nə:] n. 企业家

炫 · 知识

1. Bell Labs 贝尔实验室

贝尔电话实验室或贝尔实验室，最初是贝尔系统内从事包括电话交换机、电话电缆、半导体等电信相关技术的研究开发机构。

2. time-travel 时间旅行

时间旅行，或称时空旅行、时光旅行、穿越等，泛指人或者其它物体由某一时间点移动到另外一个时间点。

3. blue-sky 不切实际的

blue-sky的字面意思是"蓝天"，但是构成合成词之后，其意思是"不切实际的"，比喻事物和蓝天一样虚无。

阅读技能练习场

Exercises:

1. Why are transistors so important in humans' history?

A. Because they are a kind of new things in the world.

B. Because scientists know their specialty.

C. They powered the technology revolution that built today's connected world.

D. They're cheap and the mass production of them is possible.

2. What can't we get about Jon Gertner from the passage?

A. He's a writer for the *New York Times* Magazine.

B. He has a successful writing career.

C. He could make complex science intelligible to the lay reader.

D. He let people take a look at Bell Labs through his writing.

3. Which of the following is not correct according to the passage?

A. Transistors are getting smaller as time goes by.

B. Bell Labs changed our world greatly by its inventions.

C. Bell Labs is still the research arm of AT&T.

D. Claude Shannon is famous for having founded information theory.

Reading Skills

1. 根据文中信息作答 ★ ★ ★ ★ ★

　　解题时，要根据题目要求检索文中的有关信息，进行判断和选择，选项中如果含有文中没有体现，或完全推断不出来的信息时，就可以把它们排除。

> **Q1解析**：此题关于晶体管的重要性，C选项在文中有明确提及。A、B两选项与其重要性无关。而D选项说它们"便宜且可大规模生产"，这在文中并无表述。
>
> **Q2解析**：A、C、D三个选项在第三段中均有提及，但原文并没有关于他的事业是否"成功"的语句。所以选B。

2. 仔细审题 ★ ★ ★ ★ ★

　　认真读题干是解题的第一个步骤，随后可以快速浏览题目中提供的选项，按选项涉及的内容将它们归类，然后再根据原文进行判断，不过，同时也要注意选项的表述是否合理。

> **Q3解析**：A选项在第三段末尾处有体现。B项在文中也有提到，因为在贝尔实验室制造了第一个晶体管，而它powered the technology revolution that built today's connected world。C项错在根据最后一段第一句，可得知贝尔实验室现在的拥有者为Alcatel-Lucent。D项根据the father of information theory可知是正确的。

Passage 14

Infrared and 3-D Vision Systems Help Pilots Avoid Crash Landings

——红外线和3D可视技术助飞行员避免着陆撞击事故

——Feb. 8th, 2012, Scientific American

Reading Guide

飞机的出现带给了我们便利的生活，却一直以来让人担忧它的安全性。其实不仅仅是飞行过程中容易出现安全性的问题，在降落着陆的过程中也有安全问题。新技术的出现能帮助飞行员更好地预判地面情况，保证了整机人员的安全。

When large airliners approach an airport for a landing, a combination of radio signals and high-intensity lighting shows the pilot exactly where the runway is, even at night or in fog. But millions of people a year fly on smaller commercial planes and many private, which do not have such technology. The pilots of those craft must rely on less **sophisticated** instruments, along with their **cockpit** window view during landing, a situation that can be fatal in bad weather. In 2011 alone four such commercial jets crashed into terrain or an obstacle, killing 140 passengers and

当大型客机驶向机场准备着陆时，广播信号和高强度信号灯会提示飞行员哪里是跑道，甚至是在夜晚或大雾弥漫的时候。但是每年有数百万人乘坐小型的商业机和许多私人飞机，而这些飞机都没有这项技术。这些飞机的驾驶员必须依靠不太精密的仪器和对自己着陆过程中窗外情景的推测，而这种方式的致命大敌就是坏天气。根据航空设备制造人员哈尼维尔以及航空航天公司艾森德公司提供的数据，仅在2011年就有4架这种类型

---

sophisticated [səˈfistikeitid] a. 复杂的，精密的

cockpit [ˈkɔkpit] n. 驾驶员座舱

crew, according to avionics-maker Honeywell and **aerospace** research firm Ascend. The accidents are known as "controlled flight into terrain".

Landings could be safer if new **navigation** displays featuring nighttime infrared imaging and 3-D graphics that accurately portray an aircraft's surroundings become standard equipment on smaller commercial and private planes. In addition to the potential safety benefits, Gulfstream, Bombardier and other makers of small and midsize business jets are also learning that the same technology can save time and money by keeping flights on schedule even in the face of weather that would normally require runway circling or flight rerouting.

Synthetic Vision

The new technology, which this writer observed firsthand during a recent test flight, actually combines and **leapfrogs** two earlier technologies only recently being installed on smaller commercial craft. Synthetic vision systems (SVSs) use terrain data culled from actual flights and stored in a database to create a 3-D graphical interface (think Windows or Mac OS) on a screen in front of the pilot and co-pilot, enabling them to see a digital model of their surroundings even when their vision is obscured by darkness or clouds. SVSs also include information about the location of airports and runways, to help guide pilots until they can establish visual contact with their landing destinations.

的商业飞机因撞上地面或障碍物，导致140名乘客和机组人员丧生。这些事故被称为"可控飞行撞地"。

新的导航技术以夜间红外线成像和准确描绘飞机周围环境的3D图形为特色。如果这一技术成为小型商务机和私人飞机的标准配备，着陆就会安全很多。除了潜在的安全优势，湾流公司、庞巴迪公司和其他中小型商务喷气机制造者也认识到，同样的技术能够省时省钱，即使是在需要更改跑道或改变航线的恶劣天气里，也能保证航班准时。

综合视觉技术

笔者在最近的飞行测试中观察到的一手的新技术实际上综合并超越了两项早期的最近才用在小型商业机上的技术。综合视觉系统使用从实际飞行中挑选的地形数据，并储存在数据库中，在驾驶员和副驾驶前的屏幕上创造出3D图像界面（想想windows系统或是Mac OS系统），即便是黑夜或云层挡住其视线时，他们也能看到周围情况的数字模型。综合视觉系统也包括飞机降落机场和跑道的信息，来帮助引导飞行员，直到他们可以和着陆地建立可视化的联络。

---

aerospace ['eərəuspeis] n. 航天
navigation [ˌnævi'geiʃən] n. 航行

synthetic [sin'θetik] a. 合成的
leapfrog ['liːpfrɔg] v. 跃过

Combined Vision

Although SVSs can improve safety, a newer technology that incorporates the two may eclipse it. Honeywell Aerospace, which sells an SVS for several Gulfstream and Dassault Falcon business jets and is developing an EVS, is one of a handful of companies pushing the development of a "combined vision system" (CVS) in which the pilot can see a mashup of 3-D graphics and infrared imagery. Individually, SVS has limitations. Because SVS is driven by stored databases, it may not display the latest changes in terrain, obstacles and urban feature data. And the infrared cameras cannot see through clouds or fog, and they also have a limited field of view that restricts the image to a small area.

Regardless of the details of how they are designed, CVS is the future of aviation safety, even if it will take a few years before it is commercially available, Bailey says. "Synthetic and enhanced vision systems are two different technologies but they're actually complementary," he adds. "What makers of CVS technology are trying to do is to develop one display that has the best of both worlds."

综合影像

尽管综合视觉系统能提高安全性，一项更新的包含了这两项技术的技术可以覆盖它。哈尼维尔航空航天公司为一些湾流公司、达索猎鹰公司的商务机出售综合视觉系统，并且正在研发EVS，它是几个推进"综合视觉系统"发展的公司之一，这项技术中飞行员能看到混合的3D视图以及红外线图像。单独来看，综合视觉系统有许多局限性。因为它是由储存的数据库里的数据驱动的，也许不能及时更新最新的地形、障碍物和城市建筑的数据变化。红外线相机不能穿透云雾的遮挡，它们也有在视野方面的限制，把视野限制到很小的范围。

贝利说，忽略它们的设计细节，即使还需要几年它才能商业化，综合视觉系统是航空安全的未来。"综合视觉系统和加强视觉系统是两项完全不同的技术，但是它们实际上是相互补充的，"贝利补充道。创造综合视觉系统技术的工作人员正试着开发出能够充分利用两者的系统。"

炫 · 知识

1. controlled flight into terrain 可控飞行撞地

"可控飞行撞地"是指一架处于适航状态的飞机，在飞行机组控制之下，与地面、障碍物或者水面发生相撞的事故，而飞行机组却对将要发生的相撞事先毫无察觉，结果造成飞机坠毁、严重损坏和人员伤亡。

2. Bombardier 庞巴迪公司

庞巴迪公司是行业排名世界第一的交通运输设备制造商，主要产品有支线飞机、公务喷气飞机、铁路及高速铁路机车、城市轨道交通设备等。

阅读技能练习场

Exercises:

1 According to the passage, what could show the pilot exactly where the runway is?

    A. Radio signals.

    B. High-intensity lighting.

    C. Combination of radio signals and high-intensity lighting.

    D. Cockpit window view.

2 Which description is NOT right?

    A. Millions of people a year fly on smaller commercial planes and many private, which do not have such technology.

    B. Landings could be safer if new navigation displays feature nighttime infrared imaging.

    C. SVSs help guide pilots until they can establish visual contact with their landing destinations.

    D. In 2011 alone four such commercial jets crashed into terrain or an obstacle, killing 140 passengers.

3 Why is CVS more advanced than others?

    A. Through CVS, pilots can see a mashup of 3-D graphics and infrared imagery.

    B. Because SVS is driven by stored databases, it may not display the latest changes in terrain, obstacles and urban feature data.

    C. The infrared cameras cannot see through clouds or fog, and they also have a limited field of view that restricts the image to a small area.

    D. We cannot infer.

Answers:
1. C　2. D　3. A

1. 注意答案不要以偏概全 ★ ★ ★ ★ ★

　　有时，答案选项里会出现不止一个我们认为正确的答案，遇到这种情况，我们要根据文章整体分析，选出最有综合性的答案。

> 　　**Q1解析**：答案A和B都是对的，答案C也是正确的。这是一道很简单的问题，根据文章的第一自然段，我们可以发现只有C是最完整的答案，所以正确答案是C。
>
> 　　**Q3解析**：其实这道题给出的选项里，B和C也都没有错，都是出自原文。但是仔细看问题，问题主要是关于CVS，我们就应该注重从这项技术的角度选择答案，B和C说的是其他两项技术的限制性，所以正确答案是A。

2. 注意原文细节 ★ ★ ★ ★ ★

　　有一类是非题主要问的是描述或者表达是否正确，遇到这种情况，没有其他讨巧的办法，只能回到原文中再去一一核实，选择正确答案。

> 　　**Q2解析**：看过选项不难发现，4个选项出自整篇文章的不同段落。问题是要求我们找出错误描述的那一句，根据原文不难发现D选项与原文有出入，原文说的是140名乘客和机组人员遇难，D选项只提到了乘客，所以正确答案是D。

Chapter 03
科技风向 Trends

Passage 15

The Cloud Goes Hollywood
——云技术风潮席卷好莱坞
——Feb. 3rd, 2012, Fortune

Reading Guide

　　云技术进一步走进了我们的生活，这一次影响的是电影行业。紫外光格式的诞生让看电影成了生活中更加平常和方便的事情。此后要欣赏精彩的电影，只需注册一个储存空间，不必再担心电影院的拥挤，也不必再排队购买限量版的DVD，甚至不必为盗版烦恼。

Consumers who recently purchased Warner Brothers' final *Harry Potter* film on DVD or Blu-ray found a surprise in the package: a digital copy of the movie in the new UltraViolet format. Although the name is not yet familiar, UltraViolet represents Hollywood's first step into the cloud—the much-hyped idea that media will be stored on remote servers and accessed by various devices.

The idea behind UltraViolet is simple: The format allows buyers to own rights to films, which they can store in a "digital locker" and access via various Internet services. It's potentially a huge convenience for consumers, who now have a **dizzying** number of devices (phones, tablets, computers) on which they can watch video content, and indeed, some 750,000 households in the U.S. and Britain have set up UltraViolet accounts, its

最近购买了华纳兄弟电影公司发售的《哈利·波特》终结篇电影的DVD或是蓝光光碟的顾客会在包装里发现一个惊喜：紫外光格式的电子版数字拷贝。虽然这一名称还不为人所熟知，但紫外光技术代表好莱坞向云技术迈出的第一步——这个让人无比兴奋的理念意味着电影媒体将被储存在远程服务器上，而且可以被各种各样的设备读取。

紫外光技术的理念十分简单：这种格式使顾客能够拥有电影的所有权，这样他们就可以把电影储存在"数字储物柜"中，并利用各种的网络服务设备读取。这对顾客来说是极大的便利，如今他们拥有多到眼花缭乱的各种设备（例如电话、平板电脑或是台式电脑）可以用来观看视频内容。事实上，该技术的支持者表示大约有

---

dizzy ['dizi] a. 晕眩的

75

backers say.

For the studios the stakes are high: DVD sales, which peaked at $15.5 billion in 2004, have stalled as consumers have turned to streaming services such as Netflix (NFLX) or, worse, illegal downloads. The studios that have announced releases in the UltraViolet format (Fox is expected to announce soon; Disney (DIS) remains a holdout) believe UltraViolet will help goose home video sales by enabling consumers to build a remotely stored library of movies. "We know consumers like collecting movies," says Mitch Singer, president of the Digital Entertainment Content Ecosystem, the consortium that controls UltraViolet.

5 Ways the Cloud Will Change

The consortium believes the UltraViolet format addresses industry and consumer concerns around **compatibility** and **piracy**. Working with tech company Neustar (NSR) the group developed a system that operates more like an entertainment ATM. When users sign in, it **queries** a central database to see what movies they have rights to watch —much as an ATM checks how much money cardholders can withdraw.

The format isn't without its challenges. Setting up a digital locker takes time. Customers must first create an UltraViolet account; and then, to watch movies online, they sign in to Flixster, a movie site operated by Warner Bros., which like *Fortune*, is a unit of Time Warner (TWX).

But the biggest hurdle could be competition from technology companies such as Apple (AAPL),

75万个美国及英国家庭已经开设了紫外光技术账户。

对于工作室来说利益也很高：DVD的销量在2004年达到顶峰，销售量高达155亿美金，然而由于消费者转为使用例如网飞等公司提供的媒体流服务，或者更糟糕的盗版下载现象，DVD销量开始止步不前。那些已经宣布发行紫外光技术格式的影视工作室（福克斯公司有望立即宣布；迪士尼则仍在坚持）相信，通过授权消费者建立远程储存的电影图书馆，紫外光技术将使家庭视频产品的销售大幅上升。"我们知道消费者喜欢收集电影，"数字化娱乐内容生态系统董事长米奇·圣家这样说道。该集团控制着紫外光技术。

云技术将以5种方式改变行业

该集团相信紫外光格式可以解决电影业和消费者关心的兼容性及盗版问题。该集团通过与中立星技术公司合作，开发了一种操作上十分接近ATM的娱乐系统。用户一旦登录，系统就会查询中央数据库，根据该用户的权限选出可以观看的电影——这非常像ATM机检验取款人可以取用多少金额的过程。

这种格式也面临着挑战。设置一个数据存储空间也需要花费时间。用户必须先建立一个紫外光账户；然后才能在线观看电影。他们必须登录菲力克斯特网站，该网站由华纳兄弟公司运营，就像《财富》周刊是时代华纳公司的一部分那样。

不过最大的障碍还是来自于苹果这样有竞争力的科技公司，苹果有专

---

compatibility [kəmˌpætəˈbiləti] n. 兼容性

piracy [ˈpaiərəsi] n. 盗版侵权

query [ˈkwiəri] v. 询问

which has its own iTunes ecosystem for movies. Amazon (AMZN), on the other hand, has signed a deal with one studio, which it didn't name, to sell UltraViolet films.

Despite the challenges, studio executives are bullish on the format. For the first time they're able to offer on-demand video on **multiple** screens, and may even outfox pirates. Talk about a Hollywood ending.

门的系统iTunes可以用来观看电影。另一方面，亚马逊也已经与另一家没有透露名字的工作室签订了协议，出售紫外光格式的电影。

尽管挑战重重，电影工作室的高管们仍然非常看好这种格式。他们将首次在多媒体银幕上，按照用户的要求提供视频，而且这可以完胜盗版。这也算是好莱坞式的完美收场。

炫 · 知识

1. Blu-ray 蓝光光碟

蓝光光碟是DVD之后那一代的光盘格式之一，可以存储高品质的影音以及高容量的数据存储。之所以命名为蓝光光碟，是由于其采用波长405纳米的蓝色激光光束来进行读写操作。

2. Netflix 网飞公司

Netflix是一家在线影片租赁提供商。公司能够提供超大数量的DVD，而且能够让顾客快速方便地挑选影片，同时免费递送。

3. sign in 登录

sign in是指以自己在某个网站的固定会员资格登录的意思，比如微博等社交网站的登录。sign意为"签署"，有"签入"的含义。

4. bullish 看涨的

bull在英语中是"公牛"的意思，加上形容词词尾-ish，有"公牛似的"的意思。我们都很熟悉股市中常说的"牛市"就是bull market，因此bullish在这里就表示"看涨的"。

阅读技能练习场

Exercises:

❶ According to the passage, how many users have had Ultraviolet accounts now?
A. It cannot be inferred.
B. 15.5 billion.

multiple ['mʌltipl] a. 多种多样的

C. 750,000 households.

D. 750,000 customers.

2 Which devices can be used to watch UltraViolet movies?

A. Your phones.

B. Tablets.

C. Traditional DVD-players.

D. Both A and B.

3 Why are studio executives bullish on the UltraViolet format?

A. It could offer on-demand videos.

B. It could offer video on multiple screens.

C. It may outfox pirates.

D. A, B and C.

Answers: 1.C 2.D 3.D

Reading Skills

1. 避免掉入"陷阱" ★★★★

读完问题，看完选项发现正好有自己心中的答案，这时最好不要直接作答，要仔细查看这个答案是否真的正确。如果拿不准，就要再回到文中去，根据细节再确定最终的答案。以免掉入出题者设置的"陷阱"。

Q1解析：根据题目，我们可以马上排除A和B这两个错误选项，C和D虽然很像，但只要回到文中，找到It's potentially… some 750,000 households in the U.S. and Britain… 这部分，就能确定正确答案是C。

2. 不要漏掉正确选项 ★★★★★

遇到一些直接能从文中找到答案的问题时，很多人容易下意识地进行选择，其实在遇到这种情况时，应该认真把选项读完，以免漏选。

Q2解析：文章的第二自然段同时提到了选项A和选项B，C选项为干扰项，因为这种新技术的视频文件并不是储存在光盘上的。因此选D。

Q3解析：根据文章的最后一段的最后一句，可以判断A、B、C三个选项都是正确的，因此很容易选出正确答案是D。

Passage 16

Digital Age Is Making Newspaper Editors Redundant

——数码时代让报纸编辑变得多余吗?

——Apr. 22nd, 2012, Guardian

Reading Guide

数码时代的到来让我们的生活发生了日新月异的变化,而传统的许多职位也会随之发生变动。编辑是一个历史悠久的职业,无论是对于报纸,还是广播,编辑都是不可或缺的。然而,随着数码时代的到来,面对数码产品的普及程度,编辑真的会退出历史舞台吗?

Some journalists shrug at the news that BBC local radio may lose its station managers. Bon voyage, bureaucrats! But shrugs turn to shivers when it emerges that the corporation's next director general never needs to have made a program, or indeed edited anything. And now Johnston Press, commanded by a former BBC digital wizard, begins to abolish editors for individual papers themselves, merging and melding from Edinburgh to Leeds as though they were, well, managing local radio stations.

Are editors, too, on their way to a cyberspace version of journalism's knacker's yard? It's a question, of course, that excites the Society of Editors—and one that Lord Justice Leveson, back from an Easter break to examine proprietors about who controls what, may also find

BBC公司可能会取消当地广播电台经理这一职位,一些记者对这个消息不以为然。祝你一路平安,官僚们!然而,当公司下一任的领导也不再需要制作节目或是编辑内容的情况出现以后,不以为然就变成了不寒而栗。如今,前英国广播公司数字向导管理的约翰斯顿出版社开始取消单一的报纸编辑,从爱丁堡到利兹的部门全部合并,这就好像在管理当地的广播电台一样。

编辑们也要成为网络版新闻业的牺牲品了吗?这个问题当然激起了编辑协会的注意——正在度复活节假期的上诉法院法官莱韦森被要求返回工作岗位,来检查经营者们各自控制着什么,也许可以发现强迫的现象。如

compelling. Can you have editors' codes if you don't have editors? Can editors be responsible in law if they don't exist in reality? Yet the whole proposition isn't quite as **outlandish** as it can be made to seem.

Editing, through history, has been a role without a settled job description. Some great names—like CP Scott—**contrived** to combine it from Manchester with holding a Liberal seat at Westminster. Some still sweat late at night over every headline; some, in quite recent memory, preferred an early pre-prandial drink at the Garrick club. What you do, in sum, varies over time and from paper to paper. But digital rocks even our most traditional worlds.

Putting digital news first—the increasingly familiar slogan of a new dawn—means that the **editorials** are up there fast on website after website, sitting alongside the columnists of controversy, aiming to recruit unique visitors or paywall **subscribers**, the financial props of pending salvation. But is there truly a need, on the net, for some judicious, representative encapsulation of what a paper collectively thinks?

The very nature of leader writing would seem to query the proposition. One *Guardian* column from Polly Toynbee the other day produced 1,257 responses online—while five

果没有编辑，那么你有编辑代码吗？如果编辑不再存在于现实中，那他们还能负起法律责任吗？也许这个提议本身并没有看起来那么奇怪。

纵观历史，编辑一直都没有严格定义的职位描述。有一些伟大的名字设法从曼彻斯特将此与在威斯敏斯特自由党获得一席之地联系起来，比如CP·斯哥特。另一些编辑则为了每一条头版标题挥汗如雨，直到凌晨；在最近的记忆里，一些编辑早早起来，在餐前喝上一杯后，就在嘉里克文学俱乐部开始了工作。而你所做的全部就是，花大量的时间一份份地翻看报纸。但是数码技术撼动了我们这个最传统的世界。

首先来看数字新闻——新闻的标语越来越相似——这意味着社论与专家们的争论一起，在各个网站不断地快速出现，旨在吸引独立访客和付费读者，因为赞助费用的问题仍未解决。但是那些明智的、代表报纸的共同思考的封面在网络上还有必要吗？

领军人物写下的评论仿佛带有质疑这一议题的特点。几天前，波莉·托因比在《卫报》上的专栏出现了1257条在线回复——但是各类业界

---

compelling [kəm'peliŋ] a. 强迫的
outlandish [aut'lændiʃ] a. 古怪的
contrive [kən'traiv] v. 设法做到

editorial [,edi'tɔ:riəl] n. 社论
subscriber [səb'skraibə] n. 订阅者

whole days of variegated leader comment managed only 1,201 rolled together.

The dynamics are different in web world, too. For one thing—whether actively participating or not—the audience is **omnipresent**. They can respond actively, swamping the newsroom in tweets. But its rather more passive, judgmental role is always on hand as well. How many hits on story A? How much clicking interest in B and C? There'll be a list of the five or ten most-read tales up on screen and possibly in the newsroom itself. Success (in unique visitor terms) can be measured hour by hour—success with mystique and, theoretically, revenue attached.

You're not, in any traditional sense, editing the news. You're an intermediary-cum-overseer, **manipulating** it to best effect, **steering** rather than decision-making. And the advertising on which your job depends doesn't arrive from a different department beyond your ken. It is, psychologically, part of the whole operation—and the people who sell it, just like the technical staff on whom delivery depends, are all on the same, intermingled team.

Journalism, via web or app, can still be fine and probing, spurred on by great section heads, but it cannot be edited in any strict sense, any more than TV cable news churning day and night while controllers sleep. Leveson and his supplementary silks have often looked askance these past few months when an editor in their

领军人物的评论在整整五天里，只有1201条回复。

这种力量在网络世界中也是完全不同的。一方面，无论是否积极参与，观众是无处不在的。观众可以积极回应，使编辑室淹没于推文中。但这不仅十分消极，而且批判的角色随时随地都会出现。有多少人被故事A吸引？有多少人因为对B和C感兴趣而点击查看？ 5到10个最受欢迎的故事将会出现在屏幕上或者阅览室本身。成功（从独立访客的角度来说）可以以小时来计算——从理论上来说，成功是神秘且伴随着收益的。

从传统意义上来说，你不是在编辑新闻。你的角色只是媒介监工头，你操控新闻以让它产生最大的影响，操纵的成分大大地超过了决策。而你的工作所依赖的广告并非来自你无法理解的不同部门。从心理学上来看，这是整个运作过程的一部分——而出售广告的人们也在团队中，他们就像技术工作者一样，你可以把需求传达给他们。

通过网络或应用程序，新闻仍然可以制作精良且具有探索性，并由相关板块的领导者带动而发展，但从严格意义上来讲，这不再像是过去编辑在电视台播放的有线新闻节目，在管理者们睡着的时候搅动着人们日日夜夜的生活。在过去的几个月，莱文森

---

omnipresent [ˌɔmniˈprezənt] a. 无所不在的
manipulate [məˈnipjuleit] v. 操控

steer [stiə] v. 控制

81

witness box hasn't kept proper audit trails, doesn't remember the decision in question or, just flat-out, was doing something else at the time. But that's the nature of the job—a job in the throes of profound, sometimes barely realized change.

Think of Paul Dacre editing his *Mail* (as described by *the New Yorker*). Where's the terminal in his office? There isn't one. Think of Tony Gallagher at the *Telegraph* producing his paper via iPad conferencing. Think of John Paton, America's digital-first apostle: "For God's sake stop listening to newspaper people... Put the digital people in charge of everything. They can take what we have built and make it better." Think of Highfield, an appointment with added symbolism. Then book your seats, no more than a dozen years hence, for the first annual conference of the Society of Aggregators, Moderators and Administrators.

和他的精英团队经常表示怀疑：比如一名编辑在他们的证人席上没能恰当地记录、没有记住审问的结果，或是只是高速地工作，甚至同时处理多项工作。但这就是这份工作的本性——一份带来深刻痛苦的工作，有时几乎是无法进行任何改变的。

想想保罗·达克雷如何编辑他的《每日邮报》（就像《纽约客》中描述的那样）。他的工作室会在何时终结？其实这并不会终结。想想《每日电讯报》的托尼·贾拉赫如何通过iPad视频会议制作他的报纸吧。想想美国数码至上理念的宣传者约翰·佩顿："看在上帝的份上，不要再听信新闻工作者的话了……让数码工作者掌管一切吧。他们能接管我们所建立的一切，并使这一切变得更好。"再想想海菲尔德那带有象征意义的任命。用不了十几年，第一届整合者、版主和管理员年会就要召开。所以，提前给自己在大会上订个位置吧。

炫·知识

1. shrug at 对……不以为然

当我们要表现对某些事物不以为然的时候，通常会做出耸肩这个动作。因此，"耸肩"shrug这个单词就被赋予了这种引申意义，shrug at就是"对……不以为然"的意思。

2. Bon voyage. 一路顺风

Bon voyage. 是一句法语，意为"一路顺风"，这句临别前的一种祝福语在英语中也很常用。

Chapter 3

3. Liberal 自由党

自由党是英国资产阶级政党，前身是1679年成立的辉格党。1832年议会改革后，辉格党逐渐转向自由主义，要求自由贸易和自由政治。党员多数是工商资本家、律师、教师和学生。

4. beyond your ken 难以理解

ken这个单词不是十分常见，它有"视野"的意思。因此beyond your ken自然就是表示让你感觉"难以理解"。

5. cable news 有线电视新闻

有线电视cable television常缩写为CATV，是一种使用同轴电缆作为介质直接传送电视、调频广播节目到用户电视的一种系统。有线电视新闻则是有线电视台的一档固定节目。

阅读技能练习场

Exercises:

1 Why did the author say the proposition—could editors be responsible in law if they don't exist in reality—isn't too strange?

A. People do not need editors any more.

B. There are some works that can't be done by computer.

C. Through history, there is no settled job description on editing.

D. We cannot infer.

2 According to the passage, what is the current situation of editing?

A. Computer can do everything.

B. People are tired of editing.

C. Now, the situation of editing is traditional and complex.

D. The author did not mention.

3 What is the author's point towards cancelling the editing position?

A. We cannot infer from the passage.

B. It is unnecessary to change the current situation.

C. Data would replace editors in the future.

D. He is indifferent towards it.

Reading Skills

1. 细读文章揣摩作者意图 ★ ★ ★ ★ ★

在回答针对作者观点进行提问的问题时，不能根据自己的主观臆断来选择答案，而是要找到作者支撑自己观点的句子，仔细阅读，认真揣摩作者的真正意图。

> **Q1解析**：根据问题提示，我们可以发现这个问题是针对第二自然段的内容提出的，根据：Can you have editors' codes if you don't have editors? Can editors be responsible in law if they don't exist in reality?这两句话，可以判断正确答案是B，编辑是不能被电脑取代的。
>
> **Q3解析**：我们首先把答案的范围锁定在文章的最后部分。在最后一段，作者不但引用了"编辑不会消失"的观点，也提出了数码技术的先进之处，所以我们无法判断作者的真正意图是什么，但"对此表示漠不关心"显然不是答案，所以选A。

2. 有针对性地阅读文章 ★ ★ ★ ★ ★

许多问题的题干就已经帮我们锁定了答案的出处，所以要学会选择关键词，比如这道题的关键词就是situation of editing。

> **Q2解析**：读过文章，就可以知道编辑的工作十分辛苦，而编辑这个行业则有着传统性强、工作复杂的特性。因此我们可以确定正确答案是C。

Passage 17

Technology Should Help Us Share, Not Constrain Us
——科技应帮助我们分享，而非限制
——Apr. 17th, 2012, Guardian

Reading Guide

书是人类共同的朋友。而今，这个共同的朋友却显得不那么平易近人了。随着科技的发展，数码时代已然来临。电子书的盛行让阅读变得方便快捷，但一些经销商却打着保护作者的旗号限制人们的阅读。然而，分享才是这个社会发展的趋势。

I love the novel *The Jehovah Contract*, and I'd like everyone else to love it, too. I have lent it out at least six times over the years. Printed books let us do that. I couldn't do it with most commercial ebooks; it's not "allowed". And if I felt like telling the publishers to take their evil rule and stuff it, the software in e-readers has digital restrictions management—**malicious** features that restrict reading, so it simply won't allow it. And the books are **encrypted** in such a way to force you to use that malicious software.

Many other habits that readers **are accustomed to** are "not allowed" for ebooks. With the Amazon "Kindle", to take one example, users can't buy a book **anonymously**. Kindle books are typically

我喜欢《耶和华的合约》这本小说，而且我希望其他人也喜欢。这些年我已经借阅这本书至少6次了。印刷书籍让我们可以这样做。而大多数商业电子书却不允许这样借阅。如果我想要告诉发行商，他们采取了过多的可恶规则——电子书阅读器里安装的软件有数字限制管理措施，而这些恶意的功能会限制阅读，所以我们才不能多次借阅一本书。而且这些书都是加密的，以强迫你使用这些讨人厌的软件。

读者的很多其他习惯也是电子书"不允许"的。以亚马逊电子阅读器Kindle为例，使用者不能匿名购买图书。Kindle里的书也只能在亚马逊阅

---

malicious [mə'liʃəs] a. 恶意的
encrypt [in'kript] v.译成密码

be accustomed to 习惯于
anonymously [ə'nɔniməsli] ad. 匿名地

available from Amazon only, and Amazon doesn't accept cash so users must identify themselves. Thus Amazon knows exactly which books each user has read. In a country like Britain, where you can be prosecuted for possessing a forbidden book, this is more than hypothetically Orwellian.

With software, the users control the program (making such software libre, or free) or the program controls its users (non-libre). Amazon's ebook policies imitate the distribution policies of non-libre software, but that's not the only relationship between the two. The malicious features described above are imposed on users through software that is not libre. If a libre program had features like those, some users skilled at programming would remove them, and then provide the corrected version to all the other users. Users can't change non-libre software, which makes it an ideal instrument for exercising power over the public.

Any one of these encroachments on our freedom is reason aplenty to say no. If these policies were limited to Amazon, we'd bypass them, but the other ebook dealers' policies are roughly similar. What worries me most is the prospect of losing the option of printed books. *The Guardian* has announced "digital-only reads": in other words, books available only at the price of freedom. I will not read any book at that price. Five years from now, will unauthorized copies be the only ethically acceptable copies for most books?

It doesn't have to be that way. It would

读器上阅读，而亚马逊又不接受现金支付，所以使用者必须使用真名。因此，亚马逊网站清楚地知道每个用户都看了什么书。在英国这样会因持有禁书而被起诉的国家，这种情况甚至比想象中的奥威尔社会还要严重。

通过软件，既可以是用户操控程序(这类软件可以被自由使用，或者是免费的)，也可以是程序控制用户(不自由的)。亚马逊的电子书阅读政策模仿了不自由的软件的分销策略，但这并不是这两者间惟一的关联。上面描述的恶意软件的特征是通过收费软件强加到用户身上的。如果一个免费的程序具有这样的特点，一些擅长编程的使用者将会移除这些特征，然后为所有其他使用者提供一个修正后的版本。使用者不能更改不自由的软件，这种软件是对公众施加权力的理想工具。

对于任何侵犯我们自由的事物，我们都有太多说"不"的理由。如果这些政策仅限于亚马逊公司，那么我们最好避开它们。然而，其他电子书经销商的政策也相差无几。最让我担心的就是未来可能会失去纸质书这一选择。《卫报》曾经宣布"只有数字阅读"：换言之，只有以牺牲自由为代价，才能阅读书籍。我不会以付出这种代价来读任何一本书。今后五年，对于大部分书而言，是不是只有未经授权的书才是在伦理道德上能被接受的书?

情况并不一定是这样。在商店里

be easy to sell ebooks in stores for cash using a documented standard format. Digital music is still sold that way, on CDs, even though the music industry is aggressively encouraging the use of digital **restrictions** management services such as spotify. CD stores have the disadvantage of an expensive inventory, but digital bookshops would need no such thing: they could write copies at the time of sale on to memory sticks, and sell you one if you forgot your own.

The reason publishers give for their restrictive ebook practices is to stop people from sharing copies. They say this is for the sake of the authors; but even if it did serve the authors' interests (which for quite famous authors it may), it could not justify DRM, EULAs or the Digital Economy Act which persecutes readers for sharing. In practice, the copyright system does a bad job of supporting authors, aside from the most popular ones. Other author's principal interest is to be better known, so sharing their works benefits them as well as readers. Why not switch to a system that does the job better and is **compatible with** sharing?

Sharing is good, and with digital technology, sharing is easy. So sharing ought to be legal, and preventing sharing (that is, non-commercial redistribution of exact copies) is no excuse to make ebooks into **handcuffs** for readers. If ebooks mean that readers' freedom must either increase or decrease, we must demand the increase.

出售的正版标准格式的电子书接受现金支付，这是很容易实现的事情。数字音乐仍然是以CD这种方式贩售的，尽管音乐产业正在积极鼓励数字限制管理服务的使用，例如spotify。CD店会有库存费用过高的缺陷，但是数码书店不会出现这种情况：他们可以在出售的时候把副本拷贝在记忆棒里，如果你忘了带自己的，还可以卖给你一个。

出版商对于限制电子书的做法给出了防止人们共享副本的解释。他们表示这是为了保护作者；但即使他们保护了作者的利益（对于那些著名作家来说，的确如此），但是从数字版权管理、最终用户许可协议，或是数字经济法案的角度来说，阻止读者分享的做法是不合法的。实际上，版权制度并没有对保护作者起到积极作用，除了对那些有名的作者以外。对于其他作者，他们最重要的利益是被更多地了解，所以共享他们的作品使他们本身和读者都能从中获益。那么，为何不改变这个体系，使其与共享一起发挥更好的作用？

共享是很好的，而且在数字技术的支持下，共享也是很容易实现的。所以，共享应该被合法化，而阻止共享（就是以非商业的形式重新分配某个特定的副本）没有理由使电子书成为限制读者的手铐。如果电子书可以使读者变得更自由或者不自由，那我们肯定会要求变得更自由。

---

restriction [riˈstrikʃ ən] n. 限制
be compatible with 与……能共存，适宜……

handcuff [ˈhændkʌf] n. 手铐

最受关注的

炫 · 知识

1. ebook 电子书

电子书是人们所阅读的数字化出版物，区别于以纸张为载体的传统出版物。它是利用计算机技术将一定的文字、图片、声音、影像等信息，通过数码方式记录在以光、电、磁为介质的设备中，借助于特定的设备来读取、复制、传输。

2. Orwellian 奥维尔式社会

Orwellian的词源是英国小说家George Orwell。该小说家作品都是影射前苏联的政治讽刺小说。Orwellian一词可以释义为"受严格统治而失去人性的社会"，转译为"严格控制的"。

3. EULA 最终用户许可协议

EULA是End User License Agreement的缩写，意为"最终用户许可协议"。这是一种具有法律效力的协议，用以规范微软公司及与公司相应软件产品的最终用户之间的法律关系。

阅读技能练习场

Exercises:

① Why did the author mention Orwellian?

A. He thinks the malicious software such as the one used on Kindle would lead to a society like that.

B. Our society is on its way to become an Orwellian one.

C. In Orwellian society, you cannot read books at your wish.

D. He endeavored to make an Orwellian society.

② According to the fourth paragraph, what did the author care about losing the option of printed books?

A. Malicious softwares are sold in the online stores.

B. People must bear the limitations of the online stores.

C. He doesn't like ebooks.

D. The ebooks are costly than printed books.

❸ Why did the ebook dealers limit sharing according to themselves?

A. They must keep profit.

B. Because of the grim competition among ebook dealers.

C. They want to protect the interest of writers.

D. Operating an ebook store online is costly.

Answers: 1.A 2.B 3.C

Reading Skills

1. 小心偷换概念 ★ ★ ★ ★ ★

有时候出题人会根据文章作者的叙述，给出一个夸大了的结论或是没有依据的推断。在遇到这种情况时，一定要仔细思考。

> **Q1解析：**首先根据问题的提示，我们回到文章第二段寻找答案。首先D选项与作者观点相反，可以排除；B和C两个选项都是偷换概念，得到了更夸张的结论。因此选A。
>
> **Q3解析：**原文中相应的段落主要讲述经销商禁止读者分享电子书的借口，乍一看四个选项都没有什么问题，但在文中可以看到，经销商一直提及作者的利益问题，所以答案是C。

2. 选择根本的原因 ★ ★ ★ ★ ★

一些题目会考查作者做出某些决定、或者发表某些看法的原因。这时一定不要停留在表面，要挖掘出作者真正的意图。

> **Q2解析：**问题已经把范围缩小到了第四自然段，根据这段的最后一句话，可以知道作者十分反感电子书给人们带来的限制，所以选B。

Passage 18

How Is the Software Industry Being Reborn?
——软件产业如何重生?
——Apr. 30th, 2012, Time

Reading Guide

软件产业迎来了新一轮的高潮。随着新科技产品的诞生，软件产业又再次被推到了火热的位置。如今，科技产品不断人性化的发展，让软件开发人员更有热情致力于开发更方便和更人性化的软件产品。科技人性化时代即将来临。

It seems that you can't go anywhere in Silicon Valley without hearing about someone who's making an app. Apps are all the rage these days and software engineering is one of the hottest jobs all over the world. But in the not too distant past, there wasn't this much excitement around software.

In fact, I have heard from many executives who have been around a while that the excitement around software and apps today reminds them of the same excitement around software when personal computers were first gaining steam.

Starting Over

I think a strong case could be made that much of the focus of the software industry over the past few decades has been on professionals and the workplace. In my opinion, only in the last five years have we had what I would consider a

在硅谷，似乎无论你走到哪儿，都会听说有人做了什么应用程序。app最近风靡一时，软件工程师成了全世界最热门的职业之一。但就在不久以前，软件产业还没有如此地令人兴奋。

实际上，我已经从很多高管那里听说了很多次了，当个人电脑刚刚开始加速发展的时候，软件和应用程序给他们带来同样的激动。

从头再来

我认为在过去的几十年，情况本该是这样的：对软件行业的关注主要集中在专业工作者和工作地点上。在我看来，只有在过去的5年，我们才有了我认为的单纯且成熟的消费者

pure, mature consumer market. The maturity of the consumer market for personal computers is the foundation that has led to the rebirth of the software industry. If the **first phase** of the software industry was focused largely on businesses, then the next phase will be largely based on consumers.

Although we can articulate what is happening by proclaiming that the software industry is being reborn, in all actuality it's starting over. The first software phase was all about creating software for desktops and then eventually laptop computers. Both were driven primarily by mouse and keyboard input mechanisms. The software generating all the excitement today is fully around touch as an input mechanism. Given the **drastic** differences between touch computing and mouse and keyboard computing, software developers are reinventing or at the very least re-imagining their softwares around touch computing. It is this reinventing and re-imagining of the software industry—brought about by touch computing—that lead me to believe it's almost like it's starting over more than it's being reborn.

New Hardware Is Driving New Software

When I speak with software developers who are driving this new phase of software, they're largely focused on the iPad and the iPhone. These two platforms are giving software developers valuable experience in gaining expertise, making the next generation of touch software much more personal. This is important because new **platforms** incorporating touch are on the horizon based on

市场。消费者市场的成熟是个人计算机行业的基础，也是引导软件产业重生的基础。如果在软件市场的初期阶段，人们主要关注业务本身，那么在下一个阶段主要就是关注消费者。

尽管我们可以通过声明来宣布软件产业已经重生，但实际情况却是重头再来。软件行业的初期阶段是制造适用于台式电脑的软件，然后是笔记本电脑。两者都是主要以鼠标和键盘输入工具来驱动。而如今，软件业最让人激动的就是触摸取代了输入工具。考虑到触摸输入和鼠标、键盘输入之间存在着极大的不同，软件开发人员进行了彻底的改造，或者至少是根据触屏电脑重新设计了软件。这场对软件产业的彻底改变与重新设想由触摸输入方式引发——这让我相信，与其说是软件产业的重生，不如说是重头再来更贴切一些。

新硬件带动新软件

当我与那些正在为这个新阶段开发新软件的开发人员交谈时，我发现他们把大部分的精力都集中在iPad和iPhone上。这两个平台在积累专业知识的方面给软件开发人员带来了非常有价值的经验，使下一代的触摸软件更加个性化。这非常重要，因为基于Windows 8系统，新平台与触摸程序

---

first phase 初期阶段
drastic ['dræstik] a. 激烈的

platform ['plætfɔ:m] n. 平台

Windows 8.

Windows 8 presents a radical **departure from** the normal desktop/notebook operating system that Microsoft usually **churns out**. Windows 8 will be the first OS to combine a touch-based operating system (called Metro) with a mouse-and-keyboard operating system and a familiar Windows interface. These two experiences combined together will lead to a new generation of notebooks, desktops, and tablet-notebook **hybrids,** all with touch interfaces.

What's Next?

That's a great question, and my answer may surprise you. I believe the next big software craze will be around television. I know it may seem crazy to think about running apps on your TV, but that's what I think is next. Google is already going down this path with Google TV, letting software developers make apps for the big screen; Samsung is also doing this with its line of Smart TVs.

We live in extremely exciting times and things will get even more exciting. I firmly believe we will see more fascinating innovations centered around personal computing hardware and software over the next 10 years than we ever saw in the past 30 years of the PC of the industry, and I'm glad that we'll get a chance to observe them firsthand.

的结合即将面世。

Windows 8与微软系统通常大批量生产的那些常规的、应用于台式电脑或笔记本的操作系统呈现完全不同的方式。Windows 8是首款能把基于触屏的操作系统(称为米雀)与通过键盘、鼠标操作的系统结合在一起的操作系统,而且它的界面和传统的Windows系统相似。这两种体验结合在一起,将引领产生新一代的笔记本电脑、台式电脑,以及平板电脑的混合体,所有这些都将使用触屏界面。

下一个是什么?

这是一个大问题,而我的答案也许会让你吃惊。我相信下一个大的软件热潮将与电视有关。我知道对你来说,在你的电视上运行应用程序的想法也许是十分疯狂的。但这就是我对下一个软件热潮的看法。谷歌已经凭借谷歌电视走上这条道路,让软件开发人员制作适合大屏幕的应用程序;三星公司也以一系列的智能电视紧随其后。

我们生活在极为让人兴奋的时代,而事情本身也会变得更加振奋人心,我坚信,与过去30年的个人电脑产业时代相比,在未来的十年,我们在有关个性化电脑硬件和软件方面能看见更吸引人的创新。我很高兴有机会可以第一时间看到这些变化。

---

departure from 离开
churn out 大量生产

hybrid ['haibrid] n. 混合物

炫·知识

1. all the rage 风靡一时

rage除了表示"愤怒，狂怒"，还有"风行，流行"的意思。因此短语all the rage就可以表示"风靡一时"。

2. gain steam 加速

steam是"蒸汽"的意思，而gain steam的说法源自过去的蒸汽火车的加速方式。

3. consumer market 消费者市场

消费者市场是指为满足自身需要而购买的一切个人和团体构成的市场。

4. on the horizon 即将到来的

on the horizon的意思是"在地平线上"，我们可以想象一下，太阳在地平线上出现之后，马上就会升起。因此这个短语也有"即将到来的"含义。

阅读技能练习场

Exercises:

1 According to the passage, over the past few decades, what's the focus in software industry?

A. Consumer market.

B. Professionals.

C. Workplace.

D. Both B and C.

2 According to the author, what is the foundation of the rebirth of the software industry?

A. Business.

B. Personal computers.

C. Consumer market.

D. Laptop.

3 Which description of Windows 8 is right?

A. It has a touch screen.

B. It can be used in equipments that have touch screens.

C. The compatibility of Windows 8 is brilliant.

D. It can only be used in desktops.

Reading Skills

1. 大致记住细节出现的位置 ★★★★★

我们知道，要做对考查细节的问题，回到原文中找到出处是必要的。但是文章都很长，所以如果能大致记住某个细节出现的位置，就会有很大帮助。

Q1解析： 这道题考查的是过去人们对于软件行业的关注点是什么，回忆全文，在文章的前几段就有关于过去的叙述，当我们找到…much of the focus of the software industry over the past few decades has been on professionals and the workplace.这个句子时，就会知道本题选D。

Q2解析： 根据问题中的the foundation of the rebirth of the software industry，我们仍然定位到文章中start over这一部分，根据原文：The maturity of the consumer market for personal computers is the foundation that has led to the rebirth of the software industry. 可以知道，正确答案是C。

2. 选择根本的原因 ★★★★★

有一类题目的选项乍一看比较复杂，但其实细读之下是有很大不同的。有些选项属于偷换概念，有些则完全是干扰项。

Q3解析： 本题询问Windows 8系统的特性，因此要定位到文章的New Hardware Is Driving New Software这一部分。根据Windows 8 …with a mouse-and-keyboard operating system and a familiar Windows interface.这句话就可以排除A和D和C。所以正确答案是B。

Passage 19

Is Mobile the Way We'll All Be Paying?
——未来支付全用手机?
——Apr. 10th, 2012, Telegraph

Reading Guide

　　20世纪50年代以前,人们的衣食住行都离不开现金支付;50年代以后,银行卡、信用卡则开始普及,人们开始尝试刷卡消费。如今,随着技术的不断进步,手机也逐渐成为人们的支付方式之一。那么,手机支付会不会取代钞票和银行卡,成为现代社会的主流支付方式呢?

　　The cashless society has been a much-mooted concept ever since consumer credit cards were widely introduced in the 1950s. Now it seems that "mobile money" is the new gold rush.

　　The term——used to describe the way the mobile phone is used to pay for goods——yields no fewer than 126 million results on a Google search.

　　This was used to justify the £109m takeover of U.S. provider Clairmail by Monitise, the British firm claiming to be the global leader of this **burgeoning** market. There is plenty of competition, with rivals ranging from eBay's Paypal to Facebook's and Google's "Wallet" apps fighting to be kings in this brave new world. Even

　　即使是从二十世纪五十年代信用卡开始普及之后,无现金社会也一直是一个极富争议的概念。而如今,"手机货币"似乎成了新一轮的争议热潮。

　　这个说法常用来描述使用手机支付的方式,在谷歌里搜索这个词,会有不少于1.26亿条结果。

　　而这可以证明Monitise公司以1.09亿英镑的价格收购美国的供应商Clairmail是正确的。因此这家英国公司声称自己是新兴市场的全球领军者。但这个市场中存在众多竞争者,从eBay的Paypal到Facebook和谷歌的"钱包"应用软件,它们都在争夺

---

burgeoning ['bə:dʒəniŋ] a. 迅速增长的

former Tesco chief executive Sir Terry Leahy is getting in on the act as a non-executive director of mobile **coupons** and gift **vouchers** firm, Eagle Eye Solutions.

Market research firm Yankee Group believes that global mobile transactions will become a $1 trillion market by 2015. While Berg Insight says there will be 894m worldwide users of mobile banking by the same year.

Peter Ayliffe, chief executive of Visa Europe, who sits on the Monitise board, believes 50**pc** of all Visa transactions in Europe will be on a mobile device by 2020.

Alastair Lukies, the former Saracens and London Irish rugby player who co-founded Monitise in 2002 and is the firm's chief executive, says: "Everyone is looking at mobile payments because mobile... bridges both the offline and the online worlds. Lots of people are going after this space and trying to own the customer."

Monitise, which has a market capitalisation on AIM of £292m, says more than £6bn of transfers and payments take place on its system every year. One of the most advanced U.K. banks for mobile banking is the Royal Bank of Scotland, whose customers can use their Apple, BlackBerry and Android phones to move money between accounts, view mini-statements and pay bills.

Monitise expects **turnover** of $100m (£63m) this year, providing its mobile banking technology

这个美丽新世界的王者地位。甚至乐购公司的前总裁特里·利亚爵士也参与其中，出任移动优惠券及礼券公司Eagle Eye Solutions的非执行董事。

市场调研公司扬基集团相信，到2015年，全球移动交易将成为一个一万亿美元的市场。而Berg Insight公司称到那时，全球范围内将有8.94亿名手机银行用户。

Monitise公司董事会成员、Visa欧洲公司总裁彼得·艾利费认为，到2020年，欧洲的Visa信用卡交易将有一半是通过移动设备来完成。

阿拉斯泰尔·卢克斯曾是Saracens和London Irish英式橄榄球俱乐部的一名球员，他在2002年与他人一起联合创办了Monitise公司，并出任公司总裁。他说："每个人都在关注移动支付，这是因为手机……将线下和线上的两个世界连接起来。很多人都想在这一领域占领一席之地，并拥有自己的客户。"

在英国AIM创业板市值2.92亿英镑的Monitise公司声称：每年通过此系统办理的转账和支付款项超过了60亿英镑。在移动银行方面，苏格兰皇家银行是最先进的英国银行之一，其客户可使用苹果、黑莓和安卓手机来进行转账、查看迷你账单，以及付账。

向300家银行提供移动银行技术的Monitise公司预计今年的营业额将为1

coupon ['ku:pɔn] n. 礼券
voucher ['vautʃə] n. 代金券
pc=percent n. 百分之……
turnover ['tə:n,əuvə] n. 营业额

to 300 banks. Clairmail serves a third of North America's top 50 banks. Together, the combined group will provide mobile money services to 13m registered users through banks including RBS and Lloyds Banking Group.

Monitise also has a five-year partnership with Visa and is 12pc owned by Visa Inc. and 8.5pc by Visa Europe. The company operates Mobile Money Network, a joint venture with Carphone Warehouse chaired by the former Marks & Spencer chairman, Sir Stuart Rose. It enables people to **sign up** to a mobile phone application called Simply Tap and make purchases through entering a code.

Then there's a venture with Standard Chartered, allowing customers in India to buy cinema, train and airline tickets on their mobile phones through the bank's app.

"Modern-day consumers are going to vote with their thumbs," says Lukies. "They're not going to wait for someone to say, 'This is the way you should buy stuff'. If there's something innovative, they will just do it."

The mobile money market can be broken into three sectors: mobile banking, mobile payments and mobile commerce—getting an alert from a retailer and then using a mobile phone to make a purchase. Analysts see the last as potentially being the biggest market of all.

"In banking, consumers are going to use

亿美元(6300万英镑)。Clairmail为北美前50家银行中三分之一的大银行提供服务。同时，合并后的集团将通过包括苏格兰皇家银行及劳氏银行在内的银行向1300万注册用户提供手机货币服务。

Monitise还和Visa集团有着五年的合伙关系，Visa股份有限公司拥有其12%的股份，Visa欧洲公司则拥有其8.5%的股份。公司经营的"手机货币网"是与Carphone Warehouse公司一起建立的合资企业——Carphone Warehouse的总裁是玛莎公司前董事长斯图尔特·罗斯爵士。用户可以注册并安装名为"一拍即付"的手机应用程序，通过输入代码来完成购物。

还有一家与渣打银行合资的公司允许印度客户通过手机上的银行应用程序来购买电影票、火车票和飞机票。

卢克斯说："现代的客户通过拇指就能投票。他们不会等待别人告诉他们：'你们应该这样购物。'一旦有了创新的方法，他们就会这样做。"

移动货币市场可以被分成三块：移动银行、移动支付、移动商务——比如从零售商那里获得提醒，再用手机进行购买。分析家认为，最后一个，也就是移动商务，是三者中的最大的潜在市场。

卢克斯先生说："在银行业，比

sign up 登记

97

mobiles more than any other channels." says Mr. Lukies.

"Mobile payments are set to explode in the next couple of years. If you think about a group of mates going out for a curry and **splitting up** the bill or paying each other for a group holiday, I think all those will be done by mobile by 2020. Why would the next generation do it any other way? They're not going to want to go to an ATM and switch cash. And by 2020 you will have contactless terminals in most retailers in the U.K. and I think mobile will have overtaken cards in the way we pay."

In Japan, about 50pc of all grocery payments are already made by people using their mobile phones. The U.K. market has been held back by the limited number of phones enabled for near-field communications (a necessity for mobile payments) but Mr. Lukies sees that changing fast.

The reason, he says, is that, while plastic cards are "dumb terminals", mobile phones allow much more connectivity, enabling balances to be checked and payments confirmed.

"I am not one of these **techies** who think that within a couple of years we're never going to use cash again," says Mr. Lukies. "But if you get the solution right for consumers on the mobile channel, they will adopt it immediately because that's what the next generation are doing. They're **leapfrogging** a generation."

起其他支付渠道，客户将更多地使用手机。"

"过不了几年，移动支付的使用将会出现激增。想象一下，如果几个朋友外出去吃咖喱，然后分开付账单，或是组团旅游时相互为对方付账。我想，等到2020年，这些都会通过手机来实现。下一代人为什么要用其他方式来支付呢？他们不打算去找自动提款机去取现金。到2020年，英国大多数零售店都将有非接触式终端，我认为手机支付将超过银行卡支付"。

在日本，大约百分之五十的杂货店里的销售都是通过手机支付的。在英国市场，这种方式因为带有近场通讯功能（这是移动支付所必需的）的手机用户数量有限而受到阻碍。然而，卢克斯认为这种情况很快就会发生改变。

他说，原因在于塑料卡是"不能说话的"终端，而手机则具有更高的连通性，因此可以支持余额查询和确认支付的功能。

卢克斯先生说："我并不是那种相信过不了几年人们就都不会再使用现金的技术狂人。但如果你针对移动支付渠道的解决方案成功了，消费者就会立即采用，因为那是下一代人将会采取的方案。他们是跳跃着前进的一代。"

---

split up 拆开，分开算

leapfrog ['li:pfrɒg] v. 跳跃前进

techie ['teki:] n. 技工

炫 · 知识

1. gold rush 淘金热

淘金热原指在美国西进运动时期，美国移民萨特在加利福尼亚的萨克拉门托附近发现了金矿，之后这一消息扩展到全世界，很多人都前往美国寻找金子。后来这个词就被用来指代可以带来经济效益的某种热潮，在这里指"手机货币"。

2. market capitalization 市值

美语用法，在英国称为capitalization，简称market cap。公司资产的市场价值=公司现有股份数额×每股市场价值。市值是投资者选择投资品种的一个重要指标。

3. AIM 英国创业板

AIM是Alternative Investment Market(替代投资市场)的简称，由伦敦证券交易所成立。这是继美国纳斯达克市场之后，欧洲成立的第一家二板市场。英国创业板对企业没有经营年限的要求，也没有最低市值要求。

4. Standard Chartered 渣打银行

全称为Standard Chartered Bank，是一家总部在伦敦的英国银行。其业务主要集中于亚洲、印度次大陆、非洲、中东及拉丁美洲等新兴市场。在英国本土的客户反而比较少。

阅读技能练习场

Exercises:

❶ Why did the author say "mobile money" is the new gold rush?

A. People are crazy about buying new mobiles.

B. People save a lot of money for their mobiles.

C. Mobile money will be popular, and more and more people will pay with their mobiles.

D. If a mobile phone can be used to fulfill your payment, it is valuable.

2 Which is not the competitor of the mobile money market?

A. Paypal.

B. Facebook.

C. Google's "Wallet" app.

D. Eagle Eye Solutions.

3 Which is not included in the three sectors of the mobile money market?

A. Mobile using.

B. Mobile banking.

C. Mobile payments.

D. Mobile commerce.

Reading Skills

Answers: 1.C 2.B 3.A

1. 抓住文章主旨，理解表达深意 ★★★★★

通读文章之后，要对文章有大致的理解，比如作者的写作意图、表达事物的态度等，这样才能正确判断其使用修辞的作用和目的。

> **Q1解析**：这道题考查的是对文章第一段最后一句话的理解。gold rush指"淘金热"，最后一句话的字面意思是"手机货币"可能会成为新的淘金热潮。根据全文，也就是说通过手机支付生活中的开销将会形成一股新的热潮。因此，选C。

2. 仔细审题，排除错误选项 ★★★★★

在做题的时候一定要注意那些"混淆视听"的选项，不要被它们迷惑了。一旦找到干扰选项，就可以迅速将其排除。

> **Q2解析**：根据第三段内容，在手机钱包这个市场上，竞争者众多，包括eBay的Paypal，Facebook的"电子钱包"应用，谷歌的"电子钱包"应用，还有移动优惠券公司Eagle Eye Solutions。而选项B描述不准确，将修饰宾语的定语误认为宾语，因此选B。

> **Q3解析**：根据第12段内容，移动支付市场包括三个方面：手机银行、手机支付和手机商务。因此选A。

Passage 20

Lomography, an Analog Company Surviving in a Digital World
——Lomo摄影，数码世界的模拟胶片幸存者
——Apr. 26th, 2012, New York Times

Reading Guide

　　在数码设备大行其道的数码时代，拍照已经变得非常简单，只要按下数码相机的快门就可以轻松拍照。但是你是否会怀念那些握在手中的、留有岁月痕迹的照片呢？是否会怀念用胶片相机捕捉精彩画面的时刻呢？虽然胶片相机已经淡出人们的视线，Lomography公司却依然坚持着自己的道路。

　　From the death rattle of companies like Kodak to the popularity of apps like Instagram that transform cellphone snaps into vintage-looking works of art, amateur film photography seems destined for the graveyard of **obsolete** technologies.

　　Yet, Lomography, a company and organization that **champions** the use of analog film photography, has found a foothold in a rocky market.

　　Lomography got its start 20 years ago in Austria, by a group of ambitious photographers and artists who stumbled across a cheap Russian camera called the Lomo that used 35-millimeter film. The Lomo produced charming photographs

　　从柯达这类公司的垂死喉鸣，到Instagram这类将手机拍摄的照片转化为复古艺术品风格的应用程序的流行，业余胶片摄影似乎注定要进入淘汰技术的墓园。

　　然而Lomography这家拥护模拟胶片摄影的公司及机构却在震荡的市场中找到了立足之地。

　　二十年前，Lomography由一群在奥地利雄心勃勃的摄影师和艺术家们创立，他们偶然发现了这种使用35毫米胶片的叫做Lomo的廉价俄罗斯相

---

obsolete ['ɔbsəli:t] a. 废弃的　　　　　　　　champion ['tʃæmpiən] v. 拥护

that often contained artsy blurry streaks and were oversaturated with color due to the camera's body design and construction.

"Instant photography is covered by digital cameras and the iPhone," said Mr. Fiegl. "You want to share a photo of something right now, and you are covered. But our version of analog is different because it's fun and unexpected, you don't know what's coming and you won't, for a few days or a week, when you get the pictures back."

Lomography, he said, appeals to people who crave an alternative, who want a print of their photos to live outside of their mobile phones and Facebooks, and still looks pretty and interesting when hung on a wall. There's something charming about only having a set number of **exposures** on a roll of film with which to capture an event. It's a stark contrast to the seemingly infinite memory and cloud storage that let people take dozens, if not hundreds, of photographs of every single event and moment.

"We now take so many digital photographs, it's hard to **sift through** them to find vacation photos from five years ago," he said.

But a small stack of prints, he said, particularly ones that have sun spots, bleached out colors, might be something you'd make a point not to lose.

It isn't to say that the company **eschews** social media. They've embraced it, with a healthy Facebook community and by using the Web to organize Lomographer meet-ups around the world.

机。Lomo相机可以拍出富有魅力的照片，这些照片通常带着具有艺术气息的模糊条纹，而且由于机身的设计和构造，照片的颜色常常过于饱满。

"即时显影技术被数码相机和iPhone覆盖了，"菲格先生说。"如果你现在想分享某个事物的照片，就会用到那些技术。但我们的模拟胶片版就不同了，因为这样的照片有趣又出人意料，你不知道会拍成什么样子，而且要过几天或一周左右才能拿到照片，这时你才能知道结果。"

他说，Lomography吸引那些渴望尝试另外一种方式的人们，他们想把照片洗出来，让它们从手机和Facebook中走出来、挂到墙上也看起来漂亮又有趣。用一卷胶卷中的几张来拍摄一组照片，捕捉一个事件，这具有独特的魅力。记忆似乎是无限的，而云存储也可以记录某一单独事件或片刻的照片，哪怕没有上百张，也有几十张。而这与Lomography形成了鲜明的对比。

"我们现在拍了太多的数码照片，而想要从中找出一些五年前度假时的照片太不容易了，"他说道。

但如果是一小叠洗出的照片，他说，尤其是带有光斑和漂白的色彩的照片，你可能就会觉得生怕它们丢失。

这并不是说公司避免与社交媒体有交集。它们张开手臂欢迎它，通过健康的Facebook社区和网络组织全世界的Lomography爱好者们见面。

---

exposure [ik'spəuʒə] n. 底片
sift through 通过

eschew [is'tʃu:] v. 避开

"Don't get me wrong," he said. "We all love Instagram. But this is not the same thing."

Even so, Mr. Fiegl said the company had to send Instagram a letter about six months ago asking them to rename a filter that had been called "Lomo."

"Even now, I'm not sure that was a smart move," he said. "We would have 30 million, maybe 100 million people, knowing our name. But what we are trying to do is so different I don't want to confuse it."

Part of the company's longevity lies in its history. In 1998, several years before sites like Flickr, MySpace, Friendster and Facebook came on the scene, Lomography had a Web site where people could upload, tag and share their **quirky** photographs. Now, the site has collected more than 10 million pictures and attracts 3 million visits each month. Lomography was informally distributing cameras around the world and selling them in museums, but the **traction** of their early Web community eventually led the company to open a Web shop so people could place orders online.

By this time, Lomography was designing and manufacturing, with the help of manufacturers in China and Russia, its own line of analog film cameras, kitschy and cute machines with bulky plastic bodies with name like the Diana; the Horizon, a camera that captures panoramic vistas; and the Pop 9, a shiny gold camera that captures nine frames **simultaneously.**

"别误解我的意思，"他说。"我们都喜爱Instagram。但这不是一回事。"

即便如此，菲格先生表示，公司必须写信给Instagram，询问关于六个月前请他们为一个叫作"Lomo"的滤镜重新命名的事宜。

"即使是现在，我也不确定这是一个明智的举动，"他说。"大约有三千万，或许有一亿人知道我们的名字。但我们正努力去做的事情是如此不同，我并不想去混淆它。"

公司能够发展至今的部分原因是由于它的历史。在Flickr、MySpace、Friendster和Facebook出现之前的1998年，Lomography成立了一个网站，在这里人们可以上传、加标签并分享他们风格奇特的照片。现在，网站已搜集了超过一千万张照片，而且每月会吸引三百万的访问量。Lomography过去非正式性地向全世界发售相机，包括出售给博物馆。但他们早期的网络社区的吸引力最终促使公司开了一家网店，这样人们就可以在网上订购了。

到现在，在中国和俄罗斯制造商的帮助下，Lomography设计并生产了自己的模拟胶片相机系列，例如拥有笨笨的塑料机身，俗气但却可爱的Diana；可以捕捉全景远景的Horizon；以及可以同时捕捉九帧画面的、金光闪闪的Pop 9。

---

quirky ['kwə:ki] a. 古怪的

traction ['trækʃən] n. 牵引力

simultaneously [siməl'teiniəsli] ad. 同时地

A few years later, in 2006, when most companies were shifting their business to the Web, Mr. Fiegl decided it was time for Lomography to move offline. The company began opening retail stores around the world, from Hong Kong to Paris, London and New York. The stores, which sell cameras, films, photo books and accessories, also serve as places for Lomographers to meet up, host exhibitions and trade tips.

The company now has 35 stores in two dozen different countries around the world, and each year, the company sells half a million cameras worldwide. Last year, they sold 2 million rolls of film.

"We're growing year-over-year. Our retail sales are more powerful than the Web," said Mr. Fiegl. "People play around with the cameras, they understand it and it convinces them."

The company is future-proofing its business by preparing for an era when the rest of the vestiges of analog photography become extinct. They have installed film processing facilities in some of their retail stores and offer a mail-in development service for their users who don't live near a drugstore or place that processes photos.

Although Lomography regularly designs and releases new products, including a 35-millimeter movie camera called the LomoKino and different kinds of film each year, it has no plans to make or market a digital camera.

"We've considered it," said Mr. Fiegl. "But in a way, Lomography is freer. We don't have much competition and we don't have to top anyone's megapixel count. We've decided to stick with the analog side of things."

在几年之后的2006年，当时大多数公司把业务转向了网络，菲格先生却决定将Lomography转到线下的时候到了。公司开始在全世界各地开设零售店，从香港到巴黎、伦敦和纽约。这些店里不仅出售相机、胶片、相册和配件，也为摄影爱好者提供聚会、办展览和交流技巧的场所。

公司目前在全世界二十几个不同的国家拥有35家店。每年在全世界范围内销售50万台相机。去年，公司出售了二百万卷胶片。

"公司一年一年地成长起来。我们的零售额比网络更有力量，"菲格先生说道，"人们和我们的相机玩耍，他们信任它，而相机也让他们信服自己。"

公司为模拟摄影消亡的时代做好了准备，而这使它可以适应未来。他们在一些零售店内安装了胶片冲洗设备，并为那些家附近没有杂货店或洗照片的地方的用户提供邮递冲洗服务。

尽管Lomography有规律地设计和发布新产品，包括名为LomoKino的35毫米电影摄影机和每年推出的不同种类的胶片，该公司仍然没有制造或销售数码相机的计划。

"我们考虑过，"菲格先生说道，"但在某种程度上，Lomography更自由一些。我们不会有太多的竞争压力，我们不必为提高像素数而发愁。我们决定继续坚持模拟胶片技术。"

炫 · 知识

1. vintage-looking 复古样式的

时尚人士对于"复古"这个词一定不会感到陌生，那么在英语中，"复古的"可以用vintage表示；而looking在这里是"样式"的意思。此外，retro也有"复古的，重新流行的"之意。

2. stumble across 偶然发现

stumble作为动词，有"绊倒"的含义。而stumble across却是"偶然发现"的意思，across有一种"偶遇"的意味，含义类似的短语还有come across, run across等。

3. Lomo

Lomography是奥地利Lomographische AG公司的商标，该公司提供与摄影相关的产品与服务。Lomography也代表了一种摄影体验、随性的、没有任何束缚的、回归摄影本源的影像记录方式。其特色有过度饱和、失衡曝光、模糊等。

4. get sb. wrong 误解某人

短语get sb. wrong是"误解某人"的意思，而Don't get me wrong.也是一个很常用的口语句子，意思是"别误解我的意思。"

5. Diana

戴安娜相机是一种简单、低品质的塑料玩具相机。戴安娜使用120底片格式的胶卷能拍摄16张4.2x4.2cm的正方型照片，因此，底片会留下一部分没有曝光的表面。

阅读技能练习场

Exercises:

1 Which of the following can't we get about Lomography from the passage?

A. It welcomes no social media.

B. It started 20 years ago in Austria.

C. It has opened retail stores around the world.

D. It releases different kinds of film each year.

2 Which of the statements about Lomography is not true?

A. It offers a mail-in development service for their users.

B. Pixel count is also the first concern of Lomography.

C. Lomography lovers could get together at Lomography stores.

D. The Diana and the Horizon are both from Lomography Company.

3 What can we get from the passage?

A. Lomography is going to end up like Kodak.

B. As time goes by, people will have no place to develop their film.

C. The charming photographs produced by Lomo are an attraction to people.

D. Lomography plans to make or market a digital camera.

Answers: 1.A 2.B 3.C

Reading Skills

1. 做真假题要看清原文 ★★★★★

真假题的难度通常都不会很大，但是需要极大的细心才能选出正确答案。解这种题的第一步就是认真阅读原文，只有把握好文章内容，才方便解答各个题目。

Q1解析：由They've embraced it, with a healthy Facebook community and by using the Web to organize Lomographer meet-ups around the world.可知选项A的表述不正确。其他三个选项在原文中则均有表述。故选A。

Q2解析：由...offer a mail-in development service for their users...可知A选项正确；由...we don't have to top anyone's megapixel count.可知，B选项表述不当；C选项与原文中的The stores, ... also serve as places for Lomographers to meet up的表述一致。D选项中提到的两款相机均来自Lomography。所以只有B选项是错误的。

2. 运用排除法 ★★★★★

解答阅读理解题时，排除法是一个比较常用的方法。我们可以利用选项的信息，到文中寻找支持其的证据，这样可以大大地提高解题速度。

Q3解析：A选项表示Lomography公司的前景不妙，这种说法在文中并未提及。B选项与文中They have installed film processing facilities in some of their retail stores...的说法矛盾。D选项与it has no plans to make or market a digital camera矛盾，故本题选C。

Passage 21

On the Road with the Proper Gear
——带着适合的装备踏上征途

——Apr. 25th, 2012, New York Times

Reading Guide

高科技产品日新月异。不过，你是各种科技产品装备齐全的"假专家"，还是将科技产品化繁为简，以最少物品换取最大功能的"真精英"？

科技时代，一台平板电脑、一部智能手机就能搞定所有问题吗？那就让我们拭目以待吧。

Last month, I was sitting in a club lounge in Newark Liberty International Airport whcn I noticed a man in the seat across from me with this technological array in front of him:

▲ A Windows 7-based tablet (I think it was an Asus).

▲ A Bluetooth keyboard.

▲ A Bluetooth mouse.

▲ A USB hub.

▲ A USB drive attached to the hub.

Clearly, my man was no **amateur**—except maybe for that Windows tablet. He was a walking **billboard** for the latest technology. Post-PC? On it. Bluetooth devices? Got it. Solid-state memory? No doubt.

But he had it all wrong.

上个月，当我坐在纽瓦克自由国际机场的一间会员休息室休息时，我注意到坐在我对面的男人面前摆放着这些科技产品：

一台Windows 7的平板电脑（我觉得那是华硕的）。

一个蓝牙键盘。

一个蓝牙鼠标。

一个USB集线器。

一个连接集线器的USB驱动器。

很显然，这位老兄并不是电子产品爱好者——但那台Windows系统的平板电脑也许可以说明他是个爱好者。他是一个最新科技产品的流动宣传牌。后PC时代的个人电脑？有了。蓝牙设备？齐了。记忆卡？毫无疑问他也有。

但是他完全错了。

amateur ['æmətə] n. 业余爱好者，外行　　　　billboard ['bilbɔːd] n. 广告牌

His setup was like an ill-conceived version of Voltron, Defender of the Universe, that 1980s Japanese cartoon about the little robots that combine to form one superrobot. Except in his case, all his little devices combined formed an unwieldy **arsenal** of silliness. I wanted to lean across the ottoman and say, "Psst, Homes, just get a laptop."

It can be easy to get caught up in the latest tech trend and think that it will solve all your problems. But that's just not true. The next big thing is not also the only thing. Tablets, for example, can be great for some things and less great for others.

This principle is all the more important when you travel, since you want to take just as much as you need and not a device more. When I'm traveling for business, I make sure I'm equipped with the following tech items, and nothing else:

A LAPTOP: Is a tablet suitable for travel? Surely it is. If I'm **headed out** on vacation with my family and want something for e-mail, reading and emergency child **sedation**, my iPad is the first thing that goes into my carry-on. But if I intend to do some actual work, then it's my laptop by a country mile

In spite of recent "tablets will rule the world" hyperbole, there's still some life in the old laptop. I use an 11-inch Apple MacBook Air, and it has become my indispensable business travel companion. Yes, it weighs a pound more than an iPad. And yes, I'm woefully **out of shape**, but I

他的装备就像一个构思欠佳的 Voltron（宇宙捍卫者）版本，那是20世纪80年代关于小机器人组合形成一个超级机器人的日本动画片。除了他旅行箱里的东西，他所有的小玩意儿组合起来，形成了一个愚蠢而笨拙的设备库。我都想要跨过软凳去跟他说，"嘿，老兄，只带个笔记本电脑就足够了。"

想要赶上最新的科技潮流很容易，而且我们会轻易认为这会解决你所有的问题。但这并不是真实的情况。下一个大事件也并不是惟一的事。举个例子，笔记本电脑对一些事情来说非常好，但对另一些事情来说不见得那么好了。

如果你去旅行，这个原则就最重要了，因为你不想多带一个设备，只要带你所需要的东西。当我需要商务旅行时，我会确保以下科技用品都已装备好，别的什么都不要：

一台笔记本电脑——带一台笔记本在旅途中合适吗？那是当然。如果我带着家人一起去度假，我想要写些电子邮件、阅读或是想让孩子们立刻安静下来，那么我的iPad就是我随身行李中的第一件东西。但是如果我计划做一些实际的工作，那我就会把笔记本电脑放得远远的。

尽管最近有夸张的说法表示"平板电脑将会主宰世界"，但是仍然有一些人还生活在旧式的笔记本电脑时代。我用11寸的苹果超薄电脑，而且它已经成为我必不可少的商务旅行伴侣。没错，它有1磅重，比一台iPad还

---

arsenal ['ɑ:sənəl] n. 兵工厂，器械库
head out 启程

sedation [si'deiʃən] n. 镇静
out of shape 身材走样

think I can handle the **heft**.

If you're inclined to go with a Windows machine, new "ultrabooks" are basically MacBook Air knockoffs (that's a compliment, ultrabook makers).

Ultrabooks come in many shapes and sizes, but the trick for travel is to get the smallest one (Asus's Zenbook, which costs $900 to $1,100, has an 11.6-inch display, almost as small as the MacBook).

A SMARTPHONE: You need a smartphone, of course. But you need one that has a certain feature: wireless tethering (also called mobile hot spot). That way, your phone can act as a wireless modem for your laptop, avoiding the need for a USB dongle or an external wireless hot spot device like a MiFi. That's one less thing you have to carry.

Some smartphones can use superfast 4G LTE networks, which may not mean much on a phone, but can pay off nicely when wirelessly tethered to a laptop.

HEADPHONES: I carry two pairs of headphones: one noise-reducing set and one standard pair. Skip the bulky around-the-ear noise-reducing headphones and get in-ear models like AKG's K390 NC ($200) or Panasonic's RP HC55-S ($44 on Amazon) that cut down on airplane buzzing, but still fold up nicely in a bag.

For just walking around, you'll want a standard pair of in-ear headphones, preferably with a microphone and buttons to control smartphone features. Your smartphone most likely came with a pair. Many of these headphones

重。是的，我很不幸，身材走样了，但是我认为我还是能应付这个重量的。

如果你倾向于购买一台Windows系统的机器，新的"超级本"基本上可以说是山寨版的苹果超薄电脑(超级本的制造者，这可是赞美哦)。

超级本有多种形状和大小，但是想要旅行时使用，就要买最小号的(华硕的Zenbook，售价在900美元到1100美元之间，11.6寸显示屏，几乎和苹果笔记本电脑一样小)。

一部智能手机——当然，你需要一部智能手机。但是你需要一部有特定功能的手机：无线连接(也被称作移动热点)。那样的话，你的手机就能够作为你的笔记本电脑的无线调制解调器了，既不需要带USB的软件保护器，也不需要像MiFi一样的外部无线热点设备。那是你惟一要带的东西。

一些智能手机能够使用超高速4G LTE网络，这点在手机上可能算不了什么，但是当笔记本电脑能够连接无线网络时，就会起到很大的作用。

耳机——我会携带两副耳机：一副降噪版，一副标准版。环顾众多的环耳式降噪耳机，入耳式的耳机，如爱科技的K390 NC(200美元)或是松下的RP HC55-S(亚马逊上售价44美元)能够降低飞机上的嗡嗡声，仍能折叠好放入背包。

若只是走路时戴，你会需要一款标准版入耳式的耳机，最好有个麦克风和具有控制智能手机的按键。你的智能手机很有可能开始就是配耳机的。这些耳机很多都有可拆卸的橡胶

heft [heft] n. 重量

come with detachable rubber earpieces.

Do yourself a favor and go to a RadioShack or a Best Buy and spend $5 to get a pack of replacement earpieces. Those detachable buds are just that, and nothing's worse than losing one just as you traipse out onto Boulevard Saint-Germain.

BACKUP POWER FOR YOUR SMARTPHONE: If you have a smartphone with a removable battery, by all means keep a charged backup in your bag. But if you're without that option, check out Mophie's Juice Pack Reserve ($35).

VARIOUS CORDS AND MORE: You're going to need the power cable for your laptop and the cable for your smartphone (along with its wall-charging adapter).

I also like to bring an extra power strip, like Belkin's Mini Surge Protector with USB Charger (sounds like a restaurant dish, doesn't it? "Dayboat Scallops with Horseradish Aioli").

This $25 Snickers-bar-size powerstrip includes three outlets and two USB ports. It's a dream when your hotel decides that you really need only one accessible outlet in the whole room.

After that, it's all software: Want to read a book? Get the Kindle app for your computer or phone. Movies? Rent some before you go from Amazon or iTunes and watch them on the plane. Camera, calculator, voice recorder, translator, GPS unit? That's what your smartphone is for.

The goal in travel—and in life in general —is to use the fewest objects with the greatest function. That's what Mr. Platinum Elite missed

听筒。

帮自己一个忙，去趟RadioShack或是Best Buy，用5美元买一副可供替换的耳机。那些可拆卸的橡胶就是那样，没有比当你在圣日尔曼大道上游荡时，却发现丢了一支更糟糕的事情了。

为你的智能手机准备备用电池——如果你的智能手机是可拆卸的电池，务必在包里准备一个充好电的备用电池。但是如果你没有那个选择，那就要保证有个外接电池储备套(35美元)。

多种多样的线，或是更多——你的笔记本电脑会需要电源线，你的智能手机也需要数据线(与它的墙壁充电适配器一起)。

我也喜欢携带一个额外的电源板，像是贝尔金的迷你USB接口的电压保护器(听上去像是餐厅的一道菜，是不是？"山葵蒜泥蛋黄天舟扇贝"。)

这个价值25美元像士力架巧克力棒大小的电源板包括3个电源插头和2个USB端口。当你的酒店的屋子里只有一个可用的电源插头时，它就是求之不得的工具。

然后，就是软件了：想要看书吗？为你的电脑或是手机安装一个电子书阅读应用程序。想要看电影吗？临走之前，在亚马逊网站或是在iTunes上租用一些电影，然后在飞机上观看。想要照相机、计算器、录音机、翻译机或是GPS装置？你的智能手机全能做到。

旅行的目的——总的来说生活的目的——就是利用最少的物品达到最大的功能。这正是那些全副武装科技

with his **panoply** of devices. The savviest user of tech is the one who doesn't look as if he's using any tech at all.

设备的白金精英达人所忽略的地方。科技产品最聪明的用户就是那个看起来根本没有在用任何科技产品的人。

炫 · 知识

1. USB drive U盘

U盘出现在我们每个人的生活中，而USB drive就是它的英文表达。其中drive指的是"硬盘驱动器"。

2. carry-on 随身行李

carry-on作形容词可以表示"随身携带的"，作为名词则有"随身行李"的意思。我们乘坐飞机时可以随身携带的行李就可以叫作carry-on。

3. knockoff 山寨货

前几年，"山寨"的说法红极一时，指的是仿照其他品牌产品外观生产的产品。在英语中，山寨品也有对应的说法，即knockoff，这个词的原意是"名牌仿制品"。

4. wireless hot spot 无线热点

经常使用手机或平板电脑无线上网的人们对无线热点一定很熟悉，是指在公共场所提供无线局域网(WLAN)接入Internet服务的地点。

阅读技能练习场

Exercises:

❶ According to the whole passage, which is the author's idea of the man at the airport?

A. He is an expert on high technology.

B. He is a producer of a computer company.

C. He seems to know of the tech devices, but he can't use them in the right way.

D. He is fashionable to get caught up in the latest tech trend.

panoply ['pænəpli] n. 盛装

2 Which is NOT what the author needs to deal with on vacation with his family?

A. Receiving and sending an e-mail.

B. Going to a store to get a pack of earpieces.

C. Reading.

D. Emergency child sedation.

3 What's the author's opinion about the goal in travel or even in life?

A. To have fun.

B. To take a rest at an appropriate time.

C. To use the fewest objects with the greatest function.

D. To keep the latest high tech at hand.

Reading Skills

1. 找题干中的关键词，然后到文章中找关键词，找到解题线索 ★★★★★

要抓住题干中的关键词，并反溯到原文，找到与题干相关内容。

> **Q2解析**：从题干的"on vacation with his family"可以追溯到原文的第八段。可以在选项中依次排除，找出答案B。

2. 通读原文，理解作者真正意图 ★★★★★

作者为了文章生动，写作手法有很多。欲扬先抑，先扬后抑。想要真正理解作者的观点、想法，就要注意文章中的连词，通读全文，结合上下文推测作者的意图。

> **Q1解析**：为了叙述的生动性，有时作者会欲抑先扬。因此，在理解过程中，一定要注意观点转变的转折连词。从第三段的But he had it all wrong.就可以得出，作者并不认为他是一个no amateur。因此选C。

> **Q3解析**：通过全文介绍，可以了解作者并不认为拥有所有高科技产品是一件值得高兴的事，真正的内行认为能将所有先进技术融于一个小巧的设备中才是最好的科技产品。可以从最后一段找出答案C。

Chapter 04

通信与互联网
Communication&Internet

Passage 22

Why Does the Online Obsession with Reveal Every Detail of Your Life?

——社交网站为何喜欢爆料你的生活细节?

——Jan. 29th, 2012, Guardian

Reading Guide

　　如果在你的生活中有一台摄影机，全天24小时对你进行跟踪拍摄，并适时直播到电视上去——你去过哪里，你做了什么——你的一举一动都会被记录下来，并让全世界都知道。你会做何感想？这正是本文作者最近上网时遇到的烦心事——分享，到底是对是错？

Facebook and Spotify automatically want to share my every waking action, so that I'm like a character in *The Sims*. Hover the cursor over my head and watch that *stat feed scroll*.

Sharing. Now there's a basic social concept that has somehow got all **out of whack**. The idea behind sharing is simple. Let's say I'm a caveman. I hunt and **slaughter** a bison, but I can't eat it all myself, so I share the **carcass** with others, many of whom really appreciate it, such as my **infirm** 86-year-old neighbour who hasn't had a proper

Facebook和Spotify都试图自动分享我醒后的每一个行为活动，这让我有点像《模拟人生》中的人物。只要把光标停在头上，就能查看我的属性栏。

　　分享——现在的一种基本的社交理念，以某种方式，它已经让所有人感到混乱、不知所措。分享背后的概念却并不复杂。假设我是一个原始洞穴人。我猎获一头野牛，并将其宰杀，但自己又吃不完，所以我就分一些给别人，他们中很多人对此非常感

out of whack 混乱，紊乱
slaughter ['slɔ:tə] v. 屠宰

carcass ['kɑ:kəs] n. 残骸，尸体
infirm [in'fə:m] a. 体弱的

meal in weeks because he is incapable of killing anything larger than a woodlouse. Have you tried grilling a woodlouse? It's scarcely worth the effort.

But it's not all bison meat. Let's say I am still a caveman. The other thing I share is information: the thoughts inside my head or stirring tales of the things I have done. I grunt a hilarious anecdote about the time I dropped a huge rock on a duck and an egg popped out, and mime **scandalous** gossip about well-known tribesmen. I'm the life and soul of the cave-party.

All this sharing served a purpose. It kept the community fed, as well as entertained and informed. Now zip forward to the present day and, like I say, sharing has somehow got all out of whack. A small percentage of the population hoards more bison meat than it could eat in 2,000 lifetimes, awarding itself huge bison meat bonuses **on top of** its base-rate bison meat "salary". I say "bison meat". In case you hadn't noticed, I'm using it as a clever metaphor for money.

Sharing is for the rest of us. Not sharing money or bison meat, but personal information. Where we are. What we're doing. Share it! Make it public! Go on! It's fun!

激，比如那位已经86岁的年迈体弱的邻居。他几周以来都没吃过一餐像样的饭菜，因为他没有能力杀死任何大过土鳖的动物了。你曾试图烤土鳖吗？其实并没什么必要。

但是，并不只是野牛肉。假设我仍是一个原始洞穴人。我分享的另一个东西就是信息：我大脑中的思想，或是我曾经历过的某些激动人心的事。我喃喃地讲述着一个引人发笑的故事：有一次，我把一块大石头砸在一只鸭子身上，却飞出了一只鸭蛋。我还会表演哑剧，是关于部落中的名人的八卦传闻。我成为洞穴党的灵魂人物。

所有这些分享只有一个目的，那就是为社区提供食物、娱乐和信息。现在，把时间拉回到当前，正如我所说的，分享某种程度上令所有的人们都感到不知所措。在基本分配的野牛肉"工资"之外，有一小部分人为自己储藏了巨额的野牛肉"奖金"，这够他们吃2000辈子。如果您还没领悟到我所说的"野牛肉"的含义，那我就解释一下，在这儿它是一个比喻，指的就是金钱。

分享是为我们剩下的这些人准备的。并非共享金钱或野牛肉，而是个人信息。我们所处的地点，我们所做的事情，将这一切分享！将这一切公之于众！来吧！这很有趣！

---

scandalous ['skændələs] a. 中伤的　　　　　　on top of 另外

Increasingly, I stumble across apps and services that expect me to automatically share my every waking action on Facebook and Twitter. The key word here is "automatically". Take Spotify, the streaming music service. I have written before about my admiration for Spotify, about what a technical marvel it is. A world of music at your fingertips! Incredible!

The love affair was doomed. Spotify recently reinvented itself as a kind of adjunct to Facebook and has subsequently adopted some truly hideous "social features". For instance, it will tell other people what you're listening to, live. Yes, you can switch this feature off. That's not the point. The point is that it does it by **default**. By default. IT DOES IT BY DEFAULT.

When Sony launched the Walkman back in the late 70s, its main appeal was that for the first time in history you could stroll down the **high street** listening to Neil Diamond belting out Sweet Caroline and no one could judge you for it. It made you the master of a private world of music. If the Walkman had, by default, silently contacted your friends and told them what you were listening to, not only would no one have bought a Walkman in the first place, its designers would have been viewed with the utmost suspicion.

偶然间我注意到，越来越多的应用程序和服务软件期望我自主地将所有日常的每一个活动分享到Facebook和推特网上。在这儿，关键词是"自动地"。以音乐播放软件Spotify为例，音乐被不断更新。在我对该音乐播放软件大加赞赏之前，我就曾撰文表达过其所采用技术的奇妙。手指轻点，你就进入一个音乐世界，真是不可思议！

但这种爱恋注定会消亡。Spotify最近在自我创新改造，这让它看起来像是Facebook的附属产品，接着又采用了一些真正可怕的"社交功能"。例如：它会告诉其他人你正在听的歌曲是什么，直播的。是的，你可以关闭这一功能。但这并不是重点。重点是，这项功能被设置成默认状态。默认状态。**他们竟然将该功能设置成默认状态。**

时间回到20世纪70年代末，索尼公司推出了随身听。随身听的吸引力主要在于它是史上首次出现的，你可以漫步在大街上，听着尼尔·戴蒙德高歌的《甜蜜卡罗琳》，却没人会为此而对你指指点点。这让你成为一个私人音乐世界的主人。如果随身听也默认成会悄然联系你的朋友的状态，告诉他们你正在听什么歌曲，那么首先没有人会再买随身听，甚至就连设计者的人品也会受到极度质疑。

default [di'fɔ:lt] n. 默认(值)　　　　　　　　high street 主要街道

Don't get me wrong. I'm all for sharing thoughts, no matter how banal (as every column I have ever written rather sadly proves). Humans will always babble. If someone wants to tweet that they can't decide whether to wear blue socks or brown socks, then fair enough. But when sharing becomes automated, I get the **heebie-jeebies**. Online, you play at being yourself. Apply that pressure of public performance to private, inconsequential actions—such as listening to songs in the comfort of your own room—and what happens, exactly?

It'll only get worse. Here's what I am listening to on Spotify. This is the page of the book I am reading. I am currently watching the 43rd minute of a Will Ferrell movie. And I'm not telling you this stuff. The software is. I am a character in *The Sims*. Hover the cursor over my head and watch that stat feed scroll.

You know how annoying it is when you're sitting on the train with a magazine and the person sitting beside you starts reading over your shoulder? Welcome to every single moment of your future. (Might as well get used to it.) It's an experience we'll all be sharing.

Yes, sharing. A basic social concept that's somehow got all out of whack.

不要误会我的意思。我完全赞同思想分享，不论这有多么老套（正如我在每个专栏文章中不幸证明的那样）。人类总是喋喋不休。如果有人是因为无法决定穿蓝色袜子还是褐色袜子，而将其发到推特上，那么这还说得过去。但是，当分享变成自动活动时，我就不得不神经紧张了。在网上，你扮演你自己。假设将这种公共表演的压力施加给个人的、次要的行为——比如在自己的房间中舒服地听歌——那么，究竟会发生什么？

情况只会变得更糟：这是我正在Spotify上听的歌；我正读到这本书的这一页；我正在看的一部威尔·法瑞尔的电影，看到了第43分钟。而且，这些内容都不是我告诉你的，而是软件本身。我成了《模拟人生》中的人物。只要将光标停在我的头上，就能查看我的属性栏。

当你正在火车上看杂志，而坐你旁边的人越过你的肩膀，也盯着杂志看时，你知道这是多么让人讨厌吗？欢迎来到您的未来世界的每一刻。（你最好习惯于此。）这种经验我们都将会分享。

没错，分享——一种基本的社交理念已然让所有人感到不知所措。

heebie-jeebies ['hi:bi'dʒi:biz] n. 神经过敏，紧张

117

炫 · 知识

1. The Sims 模拟人生

　　《模拟人生》系列，是一套美国艺电发行的模拟普通人生活的个人电脑游戏。该系列的全球销量已经超过了一亿套，这使它成为了电子游戏史上最畅销的游戏。

2. stat feed scroll 人物属性栏

　　scroll意为"卷轴"。在玩游戏时，将鼠标停留在人物区域，就会出现该人物的属性、状态、任务等信息；将鼠标移开，信息就隐藏了。

3. fair enough 说得对

　　fair enough也可以作为句子单独使用，指"你认为合理的，你能够接受的东西"。

阅读技能练习场

Exercises:

1 Why did the author say "I'm like a character in *The Sims*"?

　　A. Someone will tell people what he was doing.

　　B. His privacy is uncovered in public.

　　C. He acts like the character in *The Sims*.

　　D. His information and every action will be published on the Internet by default.

2 What's the purpose of the "caveman" metaphor in the passage?

　　A. To tell us the author likes to share food with others.

　　B. To inform us people should share food in the old days.

　　C. To infer that ancient people didn't want to share food but they had to.

　　D. To compare with people nowadays who have to share information.

3 According to the passage, what's the opinion of the author about the sharing thing?

　　A. Agreeable.

　　B. Indifferent.

118

C. Irritating.

D. Boring.

Reading Skills

1. 领悟文章含义，灵活应对同义转述 ★ ★ ★ ★ ★

有的时候，正确选项通常变换了表达方式，需要我们仔细分析句式和句意才能找到正确答案。同义转述也是对文章理解的另一种考查形式。

> **Q1解析**：通过对第一段第一句话的理解，我们可知选项D是对第一句话的转述，意思相同。
>
> **Q3解析**：这道题是猜测作者观点。通过阅读全文可知，作者认为网站分享用户行为的举动就像有人越过你的肩膀看你正在看的报纸一样令人气愤，文中用annoying表达作者的观点态度，而irritating也是表示"令人恼怒的"，因此选C。

2. 找到关键点，抓准作者写作意图 ★ ★ ★ ★ ★

文章中常使用引用、举例、排比等修辞手法，这是作者为了写作做铺垫，起对比、连接、强调等作用。

> **Q2解析**：这个问题的答案要通读全文后才能确定。作者将原始洞穴人主动分享食物的事例与现代人被动分享个人信息做了对比。因此选D。

Passage 23

6 Words for the Modern Internet

——现代互联网的6个关键词

——Jun. 22nd, 2011, Wired

Reading Guide

科技和网络技术的发展给我们的生活带来了日新月异的变化。因为这些新事物的出现，我们的生活才更加便利和人性化。本文列举了现代互联网的6个关键词，我们借此可以更深刻地体会互联网。

Wired co-founder and Senior Maverick Kevin Kelly shared six choice words of his own at the **inaugural** NExTWORK technology conference to illustrate the major trends he sees in a world speeding towards video, mobile and the cloud.

You should take notes.

1. Screening

Screens are everywhere now—on the backs of airplane seats, on the backs of buildings, right next to us. Soon these screens will become a **filter** for reality—superimposed onto our glasses, an overlay of the digital world onto the real one.

"We're no longer people of the book," Kelly said, "we've become people of the screen."

2. Interacting

All of these screens are no longer just static objects to **stare at**—they demand our entire bodies, including our voices. Kelly retells

《连线》杂志的联合创始人凯文·凯利在NExTWORK技术大会的开幕式上用了6个精选的词汇来描述在他的观点中，世界在视频、移动技术以及云技术方面的发展趋势。

你应该记录一下。

1. 屏幕

屏幕如今无处不在——比如飞机座椅的后面、建筑物后墙，总之就在我们身边。很快这些屏幕就会变成现实的过滤器——叠加在我们的眼镜上，将数码世界覆盖到现实世界之上。

"我们将再不是阅读书本的人，我们将是阅读屏幕的人。"凯利说到。

2. 互动

所有这些屏幕将不再是静态对象——它需要我们整个身体的配合，包括我们的声音。凯利复述了他曾经

inaugural [i'nɔːgjurəl] a. 开幕的
filter ['filtə] n. 过滤器

stare at 盯着

how he watched a toddler try to interact with a photograph, obviously confused by how the image wasn't getting bigger or smaller with a pinch of his fingers.

These days, "if it's not interacting, it doesn't work," Kelly said. And it goes both ways—our screens are watching back at us as we watch them. Content is almost like a two-way mirror, adapting to our actions as we interact with it.

3. Sharing

Kelly calls this the "primary verb of this world." The web was built on sharing, and it will continue to go in that direction. He suspects that at some point we'll have one big cloud—the cloud of all clouds—which will allow us to share everything. We're already sharing things we never thought possible: friends, investments, memories, expectations.

"Anything that can be shared will be shared," Kelly said. "We're only at the beginning."

Although the rise of sharing obviously introduces privacy concerns, Kelly believes there is immense value to opening up your own personal data to the public. He imagines privacy and transparency on a slider—on one end is private and generic, the other end is transparent and personal.

"People are pushing this slider further toward transparency and personalization," Kelly said.

4. Flowing

First we had files, folders, desktops. Then came pages and links. Now we've got streams and tags and clouds. Life logs, Twitter streams, RSS feeds, Facebook walls—no past and future, just a

看着一个仍在学步的小孩是怎样尝试与照片互动的，很显然这个孩子很困惑，为什么照片不能随着他手指的点击而放大或缩小呢？

如今，"如果设备不能与你互动，那它一定是坏掉了，"凯利这样说道。这是一种相互的方式——当我们看着屏幕时，屏幕也看着我们。内容则好像一面双面镜，当我们与它互动的时候，它同时会根据我们的动作而调整。

3. 分享

凯利把"分享"称为"当今世界上最基本的动词。"互联网是基于分享而创立的，它也会继续朝着这个目标发展。他认为在某一天，我们将会拥有一片巨大的"云"——这片"云"包含了所有的"云"——能让我们分享任何事物。我们如今已经分享了许多过去我们不可能想到的东西：比如朋友、投资、记忆和期望。

"一切可以被分享的东西都将被分享，而我们只是刚刚开始。"凯利说。

尽管越来越多的分享显然会带来个人隐私方面的忧虑，凯利仍然相信个人信息的公开具有巨大价值。他设想隐私和透明度是在一个滑动条上的——一端是你的隐私和大众化，另一端则是信息透明和个性化。

"人们正在把这个滑动条推向信息透明和个性化。"凯利说。

4.（数据的）流动

一开始我们有文件、文件夹和桌面，然后有了网页和链接。如今，我们有了数据流、标签和云。生活日志、推特数据流、RSS订阅，以及

stream.

"All these streams are together actually forming the new media, the new platform." Kelly said.

5. Accessing

When everything is always there and always on, access to things becomes more important than owning them. Spotify, Amazon, Netflix all push people toward "just in time purchasing," because you might as well wait until you're ready to consume it.

"The burdens of ownership will be seen against the benefits of access," Kelly said.

6. **Generating**

"The internet is the world's largest copy machine," Kelly said. How do you create anything of value when it can be copied so easily? In this new ecosystem, things become valuable if they can't be copied easily, and if they're easy to pay for. We are willing to pay for personalization (having music tailored to the acoustics of your living room), findability (Amazon is more useful than a zipped file of every piece of music ever recorded in the world), and embodiment (concerts as opposed to **albums**). These and other "generatives" are valuable, because they have become the new fundamental economic unit.

While these are his six ways of **slicing up** the new networked world, Kelly thinks we have a long way to go.

"Whatever it is, we know that we're not late," he concludes. "We just started this."

Facebook照片墙——没有所谓的过去和未来，只有数据流。

"所有这些数据流聚在一起会形成新的媒体以及新的平台。" 凯利如是说。

5. 访问

当一切事物永远在那里，永远是开放的状态的话，访问它们比拥有它们显得更加重要。Spotify、亚马逊以及网飞都推动人们"及时购买"，因为你很有可能等到有需要的时候才去购买。

"所有权的负担将会影响访问带来的利益。" 凯利说。

6. 生成

"互联网是世界上最大的复印机，" 凯利说道。当复制如此简单，你又如何创造有价值的东西呢？在这个新的生态系统中，不容易被复制且购买方便的东西就成了有价值的东西。我们愿意为那些个性化服务(比如为客厅音响订制的音乐)、可检索性(Amazon网站比一个含有很多音乐文件的压缩包更有用)，以及具体的事物(就像音乐会相对于专辑)买单。这些以及其他"可生产"的东西都是有价值的，因为它们已经成为新的基础经济的一部分。

尽管这是凯利眼中切分新网络世界的六个方法，他认为我们还有很长的一段路要走。

"无论现代互联网是怎样的，我们知道我们都不是太迟，" 他总结说，"我们只是刚刚开始。"

---

generate ['dʒenəreit] v. 产生
album ['ælbəm] n. 专辑

slice up 把……切成片

炫 · 知识

1. Wired 连线杂志

　　Wired《连线》是美国的一份科技类月刊杂志，着重于报道科学技术如何应用于现代和未来人类生活的各个方面，以及新技术对文化、经济和政治造成何种影响。

2. static object 静态对象

　　static是"静止的"，在科技和互联网领域，这个单词可以表示"静态的"。相对地，"动态的"则是用active或dynamic表示。

3. RSS feed 简易信息聚合供稿

　　RSS是Really Simple Syndication的缩写，意为"简易信息聚合"。此外，RSS也可以代表Rich Site Summary。RSS订阅是某个站点用来与其他站点共享内容的一种简易方式。feed在这里表示"供稿"。

阅读技能练习场

Exercises:

1 Which field did Kelly NOT mention in the first paragraph?

　　A. Video.

　　B. Smart phone.

　　C. Mobile.

　　D. Cloud.

2 How do you understand the sentence—"if it's not interacting, it doesn't work"?

　　A. We and screens interacts with each other.

　　B. Screens interact with us, and then we interact with others.

　　C. All of these screens are no longer just static objects.

　　D. It cannot be used.

3 According to the fourth word, which is NOT mentioned as current productions?

　　A. Streams.

　　B. RSS feeds.

　　C. Clouds.

　　D. Folders.

Reading Skills

1. 注意文中没有出现的信息 ★★★★★

有时候问题的选项都是我们习以为常的事物，我们很容易想当然地认为它们都是正确的。但往往陷阱就设置在这些选项中，因此一定不能选择文中没有出现的信息。

> **Q1解析**：题目询问哪一个在第一自然段没有被提到，因此我们可以到第一段中寻找相关的线索，可以知道，除了智能手机以外的三项都有提到。所以正确答案是B。

2. 根据上下文推断 ★★★★★

遇到考查文章主旨的问题时，要回到文章相应的段落。仔细阅读上下文，根据文中提供的信息进行推断，然后选择答案。

> **Q2解析**：这句话出现在介绍第二个关键词的那个部分，根据第一段的内容，可以知道当今的设备大多都可以与人互动。所以可以知道C选项是正确的。A选项描述的则是屏幕与我们互动的方式。

2. 根据时间轴快速判断 ★★★★★

有时候题目可能询问一些与时代有关的信息。如果我们读完文章后能记住哪些事物分别发生在什么年代，做题时就会感到简单许多。

> **Q3解析**：问题询问哪一个不是当前的产物，看过选项之后，不难看出文件夹是在电脑出现的初期就存在的事物。而First we had files, folders, desktops. Then came pages and links.亦可支持此观点，故选D。

Passage 24

What's Eating Your Phone's Data Allowance?

——谁在"偷吃"你的数据流量?

——Apr. 22nd, 2012, USA Today

Reading Guide

智能手机和平板电脑等科技产品给人们的工作和生活带来很多便利和乐趣。但是,如何避免每月的数据通信流量"入不敷出"的窘境呢?怎样才能使手机更节电? 一起来文中寻找答案吧。

Question: Could all the spam I'm getting explain why I use up half of my phone's data cap in a couple of weeks?

Answer: Sorry, probably not. Most e-mail takes up little bandwidth, and spam—typically, several lines of text for each junk e-mail—uses even less.

Most mobile Web browsing also doesn't do much to eat up a bandwidth **quota.** To get a grasp of what apps can get you into trouble, employ a few simple data-usage tools.

Apple includes a bandwidth meter on the iPhone (open the Settings app, tap its General heading, then Network) and the 3G and 4G versions of the iPad (Settings, then Cellular Data). This will report the total data consumed by the

提问:我正在接收的所有这些垃圾邮件是否可以解释,为什么我手机的流量在几周之内就用了一半呢?

回答:抱歉,也许不能。大多数电子邮件只占据很少的带宽,而在通常的情况下——每封垃圾邮件只有寥寥数行——因此使用的带宽更少。

大多数情况下,使用手机浏览网页也不会消耗太多的带宽定额。如果你想了解哪些应用程序会给你带来麻烦,可以使用几个简单的数据使用工具。

苹果公司在iPhone(打开"设置",点击"主标题",然后进入"网络")及3G和4G版本的iPad("设置",然后进入"蜂窝数据")中都装有一个带宽计量器。这个计量器会报

---

quota ['kwəutə] n. 定额

device; third-party apps can provide the same info for WiFi-only iPads and the iPod touch.

On Google's Android, the Ice Cream Sandwich version offers a more nuanced data-usage gauge that breaks down the bill on an app-by-app basis. On earlier versions, other firms' software has to suffice; I've run the free NetCounter.

Years of **spot checks** with these tools have convinced me that Web radio—sometimes labeled a bandwidth hog—shouldn't be a problem, either. For example, I've **clocked** Pandora's Web-radio app using no more than 30 to 40 megabytes per hour of listening.

Web video, however, can get the meter spinning—especially on devices with larger screens. On an Android phone, an hour of Netflix viewing ate up almost 180 MB. But on an iPad 2, an hour of Netflix accounted for about 670 MB (though that figure may include background activity such as checking e-mail). On a new Android tablet, the same 60 minutes of the same movie chewed through 656 MB.

I've heard of even worse examples—Houston Chronicle tech columnist Dwight Silverman recently tweeted that watching two 30-minute episodes of The Big C in Showtime's app on a new iPad ate up a full one gigabyte of Verizon LTE data.

告设备使用的全部数据信息；对于无线版的iPad和iPod touch，第三方应用也可以提供同样的信息。

对于谷歌的安卓系统——"冰淇淋三明治"版本提供一个更精确的数据使用计量器，它分别计算每个应用带宽消耗量，把账单细化。对于更早的版本，该公司也有足够的应用可供选择。我使用了免费的上网管家。

多年来使用这些工具进行的抽样调查使我确信网络收音机也不应该是个问题——尽管它有时被打上带宽消耗大户的标签。例如，我记录了潘多拉网络收音机的带宽消耗情况，每小时的收听只使用不超过30—40兆的带宽。

然而，网络视频却能让计量器快速运转——尤其是在屏幕较大的设备上。使用一部安卓手机在网飞公司收看一小时的影片几乎需要消耗180兆的带宽，但如果使用iPad 2就要消耗大约670兆的带宽（尽管这个数字可能包括后台活动，例如查收邮件）。使用新款的安卓平板电脑，观看60分钟同样的影片需要656兆字节。

我听说过更糟糕的情况——《休斯顿纪事报》的科技专栏作者德怀特·西尔弗曼最近发表的一条推文说，在新的iPad上使用Showtime应用程序观看两集每集时长30分钟的《如果还有明天》需要整整十亿字节的Verizon长期演进计划技术数据。

---

spot check 抽样调查

clock [klɔk] v. 记录时间

Unusual situations can yield odd results, however. When I took a Samsung Galaxy Nexus to the SXSW Interactive conference in Austin and cruelly overused it, its data-usage gauge reported that my frequent Web use topped the leaderboard, at 117 MB for that week. Facebook followed at 56 MB, then Google's Play Store (what used to be called the Android Market) at 47 MB. That's a lot of News Feed scanning and software updates.

The easiest way to stay out of trouble with bandwidth caps, however, is not to worry about particular apps but to use Wi-Fi instead of 3G or 4G whenever possible.

In a follow-up e-mail, the reader who sent this query suggested that his frequent lookups of satellite photos and weather radar could have been at fault. I don't know whether he's right, but those theories make more sense than an overload of junk mail—not that you don't have plenty of other reasons to be annoyed at that.

Tip: Battery-saving black backgrounds on some phones. The abbreviations used to describe the screens on mobile devices usually invite yawns—if people take note of them at all. But one particular kind of display, OLED, allows for a special power-saving trick.

Organic Light Emitting Diode screens can generate brighter colors and deeper blacks than

然而，特殊的情况可能产生奇怪的结果。当我带着三星Galaxy Nexus手机去奥斯汀参加西南偏南艺术节互动会，使用了过多的带宽以后，我手机上的数据使用计量器报告我浏览网页的频率位列第一，在那一周使用了117兆。位列第二的是Facebook，使用了56兆，其后的是谷歌的Play Store(过去叫作安卓市场)用了47兆。这就是大量浏览新闻快讯和软件升级造成的结果。

最简单的避免带宽限定给自己造成麻烦的方法就是不去担心个别的应用，而是在任何可能的时候使用Wi-Fi而不是3G或4G服务。

提出这个疑问的读者在随后的一封邮件中说，他频繁地查询卫星照片和气象雷达可能对消耗一半带宽有责任。我不知道他是不是正确的，但是这些理论比那些认为是因为铺天盖地的垃圾邮件才导致宽带消耗过快的说法更有道理——就算你讨厌垃圾邮件，有的是其他原因，都能让你觉得它很招人烦。

小贴士：使用黑色背景可以节电那些用来描述移动设备的屏幕的简称通常让人们哈欠连连——如果有人注意到它们的话。但其中一种独特的显示方式——OLED——给我们提供了一个特别的节电小窍门。

相比一些其他屏幕，OLED屏可以生成更亮的颜色和更深的黑色，但

---

at fault 有责任

some other kinds, but as an analyst reminded me a couple of months ago, they also use **varying** amounts of power to produce those colors. That means that, much like plasma TVs, OLED displays need less electricity to display a dark area than a bright one.

I tested this by setting a phone with a particularly enormous OLED screen, Samsung's Galaxy Note, to use an all-white and then an all-black background. To keep wireless activity from **skewing** the results, I switched the Note to airplane mode; to give that 5.3-in. screen as much influence as possible on power consumption, I set it to stay **illuminated**.

The results: An hour of showing the white background left the Note with 87% of a **charge**, compared to 92% after an hour with the black background.

正如几个月前一位分析师提醒我的，生成这些色彩也需要耗费不同程度的电量。这意味着OLED显示屏和等离子电视非常相似，显示暗色背景所需的电量要少于亮色。

我在有着超大OLED显示屏的三星Galaxy Note手机上进行了测试，先是设置了全白屏，接下来是全黑屏。为了避免无线活动的影响，我把手机调到了飞行模式；为了给这块5.3英寸的屏幕在电量消耗上造成最大的影响，我把手机设置为永远点亮屏幕的模式。

测试结果：设置白屏的手机在一小时后剩余87%的电量；与此相比，设置黑屏的手机剩余92%的电量。

炫 · 知识

1. spam 垃圾邮件

垃圾邮件除了可以用junk email表示以外，还可以说成spam。SPAM最初是一个罐装肉的牌子，有段时间这种肉非常普及，到了无处不在、令人讨厌的程度。后来，spam就被用来称呼互联网上无处不在的垃圾邮件。

2. get a grasp of 理解

grasp除了可以表示"抓住"，还有"理解"的意思。因此get a grasp of就表示"理解某事"，这个说法十分地道。

varying ['vɛəriŋ] a. 变化的
skew [skju:] v. 歪曲

illuminated [i'lju:mineitid] a. 点亮的
charge [tʃɑ:dʒ] n. 电量

3. tap 轻触

大家在使用触屏手机时，一定会有轻触屏幕的动作。在英语中，这个动作十分形象地用tap这个单词来表示。

4. SXSW 西南偏南

西南偏南（SXSW/South by Southwest）是每年在美国得克萨斯州奥斯汀举行的一系列电影、交互式多媒体和音乐的艺术节，因希区柯克的电影《西北偏北》，其联合创始人路易斯·布莱克将这个艺术节称为西南偏南。而SXSW则是其英文名的首字母缩写词，其中X代表"乘号"，即by。

5. OLED 有机发光二级管

OLED的全称是organic light emitting diode，因其轻薄、省电等特性，这种显示设备在数码类产品上大量使用，尤其是用在手机的屏幕上。

阅读技能练习场

Exercises:

1 Which of the following is true according to the whole passage?

A. Apps could get you into a lot of bandwidth quota trouble, so you must have a bandwidth meter.

B. Larger screens eat up more data allowance when watching the same movie.

C. Web radio and web video are real "bandwidth hog".

D. Beware of your apps and use WiFi connection only.

2 Which one of the following is hot true about how to monitor your data usage to avoid running out of data allowance?

A. iPhone users can make use of the bandwidth meter on the phone.

B. Third-party apps can help meter the data usage of WiFi-only iPads.

C. The data-usage gauge on Android phone is helpful but can't show the data usage of each app.

D. There are also applications that can do this job, like NetCounter.

3 After reading the "Tip", which of the following do you think is NOT true?

A. If your phone has an OLED screen, why not set it black to save power?

B. The abbreviations describing the screens on mobile devices are interesting.

C. Plasma TVs need to consume more electricity to display a bright area than a dark one.

D. Under the same condition, the white background with an OLED screen consumes more power.

Reading Skills

1. 通过选项反向推断 ★★★★★

在迅速浏览过全文的基础上，不但可以从题干中找关键词，也可以快速阅读四个选项，提炼关键信息，然后再在文中找到出处，进行比对。

> **Q1解析：** A选项的前半句在文中有类似的表达，但后半句的you must have a bandwidth meter太过主观。第七段的内容可解释B选项，即作者比对了不同大小的屏幕，发现如果观看同样同时长的影片，带宽消耗与屏幕尺寸成正比。第六段的内容表明Web radio并非带宽消耗大户，故C选项也是错误的。D选项的"use WiFi only"说法过于绝对。故本题选B。

2. 对文章信息进行分类 ★★★★★

即使文章只涉及一个主题，也会从多个方面来展开。面对文章提供的大量信息，要清楚哪些内容分别在文章的哪个部分。这样能方便反查。

> **Q2解析：** 问题要求选出不能帮助用户监测移动设备数据使用情况的一项。这个内容在文章第四、五段。注意C选项描述...can't show the data usage of each app，而文章中的表达是...on an app-by-app basis。故选C。
>
> **Q3解析：** 解题的关键信息主要在文章后面的Tip部分。一般来说，大家对各种屏幕的术语及简称并不太感兴趣，故选B。

Chapter 4

Passage 25

"No Permission" Android Apps Can See and Share Your Data

—— "无权限"的安卓应用程序能发现并共享你的资料

——Apr. 23rd, 2012, CNN

Reading Guide

安卓应用程序存在安全隐患？手机用户在安装应用软件时要格外注意，因为没有获得权限的安装程序可能会从你手机的SIM卡中获取你的个人信息，并通过其他可能的途径传送出去。这对用户来说无疑是非常危险的。

Savvy Android users tend to be **wary** of installing apps that request seemingly unnecessary permissions. When an app wants access to data or functions on your phone, such as your contacts list or the ability to send text messages, it can signal potential security or **malware** risks.

But Android apps that request no permissions at all (such as this Magic 8 ball app) are generally considered pretty free of security risks.

But are they?

A test conducted by the Leviathan Security Group showed that even "no-permissions" Android apps can access potentially sensitive data on your phone—and transmit that data elsewhere

理性的安卓用户在安装应用程序时都会比较谨慎，尤其是对于那些在安装时要求似乎不必要权限的应用程序。当一款应用程序想要访问你手机中的数据和功能，比如你的联系人列表或者短信发送功能时，系统就会告知潜在的安全威胁或是恶意软件的风险。

但是没有要求任何权限的安卓应用程序（比如这款魔术8球应用）通常会被认为是完全不存在安全风险的。

但事情真的如此吗？

利维坦安全集团的一项测试表明：即使是"无权限"的安卓应用也能获取你手机里潜在的敏感数据，并通过手机的网络浏览器将数据传送到

---

wary ['weəri] a. 谨慎的　　　　malware ['mælweə] n. 恶意软件

via your phone's Web browser.

Specifically, Paul Brodeur of Leviathan created a test app that requested no permissions and **installed** it on some Android devices. He was able to scan the phone's memory card (SD card) and display a list of all non-hidden files on it.

"While it's possible to fetch the contents of all those files, I'll leave it to someone else to decide what files should be grabbed and which are going to be boring." he wrote.

He also could see which apps were installed on the phone, and list some files belonging to those apps. He observed that this might allow **nefarious** people to find and exploit permission-related **vulnerabilities** in certain apps. Last year the Skype Android app presented this kind of problem. (Skype fixed that problem.)

And for phones that operate on GSM cell networks (in the U.S., that's AT&T and T-Mobile), Leviathan's test app was able to read identifying information about the phone from the SIM card, plus some other information.

Finally, since no-permissions apps can launch the phone's Web browser, that provides a potential route to transmit some data from the phone.

While Brodeur's test app was designed to seek out such security lapses. "It's trivial for any installed app to execute these actions without any user interaction." he wrote.

其他位置。

来自利维坦的保罗 布罗德特地制作了一款没有权限的测试应用程序，并将其安装到一些安卓设备上。该程序能监测手机中的记忆卡（SD卡），并展示所有非隐藏文件夹的列表。

他写道："虽然获得所有这些文件夹中的内容是可以实现的，但我将这个权利留给其他人，让他们决定哪些文件夹值得查看，哪些是索然无味的东西。"

他也能看到手机中安装了哪些应用软件，还可以列出一些属于这些应用的文件夹。他发现这样可能会给恶意分子机会以发现并利用某些应用程序中与权限相关的漏洞。去年，安卓版的应用软件Skype就发生了类似的问题。（Skype现在已经将问题解决了。）

对于使用GSM蜂窝网络的手机来说（在美国就是AT&T和T-Mobile），利维坦的测试应用能够读取手机SIM卡中与手机相关的验证信息，以及一些其他信息。

最终，由于无权限的应用程序能够运行手机的网络浏览器，这就为从手机中传送数据提供了可行的路径。

然而布罗德的测试应用是为了找出这样的安全缺陷而设计。"让任何一款已经安装的应用在未与用户互动的情况下执行命令只是一件小事。"他写道。

---

install [in'stɔ:l] v. 安装
nefarious [ni'feəriəs] a. 违法的

vulnerability [ˌvʌlnərə'biləti] n. 漏洞

While this may sound worrying, don't panic. What Leviathan discovered probably should concern Android app developers and Google, rather than consumers who use Android phones and tablets.

"What this research found is really little cracks in Android—not great big security holes you could drive a truck through," said Kevin Mahaffey, co-founder and chief technical officer of Lookout Mobile Security, a leading provider of security apps and services for Android devices. "That's why this kind of research is so valuable—it ultimately helps make Android more secure."

According to Mahaffey, the bigger problem is not that people might maliciously exploit these security cracks to steal from users or compromise their phones—but rather that many app developers are "sloppy."

For instance, developers sometimes build apps that store user data (such as usernames and passwords) in ways that could be easily accessed through the security cracks Leviathan found. Or the app might open the phone's Web browser to allow functionality that could be handled other ways.

For instance, TheVerge.com reported that the photo gallery that comes pre-installed on Android phones by Samsung, LG, and some other manufacturers stores unencrypted copies of complete addresses associated with photos. They found in a completely unencrypted file "a list of locations which matched those of our home, work, family, significant other, friends, and even holiday destinations."

这听起来可能会让人担心，不过不用惊慌。与其说这会让使用安卓手机和平板电脑的消费者担忧，不如说利维坦公司的发现可能会让安卓应用的开发者和谷歌公司更加担忧。

"这个调查研究发现安卓系统真的几乎没有漏洞——没有大得让你可以开着卡车驶过的安全漏洞，这就是为什么此类研究如此有价值的原因——这最终使安卓系统更加安全。"凯文·马哈菲说道，他是手机安全守护者公司的联合创始人兼首席技术官。手机安全守护者公司是手机安全应用程序和安卓设备服务的主要提供商。

在马哈菲看来，更大的问题不是人们可能会恶意利用这些安全隐患，从用户那里盗取信息或是危害他们的手机安全，而是许多应用软件的开发者本身就很"粗心"。

例如，开发者制作能够储存用户数据(比如用户名和密码)的应用程序的方式有时能使信息通过利维坦公司发现的安全漏洞轻易被获取。还有一种情况是应用程序可能会打开手机的网络浏览器，允许使用其他方式的控制功能。

比如TheVerge网站的报道称，三星、LG和一些其他厂商的安卓手机中预装的未加密照片库存储了与照片相关的完整地址。他们在一个完全没加密的文件夹中发现了一个"分别与我们的家庭、工作、亲属、爱人、朋友完全匹配的地址列表，其中甚至还包括我们假日的目的地。"

133

These were not GPS coordinates, but rather full addresses: door number, street, town, zip code, and country. TheVerge noted that this address data apparently was generated by Picasa Web Albums. Google acquired Picasa in 2004.

"There is no reason for the application to be **caching** locations of private photos completely unencrypted," wrote Aaron Souppouris for The Verge. "This was information that we'd never given Google, either on a phone or within Picasa. To make matters worse, Picasa Web-Album **syncing** had been switched off a week before the information was found."

There's not a lot that the average consumer can do in terms of spotting whether apps are storing unnecessary data in insecure ways.

The best practice is still to notice which permissions apps require before installing them, don't install apps that seem to require too many permissions, and report to the developer any suspicious activity by an app.

If the developer is not responsive or seems evasive or shady when you report suspicious app behavior, Mahaffey advises alerting Google's Android security team by sending an e-mail to security@android.com.

"That channel is mainly used by developers, but it's worth letting them know if you have concerns about an app and you aren't getting useful responses from the developer." he said.

这些地址虽然不是全球定位系统坐标，但却相当完整：包括门牌号、街道、城镇、邮编和国家。TheVerge网站指出这些地址数据显然是通过Picasa网络相簿生成的。而谷歌于2004年收购了Picasa。

The Verge网站的亚伦·苏普瑞斯写到："应用软件没有任何理由可以存储完全未加密的私人照片的地址。这些信息是我们绝不会提供给谷歌的，无论是手机中的照片还是Picasa中的照片。更糟的是，在发现这些信息之前的一个星期，Picasa同步网络相簿已经关闭了。"

对于普通消费者来说，很难识别应用软件是否以不安全的方式储存了不必要的资料。

最好的做法仍然是在安装应用之前注意该软件请求了哪些权限。不要安装那些似乎要求太多权限的应用软件，并向应用开发者告知程序的任何可疑活动。

如果开发者并没有回应你的报告，或者似乎想要推脱，或是有可疑之处时，马哈菲建议你发送邮件至security@android.com来提醒谷歌的安卓安全团队。

他说："这个渠道主要被开发者使用，但让他们知道你是否对某个应用软件有所顾虑，而且你没有从开发者那里得到有用反馈，这是很必要的。"

---

cache [kæʃ] v. 储存

sync [sɪŋk] v. 同步

Chapter 4

炫 · 知识

1. launch 运行

如果你足够细心，可能在安装完某个程序的时候看到过立即运行的勾选框后面，写的英文正是launch，这个单词除了可以表示"发射"，还有"运行"的意思。

2. crack 漏洞

在本文中，作者形象地用crack来表示系统的安全漏洞。crack的本意是"裂缝，缝隙"。这种说法十分贴切地形容了漏洞的特点。

3. pre-installed 预装的

我们经常说的"预装软件"，在英文中可以用pre-installed这个形容词来表示。pre-这个前缀表示"在……之前，预先的"。

4. significant other 对……重要的人

短语significant other表示"对……重要的人"，通常情况下是指爱人。

阅读技能练习场

Exercises:

1 According to the passage, which saying is right?

A. The no-permission apps can't access to your data in your phone.

B. The Leviathan Security Group has made a no-permission app that could share your information.

C. Skype has fixed the permission-related vulnerabilities in certain apps.

D. Leviathan's test app can't read identifying information about the phone.

2 What's Brodeur's test app designed for?

A. To revise the security lapses.

B. To delete the no-permission apps.

C. To find out the security lapses.

D. To help install the no-permission apps.

135

3 What does "significant other" mean in the 15th paragraph?

A. Your parent.

B. Your best friend.

C. Your teacher.

D. Your lover.

Answers: 1.C 2.C 3.D

Reading Skills

1. 避免混淆概念 ★★★★★

有时因为文章过长，我们在阅读时只能匆匆浏览。但是一定要注意，不可漏掉重要信息或是混淆概念，一定要看清文章中的原本意思。

> **Q1解析**：通读整篇文章之后，与A、B、D三项相关的内容都可以在文中找到，根据原文可知，这三个选项叙述的内容都是错误的。根据第七段括号中的文字，可以知道Skype已经解决了相关问题，因此选C。

> **Q2解析**：根据第十段第一句话，Brodeur的test app的作用是seek out such security lapses，因此选C。

2. 联系上下文增加猜词准确率 ★★★★★

在特定的语言环境下，某些词汇或是短语会有特殊的含义。想要准确无误地理解文章表达的含义，就要学会利用上下文，通过推断的方法来猜测单词或短语的意思。

> **Q3解析**：首先根据字面意思，可以知道significant other意为"重要的另一个人"；结合整句话及上下文含义，可以推测该短语的意思就是"另一半，爱人"，因此选D。

Chapter 4

Passage 26

How Is Social Media Supporting People with Depression?
——社会媒体如何鼓励自闭症患者？
——Apr. 26th, 2012, Guardian

Reading Guide

生活节奏快、压力大是生活在一线城市的人们的"通病"。人们容易感到焦虑、压抑，从而产生自闭情绪和症状。其实，自闭症在大城市中是一种很常见的心理疾病。

作者通过网络与自闭症患者沟通、交流，充分发挥社交媒体的作用，引起了患者心理上的共鸣，并帮助他们走出困境，重新过上安宁的生活。

Depression is common, disabling and increasing in prevalence. Many people suffer in silence, don't get much empathy or sympathy and, if when they do ask for help, they may find medication more frequently offered than psychological therapy. This may be changing, but not fast enough.

I have just recently started responding to people's questions about depression online. While I am a doctor, I am an unusual one in that I am more interested in health than sickness and very interested in positive conceptions of mental health and human **flourishing**. So what I do may not even be medicine in the traditional sense; it's very much more a coaching, guiding approach. I am not an

忧郁是十分普遍的，它可以令人丧失意志，而其患病率正在逐渐上升。许多人只是默默忍受，没有得到足够的悲悯与同情，而且如果他们真要寻求帮助，则更多地选择药物治疗，而不是心理治疗。但这一现象也许正在变化，尽管并没有那么快。

我最近开始在网上回答人们关于自闭的提问。我是一名医生，不过我是一名不同寻常的医生，因为比起疾病，我对健康、积极的心理健康观念和人类的繁荣更感兴趣。因此，我所做的并非传统观念上的行医，而更倾向于一种训练、指导的方法。我并不是药物治疗的专家，也不会对具体的

flourish ['flʌriʃ] v. 繁荣

expert on medication, and won't be commenting about specific medications.

My role, as I see it, is to **empathize** (an almost universal good, but harder to do online than face to face), share information in a non-judgmental way, share options, and encourage feelings of **autonomy**, optimism and competence. Hope is something many people with depression lack, along with motivation—but both of these things can be increased over time via skillful conversation.

Online chat, discussion and support provides many other benefits to depressed people—feelings of connectedness, not being judged, **reassurance** that things can and do get better over time, or that the painful or empty feelings of depression can be tolerated.

Social networks have emerged as an accessible platform on which people are able to connect with **like-minded** individuals. Black Dog Tribe, the social site co-founded by Ruby Wax who has spoken publicly about her life-long battle with depression, uses this social space to encourage people to talk, share experiences and, most importantly, recognize that they are not alone in their depression.

Being part of a community provides access to information, advice and a supportive network of people who can understand and empathize with what is still, unfortunately, a largely misunderstood illness in mainstream society. For those with an illness that **exacerbates** feelings of isolation, this is **vital**.

While it is important that those with depression have a safe haven in which to share

药物疗法发表评论。

在我看来，我的角色就是引起共鸣(引起共鸣普遍来说是很好的方法，但是在网上会比面对面更难)，并以非批判性的方式分享信息、分享观点，鼓励人们自主管理感情、乐观积极且拥有能力。希望和动力是许多沮丧的人们所缺少的东西，但是通过长时间的技巧性谈话，这两者都是可以加强的。

在线聊天、讨论和支持为自闭的人们提供许多其他益处———一种心灵相通、不受任何人批判和安心的感觉，感到事情能够也确实可以随着时间的流逝变得更好，而自闭带来的痛苦或空虚感也可以忍受。

社交网络已经成为一个平台，人们可以在这个平台上与志趣相投的人相互联系。社交网站黑狗部落是由露比·威克斯与他人共同创立的，她曾公开谈论过将终生与自闭作战。黑狗部落利用这一社交空间鼓励人们进行讨论、分享经验，更重要的是让人们知道他们不是惟一的患有自闭症的人。

作为社区的一部分，该网站提供信息、建议以及互相支持的人际关系网，这些人能够理解并同情这种在主流社会中仍不幸被广泛误解的疾病。对那些患有自闭症并因此强烈感觉被孤立的人们来说，这是至关重要的。

然而对于患有自闭症的人来说，能够拥有一个安全的避难所，在这里

---

empathize ['empəθaiz] v. 引起共鸣
autonomy [ɔː'tɔnəmi] n. 自主
reassurance [ˌriːə'ʃuərəns] n. 安心

like-minded ['laik'maindid] a. 志趣相投的
exacerbate [ek'sæsəbeit] v. 加剧
vital ['vaitəl] a. 至关重要的

their issues with a trusted community, making use of the more mainstream sites of Facebook and Twitter may amplify previously hidden anguish. It brings conversations about depression out into the public sphere where information then has the potential to trickle down to people who have little understanding of the illness and also those who may not realize that they too are suffering.

But these open platforms have seen high profile people such as the former footballer Stan Collymore and the political aide Alastair Campbell bringing attention to the illness through moving personal testimonies. It all helps to raise awareness, **tackle** the stigma associated with depression and promote the message that people need not suffer in silence.

There is so much bullshit out there about mental health and mental illness, I suspect people are ready for an accessible and helpful resource where they can share experiences, concerns and feelings, learn about new things and explore issues without feeling judged or told what to do.

Psychiatry hasn't had the impact it thinks it has and we really do need to find a better way to heal troubled souls.

可以与可信的社区成员分享他们的问题是很重要的。利用更主流的网站，比如Facebook和推特，可能放大之前隐藏的精神痛苦，因为主流网站会将关于自闭症的谈话带入公众领域，这里的信息可能会潜移默化地影响那些对这种疾病知之甚少的人们，也包括那些不知道自己也已经患病的人们。

这些开放的平台中曾出现过一些公共人物，比如前足球运动员斯坦·科利莫尔和政党副手阿拉斯泰尔·坎贝尔，他们都通过个人言论吸引了更多人关注这种疾病。这一切都可以帮助人们提高认识，对抗因患有自闭症而感到耻辱的心理，促使人们明白他们不需默默忍受。

有很多关于心理健康和心理疾病废话，我认为人们并没有准备好在一个提供可用且有帮助的资源的网站中分享经历、问题和感受，学习新的事物，探讨问题，而不会感到被人评头论足或是被指使。

精神病学并没有像想象中那样影响人们，而且我们确实需要找到一个更好的方式来治愈陷入困境的灵魂。

炫 · 知识

1. Black Dog Tribe 黑狗部落

Black Dog Tribe是露比·威克斯打造的一个心理健康的社交网站。在该网站注册后，可以毫无顾忌地表达自己的感受、想法，在获得释放的同时，得到一些建议。

2. trickle down 潜移默化

trickle有"滴，细细地流"的意思，而trickle down则有"一点一滴"的含义。在本文中，这个短语有"潜移默化"的意思。

tackle ['tækl] v. 对抗

阅读技能练习场

Exercises:

1 How did the author communicate or contact with the people with depression?

A. By phone calls.

B. Via e-mail.

C. Face to face.

D. By online chatting.

2 Which is not the right description about Black Dog Tribe?

A. It is a mental health social site.

B. It was founded by Ruby Wax.

C. It provides access to helpful resources.

D. It is to encourage people to talk, share experiences.

3 What's the author's attitude towards depression?

A. Bias.

B. Empathy.

C. Sympathy.

D. Both B and C.

Reading Skills

Answers: 1.D 2.B 3.D

1. 读懂题干，了解大意 ★★★★★

在作答之前，我们要仔细读懂题干，明确问题到底询问哪些方面的信息。然后按图索骥，就可以将正确答案找出来。

> **Q1解析：**题目询问作者与自闭症患者沟通和保持联系的方式。通过第二段的第一句话，可以知道作者是以online chatting的形式在线与患者交流，因此选D。
>
> **Q3解析：**通读全文，不难发现作者很乐意解答自闭症患者的问题。而且作者作为一名医生，也在心里上对自闭症患者有认同感和同情心，认为这只是一种心理疾病，是可以通过治疗而痊愈的，因此A选项的表述有误，选D。

2. 追溯文章相关段落 ★★★★★

要想找答案，首先要追溯到原文的相关段落中。如果这样还不能确定答案，便可以仔细研究各个选项，将不相关的内容或错误表述剔除。

> **Q2解析：**关于黑狗部落的描述主要集中在第五段。根据这部分内容，可以发现选项A、C、D都是正确的，B项的说法不准确，因为这个社区并不是Ruby Wax一个人创建的。因此答案为B。

Chapter 4

Passage 27

Broadband Services 40% Slower Than Advertised?
——宽带速度比广告宣传慢40%?
——May. 12th, 2012, Telegraph

Reading Guide

你是否也曾因为网速没有广告中宣传得那么快而苦恼？在英国，这种情况也相当普遍。随着社会生活的高速发展，网络成为了我们日常工作生活中不可缺少的一部分。在网络使用越来越广泛的同时，网络本身的质量是否也应提升呢？

Broadband customers are paying for services that are more than 40% slower than advertised, with thousands complaining that they are being short-changed by their Internet service providers.

An investigation has found that customers are paying for an average of 12 megabits per second while actually receiving 7 Mbps, a gap of 42%.

Readers complained of broadband black spots in city centers, of exposed copper lines that fail in bad weather and of having to move businesses out of homes because of poor connections.

The survey found that TalkTalk and Sky customers reported a 60% shortfall, the widest gap between median advertised and actual services.

TalkTalk subscribers had been promised

宽带服务用户享受到的网络服务比广告宣传中的要慢40%，数千名的消费者投诉网络服务供应商们应该给他们退钱。

一项调查研究发现，选择平均每秒12兆网速的用户的实际网速平均每秒只有7兆，比广告中慢了42%。

浏览者投诉市中心的宽带网络故障，由于曝露在外的铜线受恶劣天气的影响而失效，导致人们因糟糕的网络连接状况而不得不外出办公。

调查发现，TalkTalk和Sky的用户报告媒体宣称的网速和实际使用网速之间最大的差额竟达60%。

TalkTalk的用户曾被承诺平均每

an average speed of 8 Mbps, but were receiving 5 Mbps, and Sky customers were promised an average 12 Mbps and received 4.8 Mbps.

Since advertising rules changed in April, Internet service providers can only claim "up to" speeds if at least 10% of users are receiving them.

Even this **threshold** was criticized as too low by the broadband companies who are now moving away from **blanket** advertising to **quoting** a different speed for each customer.

TalkTalk says its advertisements refer to average speeds, and everyone is given an individual quote before signing up. A spokesman said: "No one enters a contract with us without receiving a speed estimate tailored to them."

BT said it removed speed claims from its website. "We have provided personalized speed quotes for some years now, so our customers know exactly what they're getting before any commitment is made."

BT, whose copper network is used by every major telecoms retailer in the UK, is spending £2.5bn to upgrade the service by installing fiber optic cables from the exchange to street cabinets.

It aims to reach two-thirds of the UK by the end of 2014 and, with taxpayers' help, 90% of homes by 2017.

秒达到8兆的网速，但实际使用的只有5兆；Sky的用户曾被承诺平均每秒12兆的网速，但实际使用时也只有每秒4.8兆。

由于4月份广告宣传法规的更改，如果至少有10%的用户确实能享受这样的速度，网络服务供应商才能声称网速"最高可达到"这一速度。

但宽带服务公司评论这一限制设定得过低，因为它们现在正从没有限制的广告转变为针对每个客户提供不一样的网速。

TalkTalk公司称，广告宣传中提到的是平均网速，每个人在签定协议之前都会得到不同的报价。一名发言人表示："每个和我们签约的人都能享受为他们量身打造的预估网速。"

英国电信公司表示，它们已经从网站上移除了关于网速的声明。"多年来，我们一直提供个性化的网速报价，因此我们的客户在与我们签订合同之前，就已明确他们将会享受什么样的网速。"

几乎英国的每个主要电信零售商都要使用英国电信公司的铜线网，英国电信将花费25亿英镑为交换机及街上的宽带箱中安装光纤电缆，以此达到升级服务的目的。

这一举动的目的是在纳税人的帮助下，到2014年底，让三分之二的英国人都能用上宽带；到2017年，争取让90%的家庭都能使用宽带。

threshold ['θreʃhəuld] n. 门槛
blanket ['blæŋkit] a. 没有限制的

quote [kwəut] v. 报价

142

Customers with fiber optic cables to their street cabinet could get speeds of up to 76 Mbps, but experts say the service could still be unreliable for properties furthest away from telephone exchanges, because they rely on copper wiring for the final mile.

BT has **countered** this by including smaller market towns in its **roll-out** plans, and a competition allowed 10 harder-to-reach communities to win fiber for their exchanges.

Customers will be able to order an all-fiber line from BT from next year, although the **initial** price could be as high as £1,000, putting it out of reach of most householders and home-based workers.

Labor says the government must update the national broadband plan, with an emphasis on more fiber connections direct to homes, businesses, schools and health centers.

The shadow minister for innovation and science, Chi Onwurah, a former head of telecoms technology at OFCOM, said:"Ultimately fiber to the home is the aim."

"By 2020, we should have concrete plans in place. I do think that it is a failure of leadership that the government isn't prepared to do that."

The communications minister, Ed Vaizey, has said the UK is on track to have the "best broadband network in Europe" by 2015.

通过街上宽带箱中的光缆，用户能够体验每秒高达76兆的网速。但专家表示，距离交换机最远端的用户也许仍然无法享受这样的服务。因为这取决于传递到最远端的铜线。

英国电信公司以包括小城市在内的首次计划来反击这一说法，而这一竞争为10个更远的社区赢得了为交换机安装光缆的机会。

从明年起，用户就可以从英国电信公司订购全光纤线，可最初的价格可能高达1000英镑，这让大部分家庭和在家办公的人们望而却步。

工党称政府必须要升级国家宽带计划，强调要让更多的光缆直接进入到家庭、公司、学校以及医疗中心。

创新和科学的影子部长，英国通信管理局前任电信技术主管池·欧乌拉说："光纤入户才是我们最终的目标。"

"到2020年，对此我们将会有具体的可行计划。我认为，如果政府没有做好准备，则说明他们的领导确实是失败的。"

而通讯部长艾德·瓦伊择曾经说过，到2015年，英国将拥有"全欧洲最好的宽带网络"。

---

counter ['kauntə] v. 反击
roll-out [rəul'aut] n. 初次公开展出

initial [i'niʃəl] n. 最初的

炫 · 知识

1. short-changed 少找钱的

short-changed原本表示"少找钱的"，change在这里作"找零"的含义。在本文中则被用于幽默地表达宽带服务提供商向用户索取了过多费用的情况。

2. fibre optic cable 光缆

与铜线电缆相比，通信光缆不但拥有更大的传输容量，还有体积小、重量轻、无电磁干扰等优点。自1976年以后，已发展为长途干线、市内中继、近海及跨洋海底通信以及局域网等有线传输线路的骨干，并为光纤到户等宽带综合业务提供传输线路。

3. put... out 使……望而却步

在本文中，引申义句理解为"望而却步"。

阅读技能练习场

Exercises:

1 How much is the speed slower than advertised as for the 12 megabits per second service?

    A. 40%.

    B. 60%.

    C. 42%.

    D. 10%.

2 According to the new advertising rules, how many users at least must receive the speed as the provider promised?

    A. 40%.

    B. 100%.

    C. 90%.

    D. 10%.

3 What is the BT's purpose of network?

A. It aims to reach two-thirds of the UK by the end of 2017.

B. It aims to reach two-thirds of the UK by the end of 2014.

C. It aims to reach 90% of homes by 2017.

D. Both B and C.

Answers: 1. C   2. D   3. D

Reading Skills

1. 对数字保持敏感 ★ ★ ★ ★ ★

在写作时，人们通常喜欢用数字来证明自己的观点，因此在潜意识中，对数字要有一定的敏感。在读文章的时候，可以圈住自己认为重要的数字，方便查找。最重要的是不要把数字弄混，一定要看清题目中询问的是什么。

> **Q1解析：** 根据问题，我们可以知道答案会出现在文章开始的部分，根据第一自然段的第一句话，可以知道这一数字大于40%；根据第二段，可以确定正确答案是C。

> **Q2解析：** 问题中提到了新变更的规定。锁定文章相关部分之后，根据原文中的…Internet service providers can only claim "up to" speeds if at least 10% of users are receiving them. 可知正确答案是D。

2. 注意选项中的时间状语 ★ ★ ★ ★ ★

在做题时，一定要看清选项中的状语。有的选项从原文中断章取义，容易让人进行误导性的选择，因此在作答时一定要看仔细。

> **Q3解析：** 根据问题的提示和相关选项的暗示，我们可以回到文章的相关部分。根据原文It aims to reach two-thirds of the UK by the end of 2014 and, with taxpayer help, 90% of homes by 2017. 不难看出选项A的描述是错误的，B和C都正确，所以正确答案是D。

Passage 28

The United Nations Says Broadband Is Basic Human Right

——联合国声明宽带使用是基本人权

——Nov. 15th, 2011, Forbes

Reading Guide

同吃喝、居住以及医疗一样，宽带上网也成为了我们生命中必不可少的一部分。宽带不但使人们的生活变得更加丰富，同时也在信息传递和监管等方面起到很大作用。

With little fanfare two weeks ago, a key United Nations commission made a remarkable statement: it declared, unambiguously, that broadband access is a basic human right, right up there with the right to healthcare, shelter and food. Not merely dial-up Internet connection (the UN has **decreed** that before), but the kind of fast, seamless service Americans find at any Starbucks. Think about what that implies: Freedom of expression now mandates the ability to broadcast that expression to the entire world.

I moderated a conversation at the Techonomy conference on Sunday afternoon with the man most responsible for this declaration, Dr. Hamadoun Touré, the head of the International Telecommunication Union. The ITU is the UN

随着过去两周小小的喧闹，联合国的一个重要委员会宣布了一项引人注意的声明：该声明明确宣布，宽带连接是一项基本人权，几乎与医疗保险权利，居住权以及饮食的权利"平起平坐"。不仅仅是指拨号上网（委员会之前曾颁布过），而是指快捷的无缝服务，如同美国人在任何一家星巴克可以得到的那样。想想这意味着什么：如今，言论自由使人们拥有向整个世界表达自己的权利。

周日下午，我在Techonomy大会上与负责这一声明的人进行了一次缓和的谈话，这个人就是国际电信联盟的会长，哈马德 图尔博士。国际电信联盟是一个联合国机构，主要监管

decree [diˈkriː] v. 颁布

agency that oversees all things of communication —radio spectrum, satellite paths, global digital standards and the like.

The five minutes we spent talking about the right to broadband can be seen here:

Touré argues that broadband will be increasingly required for education and healthcare. He also equates it with political self-destiny. Social media, in this view, mirrors the printing press a half-millennia ago; people without broadband effectively have no paper, no ink. Touré has some private sector heavies backing this call for a new right: Carlos Slim Helu (who Forbes again ranks above Warren Buffett and Bill Gates as the richest man in the world), Cisco's John Chambers and Nobel Peace Prize winner Muhammed Yunus all serve with him on the ITU's Broadband Commission, which made the declaration two weeks ago.

It's a legitimate argument, which I saw up-close during a trip to Cairo. In Tahrir Square, T-shirt hawkers sell Facebook T-shirts—that's the symbol of the revolution. They are the Thomas Paines of their generation, and their pens were powered by broadband.

Touré argues that broadband will similarly keep unsavory regimes in check. "Communication is a very powerful tool in the hands of the people," he told me, "and when you take it out of their hands, it's a bomb waiting to explode."

通讯方面的所有事宜——无线电频谱、卫星的轨道、国际数码标准以及类似其他事项。

我们关于宽带权利问题的谈话进行了5分钟，谈话内容如下：

图尔认为，教育和医疗方面对宽带的需求会日益扩大。他还认为，这与政治本身的命运同等重要。从这个角度来看，社交媒体反映了500年前的印刷技术；如果人们无法连上宽带，就像当初没有纸墨一样。一些私营部门的重要人物支持图尔这项要求新权力的号召：在这项权力宣布的两周前的国际电信大会宽带委员会上，卡洛斯·斯利姆·赫鲁（在福布斯榜上排在沃伦·巴菲特和比尔·盖茨之前，是世界最富有的人），斯科公司首席执行官约翰·钱伯斯和诺贝尔和平奖获得者穆罕默德·尤努斯都对此表示支持。

在我最近前往开罗的旅途中，我看到一项合法的争论。在塔里尔广场，穿着T恤的小贩兜售FacebookT恤衫——这标志着改革。这些人是这一代的托马斯·潘恩，宽带为他们手中的笔赋予了力量。

图尔认为，宽带同样能够检验那些令人生厌的政权。"沟通是人们手中掌握的一个非常强大的工具，"他这样告诉我，"当你把它从人们手里拿走，这就变成了一颗快要爆炸的炸弹。"

radio spectrum 无线电频谱
satellite ['sætəlait] n. 卫星

unsavory [ˌʌnˈseivəri] a. 令人讨厌的
regime [reiˈʒiːm] n. 政权

Still, the idea of right-to-broadband seems increasingly legitimate. When I announced Toure's declaration at Techonomy, applause broke out in the room. I don't think that would have happened a year ago.	尽管如此，宽带上网的权力这一理念似乎变得越来越合法化。当我在Techonomy会议上宣读图尔的声明时，掌声响彻现场。我认为，哪怕是在一年之前，这样的场景都不会出现。

炫 · 知识

1. right up there with 与……相似

这个短语的意思是"与……相似"，在本文的特定语境中，可以理解为宽带上网的权利与衣食住行一样重要，可以说是"平起平坐"的。

2. mirror 反映

我们对于mirror作为"镜子"的含义都非常熟悉，但是这个单词作动词时，还有"反映"的意思。

3. Thomas Paine 托马斯·潘恩

Thomas Paine是英裔美国思想家、作家、政治活动家、理论家、革命家、激进民主主义者。其代表作是《常识》(*Common Sense*)。

阅读技能练习场

Exercises:

1 According to the passage, which one is not a basic human right?

A. Healthcare.

B. Living.

C. Dial-up Internet connection.

D. Entertainment.

2 Who is Dr. Hamadoun Touré?

A. The richest man in the world.

B. A Nobel Peace Prize winner.

C. The head of the International Telecommunication Union.

D. One of the top political bloggers.

3 According to the author, what is the situation of right-to-broadband now?

A. There are just a few people have witnessed the power of broadband.

B. Many politicians don't think it is important.

C. It seems increasingly concerned.

D. We cannot infer from passage.

Reading Skills

1. 细节题要快速回文中定位 ★★★★★

对于细节题来说，往往需要通读文章，才能得到答案。但在考试时，时间非常紧张，因此需要我们迅速回到文中寻找答案。

> **Q1解析**：文章的第一段说明，right to healthcare, shelter and food都是基本人权；而Not merely dial-up Internet connection (the UN has decreed that before)表明A、B、C三项都是正确的，惟有D选项没有提及。
>
> **Q2解析**：虽然四个选项叙述的内容在文章里都能找到，但我们可以根据Dr. Hamadoun Touré这个关键词回到文中相应位置寻找答案。根据：I moderated a conversation… Dr. Hamadoun Touré, the head of the International Telecommunication Union. 可以知道Dr. Hamadoun Touré是ITU的会长，故正确答案是C。

2. 锻炼分析及推断能力 ★★★★★

如果遇到问题和答案都比较复杂和细碎，就要有分析文章所传达的信息的能力，这样能保证不易出错。

> **Q3解析**：解答这种题目的时候，要对事物有一定的分辨能力，以及推断的能力。根据文章最后一段的I don't think that would have happened a year ago.可以知道人们现在对此比较关注；B选项表示政治家认为使用宽带的权利不重要，这一点没有提及；C选项表示越来越多人关注此事，与事实相符，故选C。

Chapter 05

环境保护
Environmental Protection

Passage 29

Solar Energy: Starting from Scratch
——从头开始发展太阳能
——Jan. 24th, 2012, Economist

Reading Guide

太阳能是大自然赐予我们的天然能源。然而，由于太阳能设备高昂的价格，使得许多非洲贫困地区国家的居民无法享受太阳能带来的便利。如今，英国的一家公司推行一个伟大的计划，使太阳能不再是一项遥不可及的高科技技术，而是能够真正贴合生活的日用必须能源。

Sunny countries are often poor. It is a shame, then, that solar power is still quite expensive. But it is getting cheaper by the day, and is now cheap enough to be competitive with other forms of energy in places that are not attached to electricity grids. Since 1.6 billion people are still in that unfortunate position, there is now a large potential market for solar energy. The problem is that although sunlight is free, a lot of those 1.6 billion people still cannot afford the upfront cost of the equipment in one go, and no one will lend them the money needed to buy it.

Eight19, a British company spun out of Cambridge University, has devised a clever way to get round this. **In return for** a deposit of around $10 it is supplying poor families in Kenya with a

阳光充沛的国家通常都比较贫穷。遗憾的是太阳能能源也价格不菲。但是，很快太阳能就会日益变得更便宜了，如今，在那些没有电网接入的地区，其价格已经便宜到足以和其他形式的资源竞争了。由于大约16亿人现在仍生活在这种不幸之中，太阳能资源存在一个非常有潜力的市场。问题在于即使阳光是免费的，这16亿人中的多数仍然不能马上预付建造太阳能设备的钱，而且也没人肯借钱给他们。

Eight19是一家从剑桥大学分流出的英国公司，该公司设计了一个精明的方式来避免这个问题。在肯尼亚，每户贫困家庭提供大约10美金的存款，作为回

in return for 作为……的回报

solar cell able to generate 2.5 watts of electricity, a battery that can deliver a 3-amp current to store this electricity, and a lamp whose bulb is an energy-efficient light-emitting diode. The firm reckons that once the battery is fully charged, this system is sufficient to light two small rooms and to power a mobile-phone charger for seven hours. Then, the next day, it can be put outside and charged back up again.

The trick is that, to be able to use the electricity, the system's keeper must buy a scratch card—for as little as a dollar—on which a reference number is printed. The keeper sends this reference, plus the serial number of the household solar unit, by text message to Eight19. The company's server will respond automatically with an access code to the unit.

Users may feel as though they are paying an hourly rate for their electricity. In fact, they are paying off the cost of the unit. After buying around $80-worth of scratch cards—which Eight19 expects would take the average family about 18 months—the user will own it. He will then have the option of continuing to use it for nothing, or trading it in for a bigger model, perhaps driven by a 10-watt solar cell.

In that case, he would then go through the same process again, paying off the additional cost of the upgraded kit at a slightly higher rate. Users would thereby increase their electricity supply—ascending the "energy escalator", as Eight19 puts it—steadily and affordably. Simultaneously, the

报，公司会为这些家庭提供一个可以产生2.5瓦电量的太阳能电池，和一个可以发射3安培电流的电池来储存这些电量，此外还有一盏装有发光二级管节能灯泡的电灯。公司认为一旦电池被完全充满，这个系统足以点亮两个小屋，并且给手机充电大约7小时。等到第二天，可以把这个系统放到外面再次充电。

公司的妙计是要求这套系统的持有者必须购买一种刮刮卡才能使用电力——这种刮刮卡只要区区一美元，上面印着一个参考号。系统持有者需要把这个号码以及太阳能装置上的序列号通过短信发送到Eight19公司。公司的服务器就会自动回复一个访问代码到设备上。

用户或许会觉得他们的电价每小时都在变化。实际上他们是在被这台设备买单。在买了80美金左右的刮刮卡之后，用户就能拥有这台设备了——Eight19公司估算，平均来说，80美元的刮刮卡够每户使用18个月。之后，用户可以决定继续免费使用 或者换购 一个发电量更大的设备，或许要通过10瓦的太阳能电池来驱动。

如果用户选择换购，他就要经历同样的过程，以相对高一点的费用来偿付这台升级套装。这样，用户将增加他们的用电供应量——乘着"能源扶梯"稳步上升，而且能够负担得起，这正如Eight19公司设计的那样。同时，公司还

be sufficient to 足以

company would be able to build a payment record of its clients, sorting the unreliable from the rest.

According to Eight19's figures, this looks like a good deal for customers. The firm **reckons** that the average energy-starved Kenyan spends about $10 a month on **paraffin**—sufficient to fuel a couple of smoky lamps—plus $2 a month to have his mobile phone charged at a nearby market. Regular users of one of Eight19's basic solar units will spend around half that, before owning it outright. Meanwhile, as the cost of solar technology falls, the whole system should get even cheaper. The company hopes to be able to supply users with a new, low-cost and robust sort of solar cell, printed onto plastic strips, within two years.

So far the scheme has been tried out among a couple of hundred Kenyan families. **With the aid of** a charitable loan to accelerate its roll-out, Eight19 is now in the process of dispersing another 4,000 solar units in Kenya, Malawi and Zambia. If its novel idea works, solar power will come within reach of a whole new set of customers—and the days of the paraffin lamp could well be numbered.

可以建立客户购买记录，将那些不靠谱的购买者与其他人区分开来。

根据Eight19公司的数据，这看起来对消费者来说很值。公司认为，在人均能源匮乏的肯尼亚，人们每个月要花大约10美元购买石蜡——这足够为一对烟灯提供能源——此外，还有2美元用于在附近的市场为手机充电。Eight19的固定用户在完全拥有最基本的设备之前，每月在能源上的花费只是上述费用的一半。同时，随着太阳能技术成本的下降，整个系统应该变得更便宜。公司有望在两年内为用户提供一款印在塑料条上面的全新的太阳能电池，这种电池成本更低、能量更强。

到目前为止，该计划已经在肯尼亚的上百个家庭中试验。慈善贷款的帮助加速了该计划的施行，Eight19公司目前正在将太阳能设备分配给另外的4000个肯尼亚、马拉维和赞比亚家庭。如果这个新奇的想法能起作用，公司就会坐收一大批太阳能的新用户。等到那一天，石蜡灯就时日无多了。

炫 · 知识

1. spin out 分离出

　　spin作为动词是"纺纱"的意思，而spin out在这里则有"抽出一根丝线"的意味，因此引申为"分离出"。

reckon ['rekən] v. 认为
paraffin ['pærəfin] n. 石蜡

with the aid of 在……的帮助下

2. light-emitting diode 发光二级管

发光二极管简称LED，采用砷化镓、镓铝砷、和磷化镓等材料制成，其内部结构为一个PN结，具有单向导电性。

3. scratch card 刮刮卡

刮刮卡是指卡上的一种覆盖数字和字母密码等文字的涂层，因此刮刮卡也叫密码覆膜卡、帐户卡或记账密码卡。

4. serial number 序列号

"序列号"是软件开发商给软件的一个识别码，是为了防止盗版而采取的保护措施，类似于身份证号。

阅读技能练习场

Exercises:

1. How much money would you pay to get a solar cell that generates 2.5 watts of electricity?

   A. $8.

   B. $3.

   C. $10.

   D. $80.

2. What should the users send by text message to Eight19?

   A. The reference number of your phone.

   B. A scratch card.

   C. The serial number of the household solar unit.

   D. Both A and C.

3. How long would a family use the scratch cards that cost $80?

   A. 1 year.

   B. 1 year and a half.

   C. Half a year.

   D. 6 months.

Reading Skills

1. 格外留意数字 ★★★★★

无论是在听力还是阅读理解题目中，数字都是经常出现的考查点。因此，所有有数字出现的地方都应该格外留意。

> **Q1解析：**根据原文In return for a deposit of around $10 it is supplying poor families in Kenya with a solar cell able to generate 2.5 watts of electricity…可以知道，Eight19公司对于人们10美金的存款的回报就是可以使用这种设备。所以正确答案是C。
>
> **Q3解析：**根据题目中的$80，我们可以在文章的第4自然段找到答案：After buying around $80-worth of scratch cards—which Eight19 expects would take the average family about 18 months… 所以正确答案是B。

2. 仔细读题避免失分 ★★★★★

有时候如果看题不仔细，很容易选到一个与正确答案相似的错误选项。此外，在做题时不要太过相信"规律"，有些人认为那些能够涵盖两个选项的选项(如：Both A and B are true.)一定是正确的，实则不然。

> **Q2解析：**根据题目，我们来看文章的相关部分。文中提到：The keeper sends this reference, plus the serial number of the household solar unit, by text message to Eight19. 由此可知，只有C正确。

Passage 30

7 Ways to Go Green in Your Small Business

——小型企业的7个绿色经营策略

——Mar. 1st, 2012, USA Today

Reading Guide

小型企业不好生存？成本太高，花费太多？选择绿色的经营方式不仅能保护地球，还能帮你节省不少钱。现在开始，抛弃你以前的旧习惯吧。绿色环保生产经营，事半功倍。

St. Patrick's Day, the first flowers of spring, the grass on baseball fields.

It's March, time to think green and time to go green in your small business.

It's smart to go green in your business regardless of your political or environmental philosophy.

Even if you're not worried about saving the planet, I'm guessing you would like to save money. It's just good business to reduce your energy and gas consumption—especially with the cost of gas going through the roof.

When you do, you'll also reduce your bills. And small businesses can have a big effect on the environment.

I've got seven easy steps you can take to save money and the earth at the same time:

圣帕特里克节、春天的第一簇花，以及棒球场上的绿草。

时间正值三月天，是时候看看绿色，也是时候给你的小企业添上一丝绿意了。

不管你的政治观或环境观是什么，给你的企业带来点绿色始终是明智之举。

尽管你并不关心拯救地球的事，但是我猜你肯定愿意省钱。这可都是能帮您减少能源和汽油消耗的好事——尤其是现在油价飞涨。

一旦你这样做，就会降低你的开销。而且小企业也能对环境产生大影响。

我给您提供7个简单的步骤，既能帮您省钱，又能保护地球：

1. Go after waste aggressively. Waste, of any kind, wastes your money.

Think of it this way: Whenever you see waste, you're looking at something you paid for and didn't consume. It might be energy—lights and heat left on over the weekend—over-ordered inventory or excessive raw materials used because of inefficient production methods.

Examine every aspect of your business to be more efficient, use fewer resources, and cut waste.

2. Reduce commutes. Frequently, the biggest energy consumption comes before anyone even arrives at the office.

Commuting **devours** an immense amount of energy and time. Encourage employees and yourself to walk, bike, carpool or take public transportation.

Reimburse or **subsidize** public transportation costs. When your lease expires, consider moving closer to your home or public transportation hubs. You'll save money on gas and car expenses.

And you can put the time you would have spent commuting into money-making activities instead.

3. Reduce "vampire" energy drain. At night, "vampires" suck up energy in your office or factory.

No, these aren't the vampires that drink blood or star in movies; these vampires are the machines and equipment continuing to work even after you've left for the day or the weekend.

1. 狠狠地检查是否有浪费现象。无论哪种，浪费都是在浪费你的钱。

你可以这样想：只要你看到浪费现象，就是看见了一些你花了钱但却没有使用的东西。这可能是在浪费能源——比如周末忘了关的灯和电热器——超过需求订购而产生的库存，或是由于低效率生产方法而被浪费的原材料。

检查你的生意中各个方面以提高效率、节约能源、减少浪费。

2. 减少出行。通常，最大的能源消耗是在你开车到达办公室之前的路上。

乘车上下班消耗了大量的能源和时间。所以要鼓励员工和自己选择步行、骑自行车、拼车或乘坐公共交通工具。

补偿或补贴公交费用。当你的租约到期时，考虑把公司搬到你家或者公交枢纽附近，这样你就可以省下汽油和车辆相关的费用了。

而且，你可以把原本花在路上的时间节省下来，用来挣更多的钱。

3. 减少"吸血鬼"般的能源消耗。晚上，"吸血鬼"会在你的办公室或工厂里吸嗜能源。

不，这不是电影中饮血的吸血鬼主角，而是当你每天下班的或是周末时，仍然工作着的机器和设备。

---

devour [di'vauə] v. 吞噬
reimburse [,ri:im'bə:s] v. 补偿

subsidize ['sʌbsidaiz] v. 资助

Your printers, fax machines, copiers and other office machines are on **standby** mode, continuing to draw down power. If you leave computers and monitors on, they use up even more. Surprisingly, this kind of vampire energy drain can account for up to 10% of your energy costs.

Turn equipment fully off before you leave every night. The extra minute it takes to warm these up in the morning isn't really that much of a hardship, is it?

4. Bring lunch. Make it easy for yourself and employees to eat at work instead of driving to a nearby restaurant or fast-food outlet.

Everyone saves money, and you won't lose so much of your employees' time while they're out of the office. If you don't already have one, set up a small kitchen or kitchenette with an office-size fridge, microwave and water cooler.

5. Go to the cloud. Using Internet-based, rather than on-premise software applications, can be very green.

Running your own servers is inefficient and costly. You not only have the cost of servers, but you have to pay for energy to keep them running and continually backed up and may have to maintain constant temperatures.

While large cloud-solution providers use lots of energy, they are able to be far more energy-efficient than you can in your own small business.

6. Use **environmentally-friendly** products. Whenever possible, choose recycled and nontoxic

你的打印机、传真机、复印机和其他办公设备待机时仍会消耗能源。如果你让你的电脑和显示器仍然开着，耗电量甚至会更高。令人震惊的是，这种能源吸血鬼可以浪费你10%的能源费用。

每天晚上离开时，务必把设备的电源彻底切断。早上花点儿时间再开机预热并不是件难事儿，是吧？

4. 自带午餐。这样可以方便自己和员工在工作日解决午餐，而不用开车跑到附近的餐馆或是叫快餐外卖。

每个人都省了钱，而且你也不用再担心员工外出就餐而耽误了许多的工作时间，如果你的办公室还没有小型厨房的话，可以建一个配有办公室专用小冰箱、微波炉和冷水器的小厨房。

5. 使用云服务器。使用基于互联网的文件来取代预置的软件应用程序，这样非常环保。

运行自己的服务器不但效率不高，而且成本很高，你不仅要支付服务器的费用，还要花费维持服务器运行的能源费用、一直存在的机器的维护费用，以及不得不使机器维持恒定温度所需的费用。

尽管大型的云计算方案提供商也消耗大量的能源，但他们远比你的小企业更节能。

6. 使用环保产品。尽量选择可回收的无毒产品。

---

standby ['stændbaɪ] n. 待命

environmentally-friendly 环保的

products.

Look for post-consumer waste products, including stationery, packaging materials, paper towels and other kitchen and bathroom supplies. These are now priced competitively with nonrecycled products.

If you're a manufacturer or use chemicals in your business, ask for nontoxic, environmentally-friendly materials.

7. Buy hybrid or electric cars or trucks. Need a new car or truck for your small business?

Make energy efficiency a priority. This is especially important if yours is a business where you or your employees drive a substantial amount of time.

One look at the price of gas, and you'll immediately understand the financial benefit as well as the environmental benefit of such a choice. Whatever you drive, however far, make sure your cars and vans are well maintained and tires are properly inflated. That reduces energy use.

Little things add up.

Reduce waste, turn off lights, wear a sweater when you're cold and open a window when you're warm. You'll have more greenbacks in your pocket when you choose to go green.

选择再生产品，包括文具、包装材料、纸巾和其他的厨卫产品。现在，与不可回收的产品相比，这些产品在价格上极具竞争力。

如果你是一个制造商，或者你的业务需要使用化学产品，那么你要选择购买无毒、环保的材料。

7．购买混合动力车辆或者电动车辆。你的企业需要一辆新车或是卡车吗？

把节能高效放在第一位。如果你和你的员工们需要长时间驾车外出的话，这一点非常重要。

一旦你看到汽油的价格，你立刻就会明白，无论是从经济还是环保的角度来说，电动车辆都是一个不错的选择。无论你驾驶何种车辆，无论你要开多远，都要确保你的车辆处于保养良好的状态、轮胎中的气是充足的。这样就可以减少能源消耗。

再补充几小条吧：

减少浪费，关灯，冷的时候多穿件毛衣，热的时候就打开窗户。当你选择绿色的方式时，你口袋里的钱也就越来越多了。

炫 · 知识

1. go through the roof 价格飞涨

go through the roof表示"价格飞涨"。大家可以想象一下价格高到冲出屋顶的势头，就会发现这个短语虽然夸张，但是十分形象。

2. carpool 拼车

拼车就是在一个小区里，或周围的几个小区，有同一目的地的，或可以顺道路过的，可以搭车一起上下班。

3. post-consumer waste products 再生产品

产品可再循环生产，再生产出的产品继续出售，这种产品充分利用了废弃物，保护了环境。

4. hybrid cars 混合动力汽车

混合动力汽车是指车上装有两个以上动力源：蓄电池、燃料电池、太阳能电池、内燃机车的发电机组，当前混合动力汽车一般是指内燃机车发电机，再加上蓄电池的汽车。

阅读技能练习场

Exercises:

1. According to the passage, why should you "Go after waste aggressively"?

   A. It could help us save more money.

   B. It could help your business more efficient.

   C. It could help you reduce energy consumption.

   D. A, B and C are all right.

2. What could you do to reduce commute?

   A. Go to work by bike or on foot

   B. Get an electric car.

   C. Work at home.

   D. Live in your office.

3. What are the "vampires" in your office?

   A. It's a kind of monster that drinks blood.

   B. It's a famous movie star.

   C. They are the devices that suck up energy in your office.

   D. It will waste your money.

Reading Skills

1. 考虑作者的意图 ★ ★ ★ ★ ★

对于考查作者意图的题目，要回到原文中结合上下文推断，不要盲目地根据自己的主观印象猜测。

> **Q1解析：** 本题询问为什么要注意浪费的现象，根据Waste, of any kind, wastes your money.这句话，可以知道A是正确的，而Examine every aspect of your business to be more efficient, use fewer resources, and cut waste.则说明B和C也正确，因此选D。

2. 巧妙地排除干扰项 ★ ★ ★ ★ ★

有些题目的选项不是存在明显的错误，就是在文中根本没有提及。这时如果有把握，可以排除干扰项，降低题目的难度。

> **Q2解析：** C、D两个选项在文中根本没有提及，B选项中提到购买电动车，这是对需要经常开车外出的公司提供的建议。根据原文：Encourage employees and yourself to walk, bike, carpool or take public transportation. 可以知道只有A选项中的方法才是作者提及的。
>
> **Q3解析：** 作者提到吸血鬼本是一个比喻，根据这一点，可以排除A和B选项。D选项没有理论性错误，但不是对"吸血鬼"的解释，而是提到了它会造成的后果，所以正确答案是C。

Passage 31

Waste Not, Want Not
——无浪费，需求少
——Jan. 20th, 2012, Economist

Reading Guide

　　水资源是人类赖以生存的能源之一。如今，随着人口的增长，水资源日渐匮乏。新技术的出现让水资源可以被循环利用。但人们的观念能否随着新科技的出现而改变，这还是一个很难回答的问题。

　　Each drop of water used by Londoners subsequently passed through the plant for reprocessing at least six times before eventually escaping to the sea. The engineer in charge was convinced that, with further refinement, the **sewage** works would be capable of recycling the same water indefinitely—with the quality improving with each treatment cycle. Offered a glass of the finished product, your **correspondent** thought it tasted a good deal better than the chalky liquid that spluttered from London taps.

　　The very idea of consuming reprocessed human, animal and industrial waste can turn people's stomachs. But it happens more than most realize. Even municipalities that do not pump waste-water back into **aquifers** or **reservoirs**, often draw their drinking supply from rivers that

　　伦敦市民使用过的每一滴水在最终被排放到大海之前，在工厂中都至少要经过6次的再处理。负责污水处理的工程师相信，随着进一步的提纯，下水道可能具有循环再生同样的水的能力——就是在处理污水的每个环节都提高水的质量。本报特约记者认为，这样的一杯最终产品喝起来比伦敦的水龙头里流出的那种灰蒙蒙的液体好多了。

　　使用这种将人类、动物和工业废水再加工的水——这个想法让人反胃。但这已经成为现实。即使市民没有把废水排到含水土层或者水库里，他们的饮用水供应也是来自河水，而河水中当然含有处理过的、来自社区上游污水。

---

sewage ['sjuːidʒ] n. 污水
correspondent [ˌkɔri'spɔndənt] n. 新闻记者

aquifer ['ækwifə] n. 含水土层
reservoir ['rezəvwɑː] n. 水库

contain the treated effluent from communities upstream.

The main problem is not changes in the weather (though global warming hardly helps), but population growth. The American population has doubled, to over 300m, since the middle of last century—and is expected to increase by a further 50%, to 450m, over the next half century. Meanwhile, households as a whole have been consuming water at an even faster rate, thanks to the housing boom and the widespread use of flushed toilets, dish washers, washing machines, swimming pools and garden sprinklers.

Then there is the ongoing migration within America from the cooler climes of the north-east and mid-west to the sunbelt of the south. Since 1970, Arizona, California, Florida, Nevada and Texas have seen their populations surge by 85% to 400%. This exodus to warmer, dryer parts of the country has **coincided with** a decline in the construction of hydrological infrastructure— dams, aquaducts, tunnels, pipelines and reservoirs —for collecting, storing and transporting water to precisely those parched places.

Conservation has also helped ease the demand for fresh water, though it comes nowhere near offsetting the thirst of the sunbelt's surging population. The only conclusion is that, like it or not, people will have to get used to drinking their own effluent.

In doing so, the least of the troubles water districts face are technological. The know-how for

最主要的问题不是气候变化(尽管全球变暖并没有起到什么作用),而是人口增长。自上世纪中期以来,美国的人口已经增长了一倍,超过3亿人——在下一个50年内,美国人口有望增加50%,达到4.5亿。同时,所有家庭也以更快的速度消耗水资源,这都是拜房屋数量的上升以及家庭大规模使用冲水马桶、洗碗机、洗衣机、游泳池和园艺洒水装置等设施所赐。

而且在美国,不断有人从较冷的东北部和中西部地区移居阳光充足的南方地区。自1970年,亚利桑那州、加利福尼亚州、佛罗里达州,内华达州和德克萨斯州的人口激增了85%至400%。大批人离开居住的地方,到更温暖、更干燥的地区生活,这与水文设施建设的放缓相吻合——水文设施即大坝、高架渠、隧道、管道以及水库,可以用来收集、储存水,并把水运送到需要的地方去。

保护措施也帮助缓解淡水资源的需求,尽管这仍然无法抵消阳光充足的南部地区激增人口对淡水的需求。惟一的结论就是不管你喜欢与否,人们都将不得不习惯于饮用自己生产的污水。

这样做的话,水资源短缺所面临的一个最小的问题是技术层面的。在美

coincide with 与……相一致

filtering and purifying waste-water is as advanced in America as anywhere, though installation still lags. In Britain and much of the rest of Europe, water authorities insist not only on primary and secondary treatment of raw sewage (to remove suspended solids and organic matter, and add disinfectants), but also require tertiary processing (to remove nutrients, biodegradable products and even traces of pharmaceuticals and other organic compounds).

This is not necessarily cause for concern. Many rural communities do not need tertiary sewage treatment. Regions with heavy rainfall may not either. The Safe Drinking Water Act of 1974 sets the same standard for potable water throughout America, irrespective of whether it is derived from pristine mountain streams, recycled effluent from sewage works, or **de facto** reuse from upstream communities.

Getting the great American public to accept having waste-water in its drinking supply is a bit of a problem, too. As the NRC report notes, people have been trained for generations to think of their water supply and their waste disposal as two quite separate, and unrelated, undertakings. No one is sure how they will **come to terms**, if ever, with the notion that the two are part and parcel of the same thing. But if only people could be persuaded to take the taste test, your correspondent is certain they, too, would find that recycled waste-water can be every bit as sparkling and tasty as the freshest mountain dew.

国，过滤和净化废水的技术和其他地方一样先进，尽管安装技术仍然落后。在英国及欧洲其他国家，水利部门不仅坚持污水处理的第一道和第二道程序(去除悬浮固体和有机物质，然后添加消毒剂)，还要求进行第三道工序(去除营养物质、生物分解的产物甚至是药物和其他有机化合物)。

这不一定会引起关注。在多数农村地区，不需要进行第三道工序。在降水量丰沛的地区或许也不需要。1974年颁布的饮用水安全法案设立了适用于全美的饮用水统一标准，不管是原始的山间溪水、在下水道中经过处理的循环污水，还是来自上游地区的再循环水。

让伟大的美国公众接受在饮用水中掺杂污水的事实也是一个问题。正如国家研究委员会所说明的，一代代的人们被训练成认为供给他们的水源和污水处理是完全不相干的、是毫无关联的两件事情。没有人确切地知道他们如何才能妥协，就算他们真的妥协，他们也不知道如何接受这两者只是同一事物的不同部分这种理念。但只要人们能够被说服，就像本报记者那样试着去尝一尝这种水的话，他们就会发现经过循环处理的废水完全和冒着汽泡的新鲜山露一样甘甜可口。

---

de facto 实际上   come to terms 让步

炫 · 知识

1. fresh water 淡水

　　fresh虽然有"新鲜的"这个含义，但是不要忘记它也可以表示"淡水的"。因此淡水就可以用fresh water表示。

2. raw sewage 原污水

　　原污水是指未经过任何处理的污水。raw在这里表示"未加工的"。

3. organic matter 有机质

　　有机物质是指除一氧化碳、二氧化碳、碳酸盐、金属碳化物等少数简单含碳化合物以外，分子较大的含碳化合物，是碳氢化合物及其衍生物的总称。

阅读技能练习场

Exercises:

1 How many times does sewage water being reprocessed in London?

　　A. It is not mentioned.

　　B. 6 times.

　　C. 3 times.

　　D. twice.

2 Which one doesn't need to use fresh water?

　　A. Flushed toilets.

　　B. Dish washers.

　　C. Washing machines.

　　D. Tap.

3 Why did the author say "Getting the great American public to accept having waste-water in its drinking supply is a bit of a problem, too"?

　　A. People think water supply is separately from waste disposal.

　　B. People would not take the taste test.

　　C. No one is sure if the citizen will come to terms.

　　D. We cannot infer.

Reading Skills

1. 寻找相关细节 ★ ★ ★ ★ ★

其实考查细节的问题通常难度不会很大，只要仔细阅读文章都能找到答案。我们可以据题目的提示词回到文章相关部分去寻找，这样就能缩小正确答案的出现范围。

> **Q1解析：** 由于问题是针对第一自然段，所以我们要找到相应的位置。根据文章提示：Each drop …at least six times before eventually escaping to the sea.可以知道正确答案是B。
>
> **Q3解析：** 问题的答案出现在文章的最后一部分，首先排除选项B，因为这其实是人们不愿接受的结果，而不是根本的原因。A和C选项乍看都是正确的，但是C选项其实是循环水真正开始应用之后可能出现的后果。所以正确答案是A。

2. 从多方面入手解决问题 ★ ★ ★ ★ ★

有时候仔细观察选项，会发现一些选项是不符合常识的，而这种选项通常就是错误答案。用这种方法可以起到辅助的作用，真正做出判断，还是要看原文。

> **Q2解析：** 本题考查的是"哪个设备不会用到淡水"。根据常识，我们知道水龙头是不会消耗淡水的，然后回到文中确认一下，可以看到thanks to the housing boom and the widespread use of flushed toilets, dish washers, washing machines, swimming pools and garden sprinklers. 所以正确答案是D。

Passage 32

New Climate Threat: Methane Rises from Cracks in Arctic Ice

——新气候威胁：北极冰层裂缝冒出甲烷

——Apr. 23rd, 2012, Independent

Reading Guide

甲烷气体在极地的冰川中被大量地发现，它的出现及增加造成了极地冰面融化、冰层破裂、北极气温升高等后果。导致气候变暖的原因有很多，而甲烷气体的出现，让科学家们加倍重视极地的气候异常现象。

A new source of methane—a greenhouse gas many times more powerful than carbon dioxide—has been identified by scientists flying over areas in the Arctic where the sea ice has melted.

The researchers found significant amounts of methane being released from the ocean into the atmosphere through cracks in the melting sea ice. They said the quantities could be large enough to affect the global climate. Previous observations have pointed to large methane **plumes** being released from the seabed in the relatively shallow sea off the northern coast of Siberia but the latest findings were made far away from land in the deep, open ocean where the surface is usually capped by ice.

科学家已经确定，在北极地区存在一个新的甲烷来源——而甲烷是一种比二氧化碳强大多倍的温室气体，遍布北极地区的甲烷气体融化了附近的海上浮冰。

研究者发现，海洋正在释放的大量甲烷气体从海上浮冰的裂缝中升起，进入到大气之中。他们表示气体释放量已经大到足以影响全球气候。而之前的观察已经指出，大量的甲烷气体流正从西伯利亚北部海岸相对较浅的海床中释放出来，但最近的发现都来自距离地面很远的辽阔深海，而且海平面上有冰雪覆盖。

plume [plu:m] n. 卷流

Eric Kort of Nasa's Jet Propulsion Laboratory in Pasadena, California, said that he and his colleagues were surprised to see methane levels rise so dramatically each time their research aircraft flew over cracks in the sea ice.

"When we flew over completely solid sea ice, we didn't see anything **in terms of** methane. But when we flew over areas where the sea ice had melted, or where there were cracks in the ice, we saw the methane levels increase," Dr. Kort said. "We were surprised to see these enhanced methane levels at these high latitudes. Our observations really point to the ocean surface as the source, which was not what we had expected," he said.

"Other scientists had seen high concentrations of methane in the sea surface but nobody had expected to see it being released into the atmosphere in this way." he added.

Methane is about 70 times more potent as a greenhouse gas than **carbon dioxide** when it comes to trapping heat. However, because methane is broken down more quickly in the atmosphere, scientists calculate that it is 20 times more powerful over a 100-year cycle. The latest methane measurements were made from the American HIPPO research program where a research aircraft loaded with scientific instruments flies for long distances at varying altitudes, measuring and recording gas levels at different heights.

来自美国宇航局位于加利福尼亚州帕萨迪纳的喷气推进实验室的埃里克·科尔特说，每次当他们研究用的飞机在海上浮冰的裂缝上空盘旋时，他和他的同事们对甲烷释放水平如此大幅度上升感到惊讶。

"当我们在整个冰冻的海上浮冰上空盘旋时，我们看不见任何与甲烷有关的东西。但当我们飞到融化的海上浮冰上空，或是有裂缝的冰面上空时，就能看到甲烷释放水平的上升，"科特博士说。"在高纬度地区看见甲烷释放水平上升，这令我们都非常惊讶。我们将海平面作为观察的资源，但所见的都是我们没有想到的。他说。

"其他科学家也都在海平面上见过高浓度的甲烷，但是没有人想到甲烷会以这种方式释放到大气里，"他补充道。

甲烷这种温室气体围住热量的威力比二氧化碳高70倍。然而，由于甲烷很容易在大气中分解，根据科学家的计算，在100年的周期甲 甲烷的威力将增大20倍。最近的甲烷测量值是由美国HIPPO机构的一个研究项目测得的。在测试中，研究飞机装载着科学仪器在不同纬度长距离飞行，测量并记录甲烷气体的在不同高度的水平。

in terms of 就……来说　　　carbon dioxide 二氧化碳

The study, published in the journal *Nature Geoscience*, covered several flights into the Arctic at different times of the year. They covered an area about 950 miles north of the coast of Alaska and about 350 miles south of the North Pole. Dr. Kort said that the levels of methane **coming off** this region were about the same as the quantities measured by other scientists monitoring methane levels above the shallow sea of the East Siberian Arctic Shelf.

"We suggest that the surface waters of the Arctic Ocean represent a potentially important source of methane, which could prove sensitive to changes in sea ice cover." the researchers write. "The association with sea ice makes this methane source likely to be sensitive to changing Arctic ice cover and dynamics, providing an unrecognized **feedback** process in the global atmosphere-climate system," they say.

Climate scientists are concerned that rising temperatures in the Arctic could trigger climate-feedbacks, where melting ice results in the release of methane which in turn results in a further increase in temperatures.

"We should be concerned because there're so many things in the Arctic where the warming feeds further warming. There are many things in the Arctic that do respond to warming." said Euan Nisbet, a methane expert at Royal Holloway University of London.

这项研究发表在《自然地球科学》期刊上，它涵盖了在一年不同时间段的多次飞行，包括阿拉斯加海岸以北950英里到北极以南350公里的地区。科特博士表示，该地区的甲烷释放量与其他科学家监测的西伯利亚北极大陆架以东地区的排放量是一致的。

"我们认为北冰洋表面的海水反应了一个潜在的重要甲烷来源，它可以证明海上浮冰的细微变化"，研究人员写道。"甲烷气体来源与海上浮冰可能轻微地改变了北极冰层的覆盖和演变过程，为全球大气气候系统的变化提供了未被察觉的反馈过程。"他们说。

气象学家担心北极地区的气温上升可能会引发气候反馈效果：冰雪的融化导致甲烷的释放，而甲烷的释放反过来会导致进一步的气温上升。

"我们应该关注，因为在北极地区有太多事物会造成这种反馈效果，会进一步导致北极变暖。在北极，有许多事物都会受到气候变暖的影响"，伦敦大学皇家霍洛威学院研究甲烷的专家尤安·尼斯贝特如是说道。

---

come off 脱离

feedback ['fiːdbæk] n. 反馈

炫 · 知识

1. shallow sea 浅海

大陆周围较平坦的浅水海域，即大陆架。其平均宽度75公里。由于浅海带始终处于海水面以下，水动力条件较弱。

2. shelf 大陆架

大陆架在英文中可以用shelf来表示。大陆架是指大陆边缘被海水淹没的浅平海底，是大陆向海的自然延伸。

阅读技能练习场

Exercises:

1 What did Dr. Kort see flow over completely solid sea ice?

A. He saw the sea ice had melted.

B. He saw methane cracked the ice level.

C. He didn't anything in terms of methane.

D. He saw the methane levels increase.

2 When it comes to trapping heat, how many times is Methane more powerful than carbon dioxide?

A. About 20 times.

B. About 7 times.

C. About 100 times.

D. About 70 times.

3 Which description is right about the study published in the journal Nature *Geoscience*?

A. It covered about 950 miles north coast and 350 south of Alaska.

B. It covered several flights into the Arctic and Antarctica at different times of the year.

C. It covered 350 miles south of the North Pole.

D. It covered 950 miles north of the Arctic.

Reading Skills

1. 看清题目所问 ★★★★★

在做细节题的时候，一定要看清问题。千万不要看到一个在文中出现的句子就误以为它是答案，要结合题干来作答。

> **Q1解析**：这道题目的四个选项都是文章中出现过的问题。这道题询问在坚固的海上浮冰上面看到了什么。根据问题，我们回到文章的第四段。When we flew over completely solid sea ice, we didn't see anything in terms of methane. But … Dr. Kort said.可以判断正确答案是C。

2. 对数字要格外留意 ★★★★★

数字经常会作为出题点，所以在遇到针对数字提问的问题时，可以马上找到文章相应位置再进行回答。

> **Q2解析**：题询问甲烷围住热量的威力是二氧化碳的几倍。回到文章相应部分：Methane is about 70 times more potent as a greenhouse gas than carbon dioxide when it comes to trapping heat.可以知道正确答案是D。

3. 不要被相似选项混淆 ★★★★★

当几个选项的描述很相近，而且句子都是在文章中出现过的话，这时一定不要慌乱。做这种题目时需要加倍小心，应该回到原文中仔细阅读，才能选出答案。

> **Q3解析**：题干询问的是刊登在杂志上的具体研究内容，根据关键字Nature Geoscience可以迅速定位。根据原文可知只有选项C是符合的。

Passage 33

We Can Have Safe, Sustainable Energy

——我们能够拥有安全且可再生的能源

——Apr. 24th, 2012, Guardian

Reading Guide

世界能源系统的开采已经快要达到极限，而人类对矿物燃料的依赖却每年都在增长。许多清洁能源技术可以避免能源枯竭带来的灾难性后果，而加速清洁能源技术的开发，提高清洁能源的利用率，既是对环境的最好保护，也是可持续发展的必经之路。

The world's energy system is being pushed to breaking point, and our **addiction** to fossil fuels grows stronger each year. Many clean energy technologies are available, but they are not being deployed quickly enough to **avert** potentially disastrous consequences.

This is the message the International Energy Agency will deliver in London at the Clean Energy Ministerial, a meeting of ministers and representatives of nations that together account for four-fifths of world energy demand. In a new report we find that achieving a more secure, sustainable energy system, **in line with** the goal of limiting the rise in global temperatures to 2C, is still possible but requires urgent action by the

世界能源系统正在被推向极限点，而我们对矿物燃料的依赖却每年都在增长。有许多可用的清洁能源技术，但它们并没有被迅速推广以避免可能出现的灾难性后果。

国际能源机构将在伦敦举行的清洁能源部长级会议上公布这个消息，出席该会议的部长和代表们来自于占全世界4/5能源需求的国家。在一份新的报告中，我们发现要达成建立更安全、更具有可持续发展性的能源系统并限制全球气温上升2摄氏度的目标仍然是有可能的，只是这需要世界主要国家政府采取紧急行动。

addiction [əˈdikʃən] n. 沉迷
avert [əˈvəːt] v. 避免

in line with 与……一致

world's major governments.

The present state of affairs is unacceptable precisely because we have a responsibility and a golden opportunity to act. Energy-related CO_2 emissions are at historic highs; under current policies we estimate energy use and CO_2 emissions will increase by a third by 2020, and almost double by 2050. This would probably send global temperatures at least 6C higher within this century.

It doesn't have to be this way. One need only look at the recent progress made by a portfolio of renewable technologies to see that rapid technological change is possible. In particular, the output from onshore wind power has grown by 27% annually over the past decade. Solar panels easily installed by households and businesses (known as solar PV) have grown 42% annually, albeit from a small base.

But other technologies with great potential for energy and emissions savings are making much less progress. Vehicle fuel-efficiency improvement is slow in many countries, and manufacturers' sales projections for electric vehicles after 2014 are a fraction of government targets. Carbon capture and storage is not seeing the rate of investment needed to develop full-scale demonstration projects. In addition, half of new electricity demand has been met by coal; and to make things more challenging, 50% of those new coal-fired power plants are still being built with inefficient technology. All these trends are going in the wrong direction.

Every day that goes by without action means higher costs down the road. Fortunately,

目前的现状恰恰是我们不能接受的。因为我们有责任，也有很好的机会来付诸行动。与能源有关的二氧化碳排放问题已经上升到历史新高；在现行的政策下，我们估算到2020年，能源的使用和二氧化碳的排放量将比现在增长1/3，到2050则几乎会翻一番。这很有可能会使全球气温在本世纪至少上升6摄氏度。

情况不是一定要这样发展。我们只需看看可再生能源技术投资组合在最近取得的进展，就可以看到科技迅速变化的可能性。特别是在过去的10年里，陆地风能产量每年增长27%。尽管太阳能电池板（也被称为太阳能光伏电池）仅从一个很小的基地收集能源，但它方便家庭和商户安装，其发电量的年增长为42%。

但其他在节能减排方面具有巨大潜力的技术却没有很大的进展。汽车的燃油燃烧效率的提升在很多国家都发展缓慢，制造商预测2014年以后的电动汽车销量也只能达到政府目标的一小部分。碳元素的收集储存和投资不成正比，需要全面建造示范工程。另外，一半的新的电力需求通过燃煤提供。更有挑战的是那些新的燃煤发电厂中的一半仍然是以低能效技术建成的。所有这些趋势都在往一个错误的方向发展。

没有付出行动就已流逝的每一天都意味着我们今后要付出更高的代

the ministers gathering in London have the power to encourage investment, innovation and reform. With that in mind, we offer three key **recommendations**.

First, level the playing field for clean energy technologies. This means ensuring that energy prices reflect the "true cost" of energy— accounting for the positive and negative impacts of energy production and consumption. It also means removing fossil fuel **subsidies** (which were at $409bn worldwide in 2010, against the $66bn allotted for renewable energy support), while ensuring all citizens have access to affordable energy.

Second, unlock the potential of energy efficiency, the "hidden fuel" of the future. The IEA has developed 25 energy efficiency policy recommendations that, if implemented globally now, could cumulatively save about 7.3 gigatonnes of CO_2 a year by 2030. That's equivalent to Europe's current energy bill, or about €850bn a year. Governments should commit to applying these measures as soon as possible.

And finally, accelerate energy innovation and public support for research, development and demonstration. This will help lay the groundwork for private sector innovation and speed technologies to market.

The ministers meeting this week have an incredible opportunity before them. It is my hope that they **heed** our warning of slow progress and act to seize the security, economic and environmental benefits clean energy transition can bring.

价。幸运的是齐聚于伦敦的部长们有能力鼓励投资、创新和改革。考虑到这一点，我们提供三点关键的建议。

第一，为清洁能源技术提供公平的竞争环境。这意味着我们要确保能源的价格可以反映能源"真正的价值"——即体现能源生产和消费的积极影响和消极影响。这也意味着取消矿物燃料的补贴（2010年的全球补贴达到4090亿美元，而分配给可再生能源的资金支持只有660亿美元），同时确保所有公民可以使用负担得起的能源。

第二，发现能效的潜力，即找到未来的"隐藏着的燃料"。国际能源机构已经制订了25条关于能效的政策建议，如果现在这些建议能够在全球范围内实行，那么到2030年，每年就可以累计减少大约73亿吨的二氧化碳排放，也就是一年节省大约8500亿欧元，这与欧洲现行的能源法案不谋而合。政府应该尽快实施这些措施。

最后，加强能源创新，提高研究、发展和示范的公众支持。这既可以为私营部门的创新打下基础，也可以加速将技术转化为产品投放市场。

这星期举行的部长级会议在他们面前提供了一个非常好的机会。我希望他们能多留意我们对科技发展缓慢的警示，并能采取行动，抓住清洁能源转型带来的安全、经济和环保的益处。

recommendation [ˌrekəmen'deiʃən] n. 建议
subsidy ['sʌbsidi] n. 补贴

heed [hi:d] v. 留意

炫·知识

1. down the road 今后，将来

这个说法在美式口语中经常出现，表示"今后，将来"。例如，Sometime down the road, we plan to have a party. 我们准备近期举办一场聚会。

2. level the playing field 创造公平的竞争环境

playing field本意指"运动场"，level作为动词，表示"弄平"。在这里用比喻的修辞手法，结合上下文，可以译为"创造公平的竞争环境"。

2. bn 十亿

bn是billion的缩写。

阅读技能练习场

Exercises:

1. According to the first paragraph, what's the current situation of clean energy technologies?

   A. Our need of clean energy technologies grows stronger each year.

   B. They are not being deployed.

   C. There are many available clean energy technologies.

   D. They can't avert potentially disastrous results.

2. According to the author's suggestion, compared with 2020, how much energy use and CO_2 emissions will increase by 2050?

   A. 2/3.

   B. 1/2.

   C. 1/3.

   D. 2.

3. Which is not one of the three key recommendations that the author offers?

   A. Leave the problem to the Clean Energy Ministerial.

B. Offer a fair platform for clean energy technologies.

C. Release the potential of the energy efficiency.

D. Increase the speed of energy innovation and public support for research, development and demonstration.

Reading Skills

1. 逐句分析，善于归纳总结 ★★★★★

在通读文章后，要对文章大意有所把握，并归纳出文章的大体结构。这样对文章的理解才不会有所偏颇。在解答这种考查细节的问题时，可以采取逐句分析的方法，以此排除错误选项。

Q1解析：解答本题需要对第一段进行逐句分析。需求逐渐增长的是燃料，而不是清洁能源技术，所以A项错误；选项B不够准确，这种技术不是没有被deploy，而是没有被"很快地"deploy，要区别其程度的不同；选项D与文章所述正好相反；因此选C。

Q3解析：通读文章后，要善于总结。将文中所列步骤、要点总结出来，才能理清文章脉络。通过第六段最后一句：With that in mind, we offer three key recommendations.可以知道，下面的几段将要说明的就是这三点建议——总结即可得出答案是A。

2. 理解是关键，对数字要敏感 ★★★★★

如果文章中列出了不同年份或者不同数字，读者就应该对这些数字保持一定的敏感度。因为答案有可能就在这些数字之间，因此弄清数字之间的关系就是解题关键。

Q2解析：这道题需要答题者进行简单的计算。根据under current policies we estimate energy use and CO_2 emissions will increase by a third by 2020, and almost double by 2050.可以将如今的能源使用量和二氧化碳排放量看作1，那么2020年则为1+1/3，即4/3；而根据almost double by 2050可知，到2050年则为2。根据题意，是以2020年的标准与2050年的使用量与排放量进行比较，那么增加量即为2-4/3，即2/3；而增加的2/3刚好占2020年使用量与排放量4/3的一半，因此选B。

Passage 34

Bright Future for Alternative Energy with Greener Solar Cells
——绿色太阳能电池为替代能源带来光明未来
——Apr. 9th, 2012, Science Daily

Reading Guide

　　太阳能对人们来说并不是一个陌生的词汇，从太阳能汽车、电池，再到热水器等，这种清洁能源广受好评。来自堪萨斯州立大学的研究生提出了更环保的太阳能电池的使用想法，为这种绿色能源提供了更光明的未来。

　　Even alternative energy technologies can sometimes be a little greener, according to a Kansas State University graduate student's research.

　　Ayomi Perera, a doctoral student in chemistry, Sri Lanka, is working under Stefan Bossmann, professor of chemistry, to improve dye-sensitized solar cells. The cells are a solar technology that use a dye to help generate energy from sunlight. By creating a less **toxic** dye and combining it with a bacteria, Perera's solar cells are friendlier to the environment and living organisms—making an alternative energy solution to **fossil fuels** even greener.

　　根据堪萨斯州立大学的一位研究生的研究，替代能源技术有时也可以变得更加环保。

　　来自斯里兰卡的亚由美·派瑞拉是一名化学专业博士生，目前正在化学教授斯蒂芬·博士曼的指导下学习，研究染料光敏化太阳能电池的改善。这种电池应用一种太阳能技术——使用染料帮助阳光生成能量。通过研发一种含有较少毒素的染料并使之与一种细菌结合，派瑞拉的太阳能电池对环境和生物更友好，提供了一种比化石燃料更绿色环保的替代能源。

---

toxic ['tɔksik] a. 有毒的　　　　　　　　fossil fuel 化石燃料

"Dye-sensitized solar cells, which are solar cells with light-absorbing dye, have been around for more than 20 years, but their highest efficiency has stayed close to 11 percent for some time," Perera said. "So the thought was that rather than trying to increase the efficiency, let's try to make the technology greener."

To make the solar cells greener and more efficient, Perera begins with the bacteria Mycobacterium smegmatis. A mycrobacterium is a type of pathogen that can cause diseases such as **tuberculosis**. Perera is using a species that is completely harmless and can be found in soil and cornflakes. It also produces the protein MspA, which can be used for numerous applications once it has been chemically purified.

After purification, Perera combines the protein with a synthesized dye that is less toxic than traditional dyes. The protein-dye mixture is coated onto individual solar cells—which form large solar panels when assembled—and is then tested with artificial sunlight to measure energy output.

"The idea is that the protein acts as a matrix for electron transfer for this dye that absorbs sunlight," Perera said. "We want the protein to be able to capture the electron that the dye gives out and then transfer that electron in one direction, thereby generating an electrical current."

Although the new dye-sensitized solar cells currently do not improve on the technology's ability to **convert** sunlight into electrical current,

染料光敏化太阳能电池是一种带有吸光染料的太阳能电池，这种电池已经出现了20多年。但这段时间以来，这种电池的最高的效率一直没有超过11%，"派瑞拉说道。"因此，我们的想法不是试图提高效率，而是试图将这种技术变得更环保。"

为了使这种太阳能电池变得更环保也更有效，派瑞拉开始研究耻垢分枝杆菌。分枝杆菌是一种病原体，可以引起例如肺结核等疾病。派瑞拉正在使用的是一种完全无害的种类，可以在土壤和玉米片中寻找到。这种细菌也可产生MspA蛋白质，这种蛋白质经化学提纯后可以用于多种用途。

经过提纯之后，派瑞拉将这种蛋白质与一种比传统染料毒性更小的染料结合。这种蛋白质染料混合物被涂在单个的太阳能电池上——这些单个的太阳能电池组合在一起，能够形成太阳能电池板，这样就可以利用人造光来测试其产能量。

"这个想法是蛋白质为吸光染料的电子转移提供一个介质，"派瑞拉说道。"我们希望这种蛋白质能够捕捉染料释放的电子，然后使电子向同一个方向传导，这样就能产生电流。"

尽管目前这种新型的染料光敏化太阳能电池并不能提高将太阳能转化为电流的能力，但这种技术位于其同类技

---

tuberculosis [tju:ˌbəːkjuˈləusis] n. 肺结核

convert [kənˈvəːt] v. 转变

the technology is the first of its kind and could help low-cost solar cells become a more **viable** option in the alternative energy field.

"This type of research where you have a biodegradable or environmentally friendly **component** inside a solar cell has not been done before, and the research is still in its early stages right now," Perera said. "But we have noticed that it's working and that means that the protein is not **decomposed** in the light and electric generating conditions. Because of that we believe that we've actually made the first protein-incorporated solar cell."

Perera was one of two Kansas State University graduate students named a winner at the ninth annual Capitol Graduate Research Summit in Topeka. She received a $500 scholarship from KansasBio and will present her poster, "Design of a 'Greener' Solar Cell using Mycobacterial Protein MspA," at the organization's **board of directors'** meeting.

Perera said the summit benefited her research because it gave her the chance to share her work with state legislators in addition to the scientific community. As a result, legislators can understand the work and how it affects Kansas.

"We know that fossil fuels are going to run out in the very near future," Perera said. "Kansas is getting a reputation as one of the central places in the U.S. for alternative energy research because of the abundance of sunlight and wind. I want to contribute to that and to the betterment of humanity with this research."

术之首，而且能将低成本的太阳能电池成为替代能源领域中的一种更可行的选择。

"之前从未进行过这种包含可生物降解或环保成分的太阳能电池的研究，而且该研究目前仍处于初期阶段，"派瑞拉说道。"但我们注意到这项研究行之有效，这也说明这种蛋白质不会在光照和有电流产生的环境中被分解。因为这一点，我们认为我们制造出了第一个含有蛋白质的太阳能电池。"

在托皮卡举行的第九届年度堪萨斯州议会研究生科研峰会上，派瑞拉是堪萨斯州立大学获奖的两名研究生之一。她得到了来自堪萨斯生物协会的五百美元奖学金。她还将在此次大会的主办单位董事会上展示自己的海报——"使用分枝杆菌MspA蛋白质的'绿色'太阳能电池设计"。

派瑞拉说，这次峰会对她的研究不无裨益，因为她得到了这样的机会，不仅能够与科学团体，还能与州立法者分享她的工作成果。最终，立法者们能够理解这项工作以及它对堪萨斯州的影响。

"我们知道，化石燃料在不久的将来将被人类消耗殆尽，"派瑞拉说。"作为美国中部地区之一，堪萨斯将因其对替代能源的研究而得到赞誉，而这得益于丰富的光照和风能。我想对此做出贡献，并让这项研究造福人类。"

---

viable ['vaɪəbl] a. 切实可行的
component [kəm'pəʊnənt] n. 成分

decompose [ˌdiːkəm'pəʊz] v. 分解
board of directors 董事会

炫 · 知识

1. alternative energy 替代能源

狭义的替代能源仅仅是指一切可以替代石油的能源；而广义的替代能源是指可以替代目前使用的化石燃料的能源(化石燃料包括石油、天然气和煤炭)，大多数的新能源都是替代能源，包括太阳能、核能、风能、海洋能等。

2. coat 涂

对于coat作为名词表示"大衣"的含义我们都非常熟悉，但是coat还可以作动词，表示"涂，覆盖"。这个用法也非常常见，比如coated biscuit，"涂层饼干"。

阅读技能练习场

Exercises:

1 Which of the descriptions is true about dye-sensitized solar cells?

A. They're extremely cheap.

B. They're friendlier to the environment and living organisms.

C. They're high in energy output efficiency.

D. They're widely used in different fields.

2 According to the whole passage, which do you think is NOT correct?

A. Dye-sensitized solar cell is a greener alternative energy solution to fossil fuels.

B. Dye-sensitized solar cells are new technology.

C. Kansas is abundant in wind and sunlight.

D. Perera's research didn't improve the energy output of the solar cells.

3 What can we know about Perera according to the passage?

A. She received a $500 scholarship.

B. She is in need of money to continue her research.

C. She comes from Kansas.

D. She's been away from her college because of the meetings.

Reading Skills

1. 先看题目再读文章 ★ ★ ★ ★ ★

有些题目的针对性较强，根据题干和选项便可直接在原文中找到对应答案。对于此类题目，注意要按照意群单位来阅读，如果可以带着问题阅读文章，便会提高解题效率，并且还能很大程度地提高自己的阅读速度和正确率。

> **Q1解析：** 此题有关染料光敏化太阳能电池，且四个选项皆围绕其展开。A项在文中并未提及。根据the new dye-sensitized solar cells currently do not improve on the technology's ability to convert sunlight into electrical current可知C项有误。文章介绍了染料光敏化太阳能电池仍在研究阶段，并未提到"广泛使用"，所以D也有误。本题选B。

2. 整合零碎信息综合分析 ★ ★ ★ ★ ★

题目要求从全文进行分析时，就要仔细阅读每个细节，并在头脑中形成一个框架。逐个分析每个选项之后，通常都能选出最合适的答案。

> **Q2解析：** B选项错在原文表述为…have been around for more than 20 years. 其他三个选项在原文均有相应的表述。

> **Q3解析：** B项错在文章没有提及这一点。由Ayomi Perera, a doctoral student in chemistry, Sri Lanka可知她并非来自美国堪萨斯，故C项错误。D项提到她离开学校很长时间，这在原文中也没有提及。所以选A。

Passage 35

Do You Believe in Climate Change?

——气候变化，你信吗？

——Mar. 23rd, 2012, Guardian

Reading Guide

冬天不再那么寒冷，新闻报道说，极地的冰雪融化。你相信气候变化吗？事实上，气候的确是在变化的，而且这和我们的生活息息相关。气候变化影响了我们的生活；同时，我们的生活也是导致气候变化的重要因素。无论你是否相信，你迟早都会体会到这种变化。那么，我们需要做些什么改变呢？

This may seem like an odd question for a climate scientist to ask, but it is one I am constantly asked now. The typical discussion starts: "I know that the climate is changing, but hasn't it always changed through natural cycles?" Then they will often give an example, such as the **medieval** warm period to prove their point.

Those asking the question include a wide range of people I meet in the pub, friends, politicians and increasingly even some of those active in sustainable development and the renewable energy businesses. What I find interesting is that I have known many of these people for a long time and they never asked me this before.

作为一名气候学家，询问这个问题确实有些奇怪，但是这也是我经常被问到的一个问题。具有代表性的探讨是这样开始的："我知道气候在变化，但气候不是通过自然循环一直在变化吗？"而后，他们通常会给出一个例子，比如中世纪气候变暖的时期，来证明他们的观点。

很多人都问过这个问题，比如我在酒吧里认识的人，我的朋友们、政客，还有越来越多的热衷于可持续发展和再生能源事业的人。我发现，有趣的地方在于我认识这些人已经有很长一段时间了，但他们之前从来没有问过我这个问题。

medieval [ˌmedi'iːvəl] a. 中世纪的

Recent studies show that **public acceptance** of the scientific evidence for man-made climate change has decreased. However, the change is not that great. The difference I find in talking to people is that they feel better able to express their doubts.

This is very hard for scientists to understand. The scientific evidence that humanity is having an effect on the climate is **overwhelming** and increasing every year. Yet public perception of this is confused. A Cardiff/Ipsos Mori study on public perceptions of climate change, published in 2010, identifies a number of possible contributory factors: the move from being a science issue to a political issue may have introduced more distrust; "cognitive dissonance"—where people modify their beliefs about uncomfortable truths—may be a factor; people may have become bored of constantly hearing about climate change; or **external factors** such as the financial crisis may have played a role. There is also increased activity among **skeptical** groups to obscure the scientific evidence in order to influence public opinion.

Around three years ago I raised the issue of the way that science can be **misused**. In some cases scare stories in the media were over-hyping climate change and I think we are paying the price for this now with a reaction the other way. I was concerned then that science is not always presented objectively by the media and interested

最近的一项研究表明，公众对于气候变化是人为因素造成这一说法的科学依据的接受程度有所降低。然而，变化并没有那么大。不一样的是在我和别人谈论的过程中，我发现他们因为能提出疑问而感觉良好。

但是科学家很难理解这一点。科学证实，人类对气候的影响势不可挡，而且每年都在加剧。然而公众对此事的认知却比较模糊。2010年，加的夫/益索普莫利的一家调查机构进行了一项民意调查以了解公众对气候变化的看法。该调查证实了好几项可能促成气候变化的因素；而这一问题在从科学问题转变为政治问题的过程中引发了更多的不信任；而"认知失调"——即人们面对让自己不舒服的真相时会调整自己的看法——也许是一个因素；人们可能会对不断听到的气候变化问题感到厌烦，或者是一些外在的因素，比如金融危机或许也发挥了作用。持怀疑态度的群体之间的活动越来越多，其目的是混淆科学依据，从而影响公众的观点。

大约在三年前，我提出了一个有关科学可以如何被误用的问题。在一些案例中，媒体用恐怖的故事大肆宣传气候变化，而我认为，我们现在就是在用相反的反应来为此付出代价。那时我就曾担心，由于媒体和利益相关人士（有时甚至是科学家自己）并不总是能客观地展示

---

public acceptance 公众接受
overwhelming [ˌəuvəˈhwelmiŋ] a. 势不可挡的
external factor 外在因素

skeptical [ˈskeptikəl] a. 怀疑的
misuse[ˌmisˈjuːz] v. 滥用；误用

parties (even sometimes scientists themselves) in important areas, like climate change. What I don't think any of us appreciated at the time was the depth of disconnect between the scientific process and the public.

Which brings me on to the question, should you believe in climate change? The first point to make is that it's not something you should believe or not believe in—this is a matter of science and therefore of evidence—and there's lots of it out there. On an issue this important, I think people should look at that evidence and make their own mind up. We are often very influenced by our own personal experience. After a couple of cold winters in the UK, the common question was "has climate change stopped?" despite that fact that many other regions of the world were experiencing record warm temperatures. And 2010 was one of the warmest years on record. For real evidence of climate change, we have to look at the bigger picture.

You can see research by the Met Office that shows the evidence of man-made warming is even stronger than it was when the last IPCC report was published. A whole range of different datasets and independent analyses show the world is warming. There is a broad consensus that over the last half century warming has been rapid, and man-made greenhouse gas emissions are very likely to be the cause.

Long-term changes in our climate system have been observed across the globe, from shifts in rainfall patterns to a decline in Arctic sea-ice. The changes follow the pattern of expected

一些例如气候变化的重要方面。在那个时候，我认为我们中的任何一个人都不能理解科学进程和大众之间已经严重脱节。

这又把我带回到了之前的问题，你应该相信气候变化吗？要确立的第一点就是这不是你应该相信与否的问题——而是一个关于科学的问题，因此是需要证据的——而且证据有很多。在这个如此重要的问题上，我想人们应该先看证据，然后确立自己的观点。我们经常会受到自己个人经历的影响。当英国经历了两、三个寒冬以后，人们通常会问："气候变化停止了吗？"。尽管世界上的许多其他地区正经历着创纪录的气温新高。而且2010年冬天是历史上最温暖的冬天。为了得到气候变化的真实证据，我们必须要把视线放得更广阔一些。

我们可以看到英国气象局的一项研究，该研究中证明气候变暖是人为造成的证据比上次联合国政府间气象变化专门委员会发表的报告中的证据更有说服力。各种不同数据和独立分析表明，世界在变暖。在过去的半个世纪，全球变暖的进程十分迅速，人为制造的温室气体排放很可能是使全球变暖的原因，这个说法得到了广泛的认同。

在全球范围内观察从降雨量模式的变化到北极海面浮冰的融化，可以看到我们气候系统的长期变化。气候变化遵循着预料中的气候变化模式，并且可

climate change and bear the fingerprint of human influence, providing the clearest evidence yet that human activity is impacting our climate. The rate of warming and ice melt varies and some regions warm faster while others don't warm at all for a while. Again, it's the big picture that's important.

Given the overwhelming evidence for man-made climate change, it could be argued that it shouldn't be necessary to keep going over old ground to prove it time after time. In fact, it's essential we move on and focus on the future, because climate change will pose challenges for humanity.

Ultimately, as the planet continues to warm the issue of whether you believe in climate change will become more and more **irrelevant**. We will all experience the impacts of climate change in some way, so the evidence will be there in plain sight.

以看到人类影响的痕迹，这提供了最清晰的证据——人类活动正影响着我们的气候。气候变暖的速率和冰面的融化不断在变化，一些地区更快地变暖，而另一些地区在一段时间之内则完全没有变暖。再次说明，以更广的视线来看这个问题十分重要。

考虑到人类对气候变化造成深刻影响的这一事实，我们可以争论的是确实没必要继续纠结于此，一次又一次地试图证明它。事实上，我们应该继续前进，并把重点放在未来，因为气候变化会给人类带来挑战。

最终，随着地球日益变暖，你是否相信这一说法开始变得越来越无关紧要了。我们都将以某种方式体会到气候变化带来的影响，所以说，证据是显而易见的。

炫 · 知识

1. cognitive dissonance 认知失调

认知失调是指一个人的行为与自己先前一贯的对自我的认知(而且通常是正面的、积极的自我)产生分歧，从一个认知推断出另一个对立的认知时而产生的不舒适感、不愉快的情绪。

2. pay the price 付出代价

pay the price这个短语中的每个单词我们都很熟悉，但它的意思并不是指"付账"，而是"为……付出代价"。

---

irrelevant [i'reləvənt] a. 不相干的

3. in plain sight 显而易见

plain可以表示"平的"，in plain sight有"就在眼前"的含义，而在本文中则引申为"显而易见"的意思。

阅读技能练习场

Exercises:

1 Why did the author feel it's interesting that his friends asked questions about climate changing?

A. Because they want to know the real answer.

B. Because they want to find a good topic to talk with the author.

C. Actually, they want to say something else.

D. They didn't ask the author this question before.

2 Which description is right about the Cardiff/Ipsos Mori study?

A. "Cognitive dissonance" is a factor that influenced the public perceptions of climate change.

B. People become interested in hearing about climate change.

C. Financial crisis has played an important role as an internal factor.

D. There is no connection between people and climate change.

3 According to the author, should we believe in climate change?

A. It's not important because it is the fact.

B. It depends.

C. We can't infer from the passage.

D. There is no exact evidence that proves climate change.

Answers: 1. D   2. A   3. A

Reading Skills

1. 理解作者的写作意图 ★ ★ ★ ★ ★

理解作者的写作意图与理解文章主旨一样重要，如果无法正确判断作者的意图，就有可能会误解文章的基调，因而也就很难做出正确的选择。在做这部分题目的时候，可以找出表达作者观点的形容词，根据这些形容词的感情基调就可以判断整篇文章的主旨。

> **Q1解析：** 根据问题的提示，可以知道答案出现在文章的开头部分。根据 What I find interesting is that I have known many of these people for a long time and they never asked me this before.可以知道，正确选项是D。
>
> **Q3解析：** 在文章的字里行间，作者都明确地告知了确实存在气候变化的现象，而在文章的结尾处更是提到Ultimately, as the planet continues to warm the issue of whether you believe in climate change will become more and more irrelevant. 根据这句话，可以知道正确答案是A。

2. 注意原文中的表述 ★ ★ ★ ★ ★

这类询问选项描述是否正确的问题都是典型的判断正误题，而我们最容易出现的问题就是根据自己的主观臆断进行判断。然而，这类问题恰恰是需要根据原文才能选出答案的。所以在选择的时候一定马上在原文中定位信息并寻找答案，这样可以把题目的范围缩小。

> **Q2解析：** 首先，根据问题我们可以确定本题针对文章第四段的内容，读过文章之后，不难发现C和D两项的内容与原文是有出入的，而B选项与这项研究无关，所以正确答案是A。

Chapter 06

医学与健康
Medical&Health

Passage 36

Why Are Families Who Eat Together Healthier?

——为何全家一起就餐使你更健康?

——Apr. 24th, 2012, Time

Reading Guide

以前，和家人一起吃饭是再正常不过的事情。但如今，随着社会的高速发展，忙碌的人们越来越少地选择在家与家人共同就餐。不过，一项研究表明，全家人经常一起用餐的家庭，其家庭成员的身体通常更健康。而在这样的家庭成长的孩子在情感和身体健康方面往往也会比较突出。

A new review of data adds to the evidence that families who eat together most often are healthier.

Problem is, many families aren't sitting down together at home very often at all. According to the research team from Rutgers, the State University of New Jersey, about 40% of the average family's budget is spent eating out, typically not together. This is particularly concerning because eating out is linked with poorer food choices—restaurant and prepared foods tend to be much fattier, saltier and higher in calories than meals made at home.

Increasingly, **obesity** and public health experts believe that such eating behavior fuels Americans' risk of obesity and nutrition

一项新的研究数据进一步证明：全家一起吃饭的家庭，其家庭成员通常比较健康。

问题是对于许多家庭来说，全家人一起坐下来，在家吃饭的机会并不多。来自罗格斯新泽西州立大学的研究团队表明，家庭平均预算的40%花在了外出就餐上，而且通常不是全家一起。还有一点特别令人担忧，外出就餐意味着你可选的食物并不多——因为餐馆里售卖的和预先加工的食品往往比家里的含有更多的油脂、盐分和更高的热量。

肥胖和公共卫生专家越来越相信，这样的饮食行为促使美国人面临肥胖和营养不良的风险。为了进一步研究，罗

obesity [əuˈbiːsəti] n. 肥胖

deficiencies. To find out more, Rutgers researchers reviewed 68 studies on the issue. They looked specifically at studies that measured the frequency and atmosphere of family meals and compared that to the quality of children's food consumption and risk of weight gain.

The data suggested that family mealtime has **a wealth of** health benefits, especially for children. Kids who ate more meals together with their families tended to eat more fruits, vegetables, fiber, calcium-rich foods and vitamins, and ate less junk food.

Social improvements were also linked to frequency of family meals. Teens who ate at the family table more often were more likely to show fewer signs of depression and feel that their family was more supportive, compared with teens who dined less often at home.

"It is very interesting that something as simple as frequently eating meals together may contribute to so many different types of benefits to all family members," says study author Jennifer Martin-Biggers, a doctoral student in the department of nutritional sciences at Rutgers.

Children in families who frequently shared meals also tended to have a lower body mass index than those who didn't, although the research did not find a conclusion between family meals and obesity.

Researchers found also that it's not just the time spent together or the act of consuming food simultaneously that matters. The quality

格斯大学的研究人员们针对这一问题进行了68项相关研究。在他们的研究中，他们详细地测定了全家一起就餐的频率和气氛，并将结果与孩子的食物摄取量和体重增加的风险进行了对比。

数据表明，家庭晚餐时间具有很多健康益处，尤其是对孩子而言。那些更经常与家人共同进餐的孩子往往可以吃到更多的水果、蔬菜、纤维、富含钙质的食物及维生素，也意味着他们更少吃到垃圾食品。

社交方面的进步也与家庭共同进餐的频率有关。相比那些不常在家吃饭的青少年，经常坐在家中餐桌前吃饭的孩子表现出自闭迹象的可能性更小，而且他们会感到更多来自家庭的支持。

"有趣的是，仅仅是经常和家人共同进餐这样简单的事，也可能给所有的家庭成员带来各种各样的好处，"研究课题的作者詹妮弗·马丁比格说道，她是罗格斯大学营养科学系的一名博士生

与那些不与家人一起就餐的孩子相比，经常与家人共同进餐的孩子的身体质量指数更低，尽管研究没有得到在家就餐和体重之间的决定性关联。

研究者还发现，不仅是一起共度时光，或是同时吃饭的简单举动，家庭成员相互交流的质量也很重要。数据表

deficiency [diˈfiʃənsi] n. 缺点　　　　a wealth of 很多的

of the interactions are important too. The data showed that families who spent time watching TV together or ate fast food out together did not have the same improved **dietary intakes** as families who ate meals together at home.

"We believe that spending that family time together may provide a platform allowing parents and children to interact and for parents to teach children healthy habits," says Martin-Biggers. "The increased focus on food and eating may be a mechanism behind the improved diets families tend to show when they eat together."

The authors note that there's no shortage of nutritional information out there for parents who want to make better choices for their families. But when will busy parent have the time to **sift through** the research? To help, the Rutgers team says it is creating at-a-glance graphics based on their findings that will visually synthesize key nutritional and healthy-eating info in an appealing way for the public.

明，家人一起看电视或是一起在外面吃快餐并不能像全家一起在家吃饭那样可以促进饮食摄入。

"我们相信，共度家庭时光可以提供一个让家长和孩子相互交流的平台，家长可以借此教会孩子健康的习惯，"马丁·比格斯说道。"家庭成员对食物和进餐越来越关注，其背后的机制就是当家庭一起就餐时，人们倾向于改善饮食。"

作者解释道，对于那些想为家庭做出更好选择的父母来说，关于营养方面的信息并不少。但忙碌的父母们什么时候去筛选这些研究呢？为了帮助他们，罗格斯团队表示，基于他们的研究结果，他们正在制作一个一目了然的图表，把重要的营养和健康饮食信息形象地结合起来，以一种有趣的形式呈献给公众。

炫 · 知识

1. prepared food 预加工食品

预加工食品指的是那些包装完好、卫生安全、便于携带、可直接(或经简单加工)食用的食品。这种食品满足了人们不愿意准备饭菜的需求，避免了开火做饭的麻烦。

2. food consumption 食物摄取量

consumption表示"消耗，耗费"，而food consumption则是"食物摄取量"的意思。食物摄取量通常是指一段时间内人体摄入的食物的量。

dietary ['daiətəri] a. 饮食的
intake ['inteik] n. 摄取量

sift through 筛选

3. junk food 垃圾食品

垃圾食品是指仅提供热量、别无其他营养元素的食品；或是提供超过人体需要的成分的食品。快餐可以说是最常见的垃圾食品。

4. body mass index 身体质量指数

身体质量指数通常简写为BMI，关注身材的人们对它一定不陌生。通过用体重的公斤数除以身高的米数平方而得出的数字，可以衡量一个人的胖瘦程度。这个标准是目前国际上通用的。

阅读技能练习场

Exercises:

1 Compared with meals made at home, how do foods sold in restaurants tend to be?

A. Fattier.

B. Saltier.

C. Higher in calories.

D. All of them are right.

2 Which is not a benefit of eating together with your family?

A. Kids would eat more fruits, vegetables, fiber, calcium-rich foods and vitamins.

B. Teens are likely to show fewer signs of depression.

C. Eating with your family keeps you away from a various types of diseases.

D. Parents and children could interact well.

3 According to the passage, which description could help improve the interactions between family members?

A. Watching TV together.

B. Eating fast food out together.

C. Playing games together.

D. None of them are right.

Answers:
1.D 2.C 3.D

Reading Skills

1. 忠于原文表述 ★★★★★

回答客观的细节题时，不要凭借自己的印象作答，要回到文章相应段落寻找答案。通常题干里会有比较明显的提示词，根据这些词就可以迅速回到文章中定位。

> **Q1解析**：问题中的foods sold in restaurants提示答案的出处在文章开头的部分。根据原文，A、B、C三个表述都是正确的，所以正确答案是D。

2. 小心文中未提及的选项 ★★★★★

经常会遇到条件反射选择正确答案的情况，而有时候问题的提问是要我们选出错误答案。遇到这种情况，避免错选的最好办法就是看清题目，只有看清了题目才能保证答案不会选错。

> **Q2解析**：问题询问哪一项不是正确的描述，乍一看A、B、C、D四个选项都是正确的，但是文章中并没有提到在家吃饭可以预防疾病。所以正确答案是C。
>
> **Q3解析**：根据interactions，锁定答案在文章的倒数第四、五、六自然段，原文中提到和家人一起看电视或外出就餐无法达到与在家共同进餐相同的效果，所以A、B都是错误的，C是干扰选项，描述的内容在文中并没有出现，所以答案是D。

Passage 37

Can Autism Really Be Diagnosed in Minutes?

——自闭症真能在几分钟内判断出来吗?

——Apr. 11th, 2012, Time

Reading Guide

根据新的诊断方法,仅在几分钟之内就能判断一个孩子是否患有自闭症。不同于传统方法的繁琐复杂,这种新方法更方便、也更快捷。然而,许多人对此也表示质疑,通过如此公式化的方法,得到的结果真的准确吗?

Autism is an extremely complex diagnosis. Parental insight, physician observations and hours of data can factor into determining whether a child actually has the condition or is just a little on the quirky side.

Now a Harvard researcher, Dennis P. Wall, has published research about a Web-based tool he developed that promises to diagnose autism in minutes, not hours—a proposition that Wall has floated for some time now and has some autism experts so skeptical they're not even willing to speak **on the record** about it.

Wall, director of the computational biology initiative at the Center for Biomedical Informatics at Harvard Medical School and associate professor of pathology at the school, combines computer

自闭症的确诊是一个十分复杂的过程。父母的洞悉,医师的观察以及数小时的数据都是确定一个孩子到底是患上了自闭症还是仅仅有些古怪的依据。

如今,哈佛大学的一名研究者丹尼斯·P·沃尔发表了一项研究:他发明的一种基于网络的工具有望在数分钟内完成自闭症的确诊,而不用几个小时那么久——沃尔已经将这个提议公布了一段时间,但一些相关的专家对此表示质疑,他们甚至不愿意正式谈论这一提议。

沃尔是首创了计算生物学的哈佛医学院生物医学资讯中心主任,同时也是学校的病理学副教授。他将计算机算法、针对父母的7个问题的问卷调查及家

on the record 记录在案

algorithms along with a seven-point parent **questionnaire** and a home video clip to make a speedy online assessment of whether a child has autism.

Wall's reliance on a quick questionnaire and video of the child playing could supplement or replace more comprehensive exams such as the commonly used behavior-based Autism Diagnostic Observation Schedule (ADOS), which evaluates social interaction, language impairments and autism-specific behaviors, and the more intensive, 93-question Autism Diagnostic Interview, Revised (ADI-R). Together, these evaluations can take four hours or even longer, which Wall says is simply too long. Instead, Wall's method would not even require the child to be seen by a clinician; it relies on seven questions that parents answer via an online portal and on an examination by a trained analyst of a two- to five-minute home video of the child in a play environment. The diagnosis is completed by the end of the video using the parent's answers to the seven questions and the video analyst's answers to eight additional questions.

When Wall compared diagnostic results from his artificial-intelligence method with more conventional exams, he found his method's accuracy—asking seven questions versus 93 —**stacked up** favorably, according to research published in *Nature Translational Psychiatry*. He compared **diagnostic** results from his method with results from more than 2,700 people who took the ADI-R. "I want to enable every family to get

庭录影带剪辑结合在一起，在线就可以迅速判定一个孩子是否患有自闭症。

沃尔凭借快速作答的问卷调查以及孩子玩耍的录像可以作为补充手段，或者取代更综合的测定，例如普遍使用的自闭症诊断观察量表，这种方法以行为举止作为参考，能判断出测试者的社会互动水平、语言损害程度以及自闭症特有的行为举止。此外还有更强大的包含93道题目的修订版自闭症诊断视察量表测试。得出评估需要将两个测试结果综合在一起，需要4小时或者更长时间，沃尔表示这个时间太长了。相反，如果采用沃尔的方法，临床医生甚至不需要观察孩子；只要家长通过网络上回答的7道题，并由一位经过训练的分析员观看2至5分钟孩子在游戏环境的家庭视频，就能诊断出孩子是否患病。最终确诊则要等到视频播放结束后，将父母对7个问题的回答以及视频分析员对另外8个问题的回答结合在一起。

当沃尔将他的人工智能诊断法的结果与更传统的测试结果进行对比时，他发现回答7个问题和93个问题相比，自己的方法十分精准，而且更容易计算，该研究已发表在《自然转移精神病学》杂志上。他将使用自己的方法得到的诊断结果与超过2700人参与的ADI-R测试的结果进行了比较。"我希望所有家庭都能得到诊断，无论是在候诊室还是通过

---

questionnaire [ˌkwestʃəˈneə] n. 问卷
stack up 累加

diagnostic [ˌdaiəgˈnəustik] a. 诊断的

access to diagnosis, whether that's in a waiting room or via an iPad," says Wall.

Of course every family should have access, says Catherine Lord, who developed the ADOS and serves as director of the Center for Autism and the Developing Brain at N.Y. Presbyterian Hospital. But she and other experts are skeptical that administering a quickie version of the more standard exams is a sound way to reach a diagnosis.

Focusing on the actual diagnostic exams overlooks the fact that most initial autism diagnoses are made in the course of office visits, via observation and not via formal exams. Children are then referred for confirmation to specialists——developmental pediatricians, for example, or psychologists or psychiatrists. Although there are indeed waitlists at the most **prestigious** clinics, many states and school systems have mandated periods of time between referral, assessment and the onset of treatment.

It's challenging to develop a reliable substitute for face-to-face evaluation, says Lord. "There is something about sitting down with a family and hearing what the child is like in various circles." she says,

For his part, Wall is more than aware of the dubious reaction his test has evoked in leaders in the autism field. Yet he's hopeful they'll be open-minded for the good of children who have autism but don't yet know it. Says Wall: "I think there's a way for us to all play together."

iPad。" 沃尔说道。

开发了ADOS测试的纽约教会医院自闭症及大脑发育中心主任凯瑟琳·洛德表示，诚然，每个家庭都应该有得到诊断的机会。但是她和其他的专家怀疑使用这种比标准化测试仓促而成的方法来诊断忧郁症是否可靠。

对实际诊断测试的关注忽略了自闭症最初的诊断方法，当时的诊断需要在医生办公室中，通过观察而得到，而不是通过标准化的测试。之后，孩子们被送到专家那里确诊——比如发育儿科医生、心理学家或精神病学家。即使最有名望的诊所中的确有相关专家，但许多州和学校体系在转诊、评定和发病治疗期间仍有过渡时期。

目前来说，发展能够取代面对面评估的方法仍是一个挑战，洛德说。"有些事需要多次和家人一起坐下来，讨论并听取孩子在多种环境中的表现"

对沃尔而言，他完全知道自己的测试在自闭症研究领域的领军人物中引发了质疑。但他希望他们为了那些身患自闭却不知情的患儿的利益，这些人能够不带偏见地看待他的方法。他说："我想肯定有一种方法，能让我们所有人和平共处。"

---

prestigious [pre'stidʒəs] a. 有声望的

炫 · 知识

1. computer algorithm 计算机算法

algorithm表示"算法",计算机算法可以理解为由基本运算及规定的运算顺序构成的完整解题步骤,可以用来解决一类特定的问题。

2. face-to-face 面对面的

从字面意思上看,就可以知道face-to-face表示"面对面"的含义,这样通过连字符连接几个单词构成形容词的用法会使表达更生动。

3. open-minded 不带偏见的

open-minded "思想开明的"这一含义我们都很熟悉,但是在本文中,它表示"不带偏见的"之意。

阅读技能练习场

Exercises:

① According to the passage, what kind of attitude does the author holds to quickly diagnosis?

A. Supportive.

B. Neutral.

C. Objective.

D. Critical.

② What is the shortage of traditional method according to Wall?

A. It takes too much time.

B. It's not accurate.

C. It would hurt the children's feeling.

D. It's too expensive.

③ How long will a traditional exam last?

A. 93 minutes.

B. 4 hours or more.

C. 7 minutes.

D. About an hour.

Reading Skills

1. 留意表示强烈态度的选项 ★★★★★

对于那些询问作者态度和文章主旨的问题，不能仅通过文章的某个段落就做出判断。此外，对于那些过于强烈的表达作者观点的词，我们也要留意，因为通常作者的观点不会过于强烈。

> **Q1解析**：题目询问作者对沃尔的方法持何种态度，当我们读过文章，有了整体的了解之后，不难看出作者还是比较中立的，所以正确答案是B。

2. 排除不相干的选项 ★★★★★

在我们答题的时候，可以看到有些选项与文章所描述的内容根本没有关联。对于这种情况，可以大胆地排除这些选项，节省时间。

> **Q2解析**：题目询问传统方法具有的缺点，因此可以排除C和D，因为这两个选项与文章中讨论的内容没有关联。再看剩下的两个选项，文中并没有说使用传统方法得到的答案不准确，只是这种方法繁琐费时，所以正确答案是A。

> **Q3解析**：这是一道非常简单的问题，93这个数字出现在介绍传统方法的部分，即这种测试中含有93道题目；7则是Wall的方法中，有7道针对家长的题目，D选项则没有提到，所以正确答案是B。

Passage 38

Beauty Might Be a Matter of Dietary Makeup?
——美丽是吃出来的?
——Apr. 21st, 2012, L.A. Times

Reading Guide

不用化妆、不用整形也能变漂亮吗？科学研究表明，多吃水果蔬菜，相关色素的颜色就能表现在你的脸上。虽然对于摄取量的控制尚无明确定论，但对于想要健康又爱美丽的人们来说，这也是一个好消息。

Please don't take this wrong. You look absolutely fine the way you are. It's just that ... well, with a little work, you might look even better.

We're not talking plastic surgery. Just the daily grind of buckling down and trying to eat better. Fresh from the the journal PLoS ONE comes word that scarfing down a few extra fruits and vegetables—yes, those again—could give you a significant leg up in the attractiveness department.

Scientists have known **for a while** that the same pigments that give fruits and vegetables their color—carotenoids—can accumulate in your skin and give it color too. What they didn't know was this: How many fruits and vegetables do you

请不要误解。你现在这个样子看起来很不错。只不过……好吧，做点小功课会让你变得更美。

我们不是在讨论整形手术。只是要认真对待日常功课，并努力吃得更好。刚刚，《公共科学图书馆》上刊登的文章表示，多吃些额外的蔬菜和水果——是的，还是这些——这样就能大大地帮助你增加吸引力。

科学家们很早之前就已经知道，赋予水果和蔬菜颜色的种色素成分——类胡萝卜素——可以在你的肌肤中累积，并让你的肌肤拥有同样的颜色。科学家们尚未得知的是究竟要吃多少水果蔬

for a while （过了）一阵子

199

have to eat for how long in order for people to notice the difference in your coloring? And what, if anything, will people think of the difference?

Researchers at the University of St. Andrews in Scotland did two studies to try to find out. In the first, they analyzed natural changes in the fruit and vegetable intake of 35 undergraduates who filled out questionnaires about their diet three times: at an initial session, three weeks later and again three weeks after that.

On those same three occasions, researchers measured the students' skin color **in terms of** lightness, redness and yellowness using a spectrophotometer—a machine designed to do that sort of thing. (To be included in the study, students could not have a recently acquired **tan** from sun, salon or chemical product, and they could not be wearing facial makeup.)

The researchers didn't ask the students to make any changes in what they ate. And they didn't betray any special interest in any particular foods. But during the six weeks, some students spontaneously increased their produce consumption, and such increases were significantly associated with increased redness, yellowness and overall darkness of skin color. From the machine's perspective anyway.

But that didn't mean mere human beings could detect any difference or would like what they saw if they could.

So the researchers did another study. This time they showed 24 undergrads pictures of two

菜，以及要吃多久，才能让人们注意到你的肤色差别？还有就是，会有人注意到这种不同吗？

苏格兰圣安德鲁学院的研究人员进行了两项研究以找到答案。首先，他们分析了35名本科生摄入水果和蔬菜后的自然变化，并他们让填写了三次关于他们饮食的调查问卷：时间分别是刚刚开学、三周过后、以及又过了三周之后。

在同样的三种情况下，研究者使用专门用于此类研究的分光光度计，以明亮、红润、暗黄三个标准测量学生的肤色。（参与研究的学生最近不能被太阳晒黑，不能进行美容保养或使用化学品，也不能化妆。）

研究员没有要求学生们改变他们的饮食，他们也不用控制自己对任何一种特定食品的兴趣。但是在6个星期内，一些学生自发地增加了他们的食物摄取量。值得注意的是，这种现象还伴有肤色显著的红润或暗黄，或者整体的肤色变黑。总之，从机器的角度来说事实就是这样。

但这并不能说明只有人类能发现变化，或者喜欢他们的改变——如果他们能看到的话。

于是研究员进行了另一项研究。这一次，他们展示了每组2男2女、共24名

---

in terms of 依照　　　　　　　　　　　　　　　tan [tæn] n. 棕褐色

men and two women that had been manipulated color-wise to correspond to how they would look if they ate various quantities of fruits and vegetables.

Students were asked to choose between pairs of faces—22 were created for each face—according to which looked healthier or, in a separate task, more attractive.

It's really not a **draconian** move. In fact, study lead author Ross Whitehead, a psychology professor at the University of St. Andrews, calls it "relatively small." She has a point too, when you consider that the recommended quota of fruits and vegetables for someone consuming 2,000 calories is nine servings a day not including potatoes. And a serving isn't very big: about half a cup.

It's possible to go overboard, though. On carrots, for instance. Eat too many of those, Heber warns, and your skin, especially on your palms, can turn orange to a not necessarily lovely extent.

曾经控制过肤色的大学生的照片，想要知道如果他们摄取不同数量的蔬菜和水果之后将会呈现什么样的肤色。

学生们被要求在一组面孔中进行选择——每张脸有22个不同的颜色。选择的依据是哪个看起来更健康，而在另一项任务中，则需要选出哪个看起来更有吸引力。

这一步的确不够严谨。事实上，研究的主要作者，来自圣安德鲁大学的心理学教授萝丝·怀特海德称这种影响"相当微小"。她也有自己的观点，因为你要考虑到推荐给那些每天消耗2000卡路里的人每天的蔬菜和水果摄取量只有9份（不包括土豆），而且一份并不大：也就是半杯而已。

尽管如此，仍然很有可能会走极端。希波提示道，以胡萝卜为例，如果吃了太多的胡萝卜，你的皮肤就会变成橘红色，尤其是手掌，而且这种程度的橘红色不一定好看。

炫 · 知识

1. plastic surgery 整形手术

plastic除了有"塑料"的意思，还可以表示"整形"。plastic这个单词来自于古希腊语plastikos，意为"塑造、定形"。所以"整形手术"通常用plastic surgery表示，此外，facelift也可以表示这个含义。

---

draconian [drə'kəunjən] a. 严厉的

2. daily grind 日常功课

grind除了有"磨"的意思以外，作名词还有"苦工"的意思。所以daily grind就是指每天都要做的"日常功课"，而这种事情通常是有点麻烦的。

3. buckle down 开始认真做

buckle作为动词，有"扣住"的含义，而buckle down则是"开始认真做某事"的意思。

4. leg up 帮助

在汉语中，我们常说"助……一臂之力"，但在英语中，却是用leg来表示这个含义。leg up在英语中可以表示"为……提供帮助"，这种说法原指在上马或跨跃障碍时提供帮助。

5. serving 一份食物

serve有"招待，供应"的意思，其ing形式的名词serving则有"上菜"的意思。在本文中，这个词还可以表示"一份食物"。

阅读技能练习场

Exercises:

1 According to Paragraph 2, what may help us get a better skin color?

A. To eat more fruits and vegetables.

B. To take plastic surgery.

C. To make up before you are going to out.

D. To dress well.

2 From now on, which description didn't the scientists know?

A. Carotenoids can accumulate in your skin and give it a certain color.

B. It is the same pigments that give fruits and vegetables color.

C. How many fruits and vegetables and how long should you eat to change your skin color.

D. People would not notice their skin color.

3 What do you think the students who attend the study can do after reading the passage?

A. Be tanned.

B. Do salon or chemical product.

C. Using facial foam.

D. The above all.

Reading Skills

1. 根据原文回答问题 ★ ★ ★ ★ ★

有时题目选项给出的信息都是原文中提及的，遇到这种情况时，一定要再次回到原文确认一下，避免选错答案。

> **Q1解析**：阅读文章后可以发现C和D是干扰项，可以首先排除；再看A和B，原文第二自然段的开头就提到了作者不打算谈论整形手术，所以B也是错误的，正确答案就是A。
>
> **Q2解析**：首先，问题询问科学家还不知道的信息是哪个，明确了我们要选出一个否定的答案。D选项的内容在文章并未提到，所以直接排除。再看原文，A和B描述都是科学家已经了解到的信息，所以选项C是正确答案。

2. 定位原文，巧用排除法 ★ ★ ★ ★ ★

经常会遇到条件反射选择正确答案的情况，而有时候问题的提问是要我们选出错误答案。遇到这种情况，避免错选的最好办法就是看清题目，只有看清了题目才能保证答案不会选错。

> **Q3解析**：根据问题，我们可以知道这道题是针对第一个研究实验而出的。回到文章中的相关部分，根据To be included in the study, students could not have a recently acquired tan from sun, salon or chemical product, and they could not be wearing facial makeup. 这句话可以知道，除了C选项没有提及之外，A和B都是禁止的。所以选C。

Passage 39

Fighting Fat with Your Mirror
——用你的真实写照与肥胖斗争
——Jan. 5th, 2012, USA Today

Reading Guide

随着社会的飞速发展，我们的体重也日益上升。许多人开始自暴自弃，把肥胖的原因归结到各种不能改变的因素上。但如果我们开始关心自己的身体，注意饮食、加强运动，记住关爱自己，肥胖终将离我们远去。

Recently, journalists and scientists have attempted to explain why Americans are bursting at the seams. While they movingly described the challenges and issues in fighting fat, they may have **left out** one of the critical components of those who succeed.

In the *New York Times* Magazine story, "The Fat Trap," Tara Parker-Pope shared her heartfelt and personal account on the profound impact genetics and the home environment play. Parker-Pope conveyed her **frustration**: "What is clear is that some people appear to **be prone to** accumulating extra fat while others seem to be protected against it."

In other words, there is science behind why obesity may run in the family. If obese parents raised you and their **pantry** was stocked with fat-

最近，新闻记者和科学家们试图解释为何美国人突然胖得要把衣服都撑爆了。当他们用那感人的话语阐述与肥胖斗争时面临的挑战和问题时，他们可能忽视了一个关键因素，而正是这个因素使一些人减肥成功了。

在《纽约时报》的一个故事里，"肥胖圈"塔拉·帕克蒲波真诚地分享了她自己肥胖的原因——遗传和家庭环境带来的深刻影响。帕克蒲波表达了她的挫败感："显然，一些人倾向于积累额外的脂肪，然而另一些人却免受这种困扰。"

换句话说，在肥胖盛行整个家族的现象背后是有科学依据的。如果你被肥胖的家长抚养大，而他们的食品室里储

leave out 忽视
frustration [frʌ'streiʃən] n. 挫败

be prone to 倾向于
pantry ['pæntri] n. 食品室

and sugar-laden foods, there is a greater chance that you too have struggled with your weight. But there are people who grew up in similar environments and have managed, with difficulty and diligence, to wear a trim frame.

She also noted the results of a study that showed, "some people were more likely to eat fatty foods, presumably because they thought being fat was their genetic destiny and saw no sense in fighting it." That approach is like putting out a welcome mat to heredity-related diseases like diabetes and heart disease when in fact, we may not be able to pick our parents, but we can pick what goes on our plates.

In his *Huffington Post* piece, Dr. David Katz, Director of Yale's Prevention Research Center eloquently wrote that he believes, "obesity is neither a psychological nor a biological disease, if it is a disease at all—it is a social disease." Katz reminds us, "Since our genes and hormones have not changed appreciably in 50 years, we must attribute the advent of epidemic obesity to environmental change." Becoming more familiar with the stove in your kitchen than the drive-through restaurant in your neighborhood, or remembering not to leave cookies on the counter or perhaps not buying cookies at all, would certainly cut the cues that stimulate us to overeat. For many, the answer may in fact be an "out of sight, out of mind" approach.

We do know that fad dieting doesn't work. In an Ontario Morning Show radio interview, Jacqui Gingras of the Ryerson School of Nutrition and supporter of the Health at Every Size Movement, tells us that extreme dieting and its

藏着脂肪和糖含量过多的食物，这样你需要和体重斗争的几率就更大了。但是一些在类似家庭环境中成长的人们已经克服困难，努力甩掉脂肪了。

她也指出，一项研究的结果表明，"一些人可能更愿意吃脂肪含量高的食品，大概是因为他们认为肥胖是命中注定的基因造成的，反抗也没有意义。"而这种方式好像铺着"欢迎光临"的地毯来迎接遗传病，比如糖尿病和心脏病。但实际上，我们虽然不能选择父母，但是我们能选择盘中的食物。

耶鲁大学疾病预防研究中心主任大卫·凯茨博士在自己在《哈芬顿邮报》的版块中发表了极富说服力的文章。他相信"肥胖既不是心理疾病，也不是生理疾病，如果非要说它是一种病——那么它是一种社会病。"凯茨提醒我们，"由于我们的基因和激素已有将近50年没有出现变化，所以我们必须把肥胖的盛行归结为环境的变化。"你应该对你厨房里的炉子越来越熟悉，而不是你家附近的得来速餐厅，或者你要谨记，不要把曲奇放在台面上，或者压根就别买曲奇，这样就减少了那些刺激我们吃得太多的诱惑。对于许多人来说，实际上答案就是这种"看不见就不会想"的方法。

我们当然知道，疯狂的节食是没有用的。在安大略晨间秀广播节目的一段采访中，瑞尔森营养学校的雅基·金格拉斯是"不同体型人群健康运动"的支持者。他告诉我们，极端节食会造成循

resulting weight cycling, or yo-yo syndrome, can actually lead to conditions like insulin resistance and hypertension. She encourages ditching the guilt that may result from obsessing about the numbers on the scale and instead, "eat according to hunger and fullness signals from inside your body." I appreciate and encourage the concept of maintaining a more mindful approach, but most of the people I counsel haven't felt hungry in years. Even the thought of that **rumbling** stomach sensation makes them feel uncomfortable, **agitated** and insecure.

After counseling patients for more than three decades and battling the burden of an overweight body as a teen myself, my response to the above accounts is that an essential component must be present to promote healthier eating and for long-term weight loss to occur. That is, the key may be an internal dialogue with respect, trust and compassion for oneself.

When patients tell the tales of how they overdid it at a holiday party, it's not the specific foods they consumed that I'm interested in as much as the answer to the one question I often ask: "What were you thinking of when you saw that food and what kind of conversation did you have with yourself while you were eating?" Sadly, the most common response is, "I wasn't saying anything."

The patients I see that are the most successful are those that not only learn the benefit of reading a food label or choosing wisely from a restaurant menu or accepting that the cards they

环增重，也就是"悠悠球综合征"，而这最终将造成胰岛素耐受性和高血压。她鼓励人们甩开体重称上的数字带来的罪恶感，而是要"根据身体内部的饥饱信号来进食。"我认同并鼓励人们维持更加警惕的做法，但是向我咨询的大部分人多年都没有饥饿感。甚至是想到肚子咕咕叫的感觉都会让他们感觉不适、焦虑以及不安全。

在为病人咨询三十多年，以及自己年少时与超重的身体负担斗争之后，我对上述原因的回答是：为了促进更健康的饮食，为了能够长期的减肥，有一个必须要告诉大家的重要因素——关键是要心怀尊重、信任以及同情来与自己的内心对话。

当病人们告诉我他们如何在假日聚会上摄入过多食物的时候，他们究竟吃了哪些食物我不是很感兴趣，我更感兴趣的是他们对我常问的一个问题的回答："当你看到食物的时候，你在想什么？当你吃东西的时候，你和自己对话的内容又是什么呢？"令人感到悲哀的是，他们通常的答案都是"我什么都没说。"

我看到的最成功的病人是这样的一群人：他们阅读食品标签。面对餐馆菜单时能做出明智选择，也会接受自己造成的不良后果——他们不仅知道这样做

rumble ['rʌmbl] v. 隆隆作响

agitate ['ædʒiteit] v. 鼓动

were dealt created a tough hand to play. They come to value themselves and care about how they look and feel. They want to make better choices—life-saving choices.

的好处，而且会开始重视自己，也会关注自己看起来如何，感觉如何。他们希望做出更好的选择——也是可以救命的选择。

炫 · 知识

1. burst at the seams 衣服要被撑破

seam就是衣服的接缝部分，burst则是"爆发"的意思。这样我们很容易猜到这个表达的意思了，就是"胖到衣服都要撑破了"，这种说法体现了作者的幽默。

2. welcome mat "欢迎光临"脚垫

通常在宾馆或饭店的门前，都会铺上一块印有"欢迎光临"字样的脚垫。在本文中作者用它来比喻肥胖症的坏习惯，显得幽默有趣。

3. heredity-related disease 遗传性疾病

heredity是"遗传"的意思，那么heredity-related就可以表示"与遗传有关的"。遗传性疾病是指因遗传物质异常或生殖细胞所携带的遗传信息异常而引起的疾病。

4. drive-through restaurant 得来速餐厅

得来速是drive-through的谐音，这种餐厅在美国十分常见，人们可以在不用下车的情况下购买快餐。其最大的优点就是可以节省时间。

5. weight cycling 循环增重

这是指"节食—反弹—再节食—再反弹"，在节食减肥的人身上经常出现。因此用cycling这个词来形象地表示这种现象。

6. yo-yo syndrome 悠悠球综合征

悠悠球综合征与weight cycling相同，是指减肥者的体重如同悠悠球一样忽上忽下，用它来做比喻，十分生动形象。

阅读技能练习场

Exercises:

1 According to the passage, how can we understand the meaning of "welcome mat"?

A. Some fat people thought being fat was their destiny, so they don't take any measures.

B. We may not be able to pick our parents.

C. We could choose healthier foods.

D. Some people welcome all kinds of foods to satisfy their hunger.

2 Why did Dr. David Katz say that obesity is a social disease?

A. Our genes changed.

B. Our hormones changed.

C. Our living environment changed.

D. Many people in our society are obese.

3 According to the author, which is not an element to succeed in losing weight?

A. Learn the benefit of reading a food label and choosing healthy food.

B. Be willing to deal with the fact of being obese.

C. Want to make life-saving choices.

D. Creat a hand of cards to play.

Answers:
1.A 2.C 3.D

Reading Skills

1. 注意选项中变换的说法 ★★★★★

　　在做客观选择题的时候，了解作者意图至关重要。通常，读完文章就可以直接了解作者的观点和意图，但在有些时候，选项中的叙述可能与原文说法不同，但其实叙述的还是同一件事物。

Q1解析：根据文中welcome mat这个提示，我们来看文章第四自然段。根据这句话前面的句子Some people were more likely to eat fatty foods, presumably because they thought being fat was their genetic destiny and saw no sense in fighting it. 可以知道saw no sense in fighting it就是选项中说的don't take any measures，故选A。

Q3解析：根据文章的最后一段，可以知道A、B选项都是正确的。根据：accepting that the cards they were dealt created a tough hand to play可以知道原文使用了比喻，将肥胖的恶果比作"一把不好的牌"，所以这句话的意思就是deal with the fact of being obese。D选项在这里自然就是不正确的了。

2. 注意题目的提示 ★★★★★

阅读题目本身通常可以看作答题的一点提示，根据这些提示来回答问题是个非常巧妙的方法，可以帮助排除错误选项，并在短时间内缩小正确答案的范围。

Q2解析：题目已经提到了Dr. David Katz said that obesity is a social disease，所以马上就可以排除A、B两个选项，因为这两个选项都是关于人类自身的改变。D选项在文章中没有确切指出，所以正确答案是C。

Passage 40

Berries Can Slow Down Cognitive Decline
——浆果能减缓认知衰退
——Apr. 26th, 2012, Time

Reading Guide

蓝莓、草莓等浆果类食物不仅美味，在某种程度上也能延缓认知衰退的情况。尽管食用浆果与减缓大脑衰老之间的联系还需要进一步的研究，但食用这种水果对人们来说也没有坏处。

It's spring, which means it's the season for fresh, juicy berries. And that's good news for your brain.

Researchers report in the journal *Annals of Neurology* that women who ate berries more frequently over a period of years showed slower **decline in** brain functions such as memory and attention when they got older than women who ate them less often. The findings don't confirm that eating berries can prevent **dementia** associated with aging, or slow down Alzheimer's, but they suggest that the fruits may play a part in keeping brains healthy.

The protective effect of blueberries and strawberries isn't an entirely new finding. But previous studies have involved animals and only a small number of people, which left open the possibility that it wasn't the berries, but something

春天是新鲜多汁的浆果成熟的季节，这对你的大脑来说是个好消息。

研究者们在《神经学年刊》上的报告中称，在数年之内，与那些食用浆果较少的女性相比，更频繁地食用浆果的女性在逐渐衰老的过程中，其脑功能的衰退出现放缓，比如记忆力和注意力方面的衰退。这项研究并没有确定食用浆果能够防止因年龄增长造成的痴呆，或者减缓老年痴呆症的发生，但是他们称这种水果也许能起到维持大脑健康的作用。

蓝莓和草莓的保护作用并不是一项全新的发现。但之前的研究只涉及动物和一小部分人群，因此造成了开放的可能性：也就是说，也许并不是浆果，而是一些其他的东西影响了大脑丧失执行

---

decline in 在某方面逐渐衰弱   dementia [dɪˈmenʃiə] n. 痴呆

else that might be influencing how quickly the brain lost its executive functions.

In the current analysis, Elizabeth Devore, an instructor in medicine at Brigham and Women's Hospital, and her colleagues addressed the gap in the research by reviewing the eating habits of a single cohort of 16,000 women participating in the Nurses Health Study. During their 50s and 60s, every four years the women answered questions by phone about what they ate. And in their 70s, they came into the lab for six different cognitive function tests. Devore and her team also had information on the women's education, income and other socioeconomic factors that can affect cognitive function.

Their findings confirmed that women who ate berries at least once a week were able to slow down their cognitive decline by about 1.5 to 2.5 years. For blueberries, the effect started with about a half cup of berries each week; for strawberries, it took about a cup of the fruit per week. This effect persisted even after the scientists accounted for the fact that berry-eaters might also have other brain-healthy habits or characteristics, such as having more education and engaging in intellectually satisfying pursuits such as learning new languages or maintaining a rich network of social connections. "In the end, we did not see a lot of confounding from these factors," says Devore.

She and her colleagues focused their attention on berries because rodent studies showed that the key compound in berries, a flavonoid called anthocyanidin, could seep through the blood

功能的速度。

在当前的分析中，伯明翰医学院及女性医院的教员伊丽莎白·德沃尔和她的同事们查看了一组16000名参与 "护理健康研究" 的女性的饮食习惯，填补了该研究的空白。在这些参与研究的女性50多岁到60多岁之间，每隔四年就要通过电话回答她们通常食用哪些食物。在他们70多岁的时候，她们要到实验室接受六种不同的认知功能测试。德沃尔和她的团队也了解那些影响认知功能的因素，包括受教育的程度、收入及其他社会经济方面的信息。

他们的发现证明，每周至少食用一次浆果的女性，其认知功能的衰退会减缓大约1.5到2.5年。对于蓝莓这种浆果，一周食用半杯才会奏效；至于草莓则需要每周食用一杯。即使是在科学家宣布浆果食用者也许还有其他维持大脑健康的习惯或特征之后，这种效果仍然存在。其他维持大脑健康的习惯或特征包括更高的受教育程度，参与能够满足智力的活动，比如学习新语言或是维持丰富的社会关系。德沃尔说，"最后，从这些因素中，无法得出认知功能衰退的减缓是由于多种因素混杂的结果"。

德沃尔和她的同事们专注于研究浆果，因为针对啮齿类的动物研究表明，浆果中含有的主要化合物———一种名为花青素的类黄酮可以渗入到血液，并进

---

confound [kənˈfaund] v. 使混乱　　　　　seep [siːp] v. 渗

and into brain **tissues**—specifically concentrating in the hippocampus, which is responsible for learning and memory. As an antioxidant, flavonoids also fight inflammation and oxidation, both processes that affect aging brain cells.

The study is only the first to track berry consumption for a long term until cognitive decline set in, and the findings will need to be repeated and confirmed. But **in the meantime**, says Devore, it makes sense to add blueberries and strawberries to your diet, frozen or fresh. "I don't think there are many downsides to that. The availability of berries and access to this kind of intervention is great as a public health message." And a tasty one too.

入大脑组织，特别是集中进入到海马体中去。而海马体正是负责学习和记忆的部分。作为一种抗氧化剂，类黄酮也可以消炎和抗氧化，而这两个过程都能影响脑细胞的衰老。

这项研究是针对长期食用浆果影响认知能力的初步探索，这项研究结果还需要不断地重复和确认。但德沃尔同时也说，在饮食中加入冰冻或新鲜的蓝莓和草莓是很有意义的。"我不认为这有什么坏处。浆果的实用性以及放缓认知衰退的特性是很好的公共健康信息。"而且浆果也十分可口。

炫 · 知识

1. Alzheimer 老年痴呆症

老年痴呆症也叫作"阿茨海默症"，即Alzheimer的音译，即所谓的老年痴呆症。这是一种进行性发展的致死性神经退行性疾病，临床表现为认知和记忆力的不断恶化，并且伴有行为障碍。

2. cognitive function 认知功能

认知功能是指人脑加工、储存和提取信息的能力，即人们对事物的构成、性能与他物的关系、发展动力、发展方向及基本规律的把握能力。

3. network of social connections 社交关系网

social connections指的是"社会联系"，而network通常指抽象的网，比如网络、关系网等等。社交关系网就是指以一个人为中心，延伸到所有他曾经接触过的人而形成的人际间的联系。

tissue ['tiʃjuː] n. 组织   in the meantime 在此期间

阅读技能练习场

Exercises:

1 Which of the following descriptions is true?

A. Women eat berries every day wouldn't suffer from Alzheimer.

B. Women eat berries can prevent dementia associated with aging.

C. Women who eat berries more frequently showed slower decline in brain functions.

D. Women would be much happier if they eat berries every week.

2 According to the passage, if women eat berries at least once a week, by how long were they able to slow down their cognitive decline?

A. 1.5 years.

B. 2.5 years.

C. 1.5 to 2.5 years.

D. Half a year.

3 Which of the following descriptions of anthocyanidin is wrong?

A. Anthocyanidin could seep through the blood and into brain tissues.

B. Anthocyanidin is a kind of antioxidant.

C. Anthocyanidin is a flavonoid.

D. Flavonoid could help us become smarter.

Answers:
1. C 2. C 3. D

Reading Skills

1. 注意太绝对的叙述 ★★★★★

有时候出题人会把作者的原话变成过于肯定的描述，导致意思发生改变。这类题目看似容易，但在比较紧张的环境下总是会迷惑答题者。所以一定要注意看清表示程度的词，比如can，could，may等。

Q1解析：题目问的是哪个选项的描述是正确的。D选项是干扰项，首先排除它。再看A和B，这两个描述都是与原文描述程度不同的，所以正确答案是C。

2. 注意数字和时间 ★★★★★

数字和年份是最容易出题的地方，一时选不出答案的话，要根据数字这个关键词回到文章中去找相应的句子，通常很快可以选出答案。

Q2解析：根据原文提示：Their findings confirmed that women who ate berries at least once a week were able to slow down their cognitive decline by about 1.5 to 2.5 years. 所以正确答案是C。

3. "尊重"文中事实 ★★★★★

在做选择正确选项的问题时，除了上面提到的出题者有可能会夸大事实以外，有些内容可能完全就是"凭空想象"的。

Q3解析：这道题让我们选出错误的描述。虽然花青素能够防止大脑功能退化，但文中并未提到是否能使人们变得更聪明，所以选D。

Passage 41

Myths about Exercise Can Hamper Efforts to Shape up
——运动有碍塑形的误解

—— Apr. 16th, 2012,Washington Post

Reading Guide

你是否对运动存在误解？白开水和运动饮料应该在什么时候饮用呢？想瘦哪里就能瘦哪里可能实现吗？每天坚持运动偶尔偷偷懒是不是一种健康的健身方式呢？本文作者逐个破解了常见的关于运动的误区。让我们一起来看看如何运动才更健康吧。

Misconceptions about exercise can **sabotage** your efforts to get in shape. Here are some common myths—and the facts.

MYTH: Your routine isn't working if you're not losing weight.

Do yourself a favor and pay less attention to the scale. Exercise has a small impact on weight loss over the short term. While wanting to look good is a reasonable goal, exercise also provides numerous health benefits, including a lower risk of heart disease and stroke. If you want to **shed** pounds in addition to getting in shape, try cutting calories while you step up your workouts.

MYTH: A pedometer is all you need to track your exercise.

一些关于锻炼的错误想法可能会破坏你为了保持美好身材而付出的努力。下面就来说说那些常见的误解和一些真相吧。

误解：如果你的体重没减轻，那么就是你的计划没起作用。

就当是帮帮你自己吧，不要那么关注秤上的数字。短时间内，运动对减轻体重的影响并不大。虽然想看要看上去很好是一个合理的目标，但运动也会带来许多健康方面的益处，包括降低心脏病和中风的风险。如果你除了保持体型之外，还想要减重，那么你可以在加大运动量的同时尝试减少卡路里摄入。

误解：只需一个计步器就能记录你的运动量。

---

sabotage ['sæbətɑːʒ] v. 蓄意破坏　　shed [ʃed] v. 摆脱

Pedometers are an excellent way to monitor overall daily activity and help keep you motivated. But counting steps isn't a reliable way to measure exercise intensity or quality. It's better to use a heart-rate monitor to track intensity, and aim for a target heart rate for a set number of minutes rather than a certain number of steps.

MYTH: You don't have to lift weights.

Actually, strength training is critical for older adults to help prevent age-related bone and muscle loss, both of which can lead to falls and other serious injuries. Strengthening your muscles also decreases your body-fat percentage and increases the rate at which your body burns calories, which can help with weight management. Women in particular shouldn't worry that they'll pack on too much muscle mass by lifting weights because they have relatively low levels of the male hormone testosterone, which affects muscle growth.

MYTH: As long as you get regular exercise, it's fine to be a couch potato at other times.

Research has found that sitting for long periods actually causes a slight increase in the risk of several diseases, including heart disease, Type 2 diabetes and possibly cancer—even among people who meet recommended levels of daily exercise. Find ways to spend less time sitting. A useful goal is to replace six to seven hours a week of sitting time with something you do on your feet, whether it's walking, playing a sport or just puttering around your home or office. And try to cut your evening screen time.

MYTH: You can lose fat from specific parts of your body.

用计步器监控每日锻炼的总量是一个非常好的方式，而且可以让你一直都有动力。但计量步数对于测量锻炼的强度或质量来说并不是一个可靠的方法。使用心率监测仪来记录锻炼强度更好，而且你的目标应该是固定几分钟内的心率，而不是一定数量的步数。

误解：你不必练习举重。

事实上，力量锻炼对老年人预防和衰老有关的骨骼脆化和肌肉萎缩十分关键，而这两者都可能导致跌倒和其他的严重伤害。加强肌肉锻炼也可减少体内脂肪含量的百分比，增加身体燃烧卡路里的速率，而这对控制体重很有帮助。女性尤其不该担心举重会导致过多肌肉的产生，因为女性的睾丸激素水平相对较低，这会影响肌肉的生长。

误解：只要你有规律地锻炼，那么其他时间也可做做"沙发土豆"。

研究发现，长时间保持坐姿会略微增加几种疾病的患病风险 包括心脏病、II型糖尿病，甚至有可能患上癌症——即使是那些达到了每日建议运动量的人。找一些方法来减少坐着的时间。一个有用的目标就是每周将6至7个小时采取坐姿的时间改为一些必须站立完成的活动，不管是散步、做运动或是仅仅在家或办公室附近走动。并尝试减少晚间面对屏幕的时间。

误解：你可以减少身体特定部位的脂肪。

There's no such thing as "spot reduction." The calories you expend during exercise help burn fat from your entire body, including whichever areas you're targeting. What's more, concentrating your exercise on a specific body part can actually limit the benefits of training, since other muscle groups might be neglected.

MYTH: You should stretch before a workout to avoid injuries.

Researchers have discovered that's not the case. In terms of increasing **flexibility**, your muscles will benefit more from stretching when they're warm, after your workout. Stretching cold muscles could actually injure them.

MYTH: It's better to have a sports drink than plain water during excrcise.

A sports drink is necessary only when you've lost a substantial amount of **sodium** and other electrolytes through sweating or if you need extra **carbohydrates** to burn for energy. Aim to drink 17 to 20 ounces of water during the two to three hours before a demanding workout and another seven to 10 ounces every 15 minutes while exercising. Continue to rehydrate with plain water afterward.

MYTH: Exercising before bedtime will help you sleep better.

Sleep experts don't recommend working out close to bedtime, even up to three hours before, according to the National Sleep Foundation. Exercise has a stimulating effect and elevates body temperature, both of which can make it difficult

并没有"定位减肥"这回事。在锻炼过程中消耗的卡路里会帮助燃烧全身脂肪，包括想减肥的身体部位。而且，专注于某个特定身体部位的锻炼事实上限制了锻炼的益处，因为其他的肌肉组织可能被忽略掉了。

误解：为了避免受伤，你应该在锻炼前进行拉伸运动。

研究者已经发现事情并非如此。就增加灵活性而言，当你锻炼过后，身体很暖和时，你的肌肉从拉伸运动中可以获得更多好处。事实上，在身体较冷时拉伸肌肉可能造成伤害。

误解：运动时，运动饮料要比白开水好。

只有当你因流汗，身体流失了大量的钠和其他电解质，或者你为了补充能量而需要额外的碳水化合物时，才需要喝运动饮料。在高强度的锻炼2到3个小时前，饮用17到20盎司的水；在运动时，每15分钟饮用7到10盎司的水，运动后，继续为身体补充白开水。

误解：入睡前运动可以让你睡得更香。

睡眠专家并不建议在马上就要睡觉之前做运动，据国家睡眠基金会称，甚至在临睡前的三个小时也不要这么做。运动有刺激的效果，并且会提高体温，而这两者都会导入睡困难。但在锻炼

flexibility [ˌfleksəˈbiləti] n. 柔韧性
sodium [ˈsəudiəm] n. 钠

carbohydrate [ˌkɑːbəuˈhaidreit] n. 碳水化合物

to sleep. But the corresponding fall in temperature in five to six hours after exercise actually makes it easier. So aim for a workout earlier in the day if you have trouble sleeping.

MYTH: Calorie counters on exercise machines are accurate.

Don't count on it, especially if the machine doesn't ask for your weight, height and sex. According to the American Council on Exercise, manufacturers use **formulas** to account for intensity and duration. If you want to make sure you're using the most up-to-date formula, call the manufacturer to see if someone can walk you through an upgrade over the phone. Experts suggest trying to burn at least 1,000 calories a week through exercise, though less than that can still have benefits. Any exercise is better than none.

后的5到6小时，体温会相应降低，这使入眠变得更容易。那么，如果入睡困难，不妨在早一些的时候进行运动。

误解：健身器材上的卡路里计量器十分精确。

不要相信它，尤其是在机器没有询问你的体重、身高和性别的时候。据美国运动协会称，制造商使用公式来计算运动的强度和持续时间。如果你想要确定你是否正在使用最新的公式，可以打电话给制造商，看看是否有人能通过电话帮你升级。专家建议每周尽量通过运动燃烧至少1000卡路里，即使达不到这个水平也仍有益处。任何运动都比不做运动好。

炫 · 知识

1. calorie 卡路里

卡路里（缩写为cal），简称卡，其定义为将1克水在1大气压下提升1摄氏度所需要的热量。

2. couch potato 沙发土豆

此俚语指长时间坐或卧的人，通常他们总是在看电视，窝在沙发里、胖墩墩的样子就像土豆一样。

3. screen time 坐在屏幕前的时间

screen time这种用法十分口语化，用名词+time表示"做某事的时间"，而screen time就是指"坐在屏幕前的时间"，这里的屏幕可以是电视或电脑的屏幕。

formula ['fɔ:mjulə] n. 公式

4. plain water 白开水

　　每天都要喝的白开水在英文中，可以表示为plain water。plain有"简单的，朴素的，原味的"等意思，非常符合白开水的特点。

阅读技能练习场

Exercises:

1 Which of the following sentences is correct according to the passage?

　　A. A pedometer has no value at all.

　　B. Women don't have to worry about building too much muscle by lifting weights.

　　C. Sports drink is always the first choice for people while exercising.

　　D. The more you exercise, the better you'll sleep.

2 Why isn't exercising close to bedtime recommended?

　　A. It makes you feel too tired to sleep.

　　B. It makes you excited and elevates body temperature.

　　C. It's bad for your heart and may cause a heart disease.

　　D. It makes you hungry and therefore you may eat and gain weight.

3 Which of the following do you think is a healthy way of living according to the passape?

　　A. Do exercise everyday and so it doesn't matter what and how much one eats.

　　B. If one can't do exercise regularly, he needn't to do it at all.

　　C. Exercise for health and don't care much about your weight.

　　D. Sitting before TV or computer screen 6 to 7 hours a week.

Answers: 1.B　2.B　3.C

Reading Skills

1. 细读原文，客观答题 ★★★★

我们要在认真阅读原文后，客观理性地分析选项里的信息。如果是与文中表达不一致的选项，通常不会是正确答案；而一些不够客观的表达，通常也是错误的。

> **Q1解析**：A选项太过绝对，原文为Pedometers are an excellent way to monitor overall daily activity and help keep you motivated. C选项的错误之处参见A sports drink is necessary only when you've lost a substantial amount of sodium and other electrolytes… D选项说"运动越多，睡眠越好"，而文中称如果运动时间不当，就会影响睡眠。

2. 浏览全文后将信息归类 ★★★★★

本文格式清晰，段落分明，因此很容易找到解题的关键点。对于这样的文章，不妨先快速浏览，之后阅读题目，然后再带着问题回到文中寻找答案。

> **Q2解析**：选项A与D在文中并未提及。B选项正是文中说到的使人入睡困难的两个原因。C选项错，文中说到运动可以带来a lower risk of heart disease and stroke。

> **Q3解析**：题目要求选出符合文中观点的健康生活方式。A项错在"只要每天运动，吃什么、吃多少都不重要"。根据文中最后一句Any exercise is better than none. 得知B项表述不当。原文中说的是每周花6~7小时站起来活动，而不是坐在屏幕前，因此D错误。本题选C。

Passage 42

Vitamin E in Diet Protects Against Many Cancers
—— 维生素E能抵抗多种癌症
—— Apr.23rd, 2012, Science Daily

Reading Guide

研究发现，维生素E具有抗癌的功效。然而，不同形式的维生素对于癌症来说，也有着不同的影响。如果想要补充维生素，要选择那些与我们日常饮食中所含的维生素形式相似的，这样的维生素才是首选。

Next time you need to choose between vegetable oil and **margarine** in that favorite recipe, think about your health and reach for the oil.

While the question of whether vitamin E prevents or promotes cancer has been widely debated in scientific journals and in the news media, scientists at the Center for Cancer Prevention Research, at Rutgers Ernest Mario School of Pharmacy, and the Cancer Institute of New Jersey, believe that two forms of vitamin E—gamma and delta-tocopherols—found in soybean, canola and corn oils as well as nuts do prevent colon, lung, breast and **prostate** cancers.

"There are studies suggesting that vitamin E actually increases the risk of cancer and decreases bone density." says Chung S. Yang, director of the

下次当你需要在植物油或者人造黄油中做出选择，加入你最喜欢的食谱的话，考虑一下你的健康再做出选择。

尽管关于维生素E到底是能增进还是抑制癌细胞的问题已在学术期刊和新闻媒体中得到广泛的讨论，来自癌症预防研究中心、罗格斯·厄内斯特·马里奥药学院以及新泽西癌症研究中心的科学家们相信，从大豆、菜籽油和玉米油中以及坚果中提取的两种形式的维生素E——伽马和德尔塔形式的维生素E可以预防结肠癌、肺癌、乳腺癌和前列腺癌。

"一些研究表明维生素E增大了癌症的风险，同时降低了骨密度，"中心主任杨中枢说道。"我们在信息中提到的

---

margarine [ˌmɑːdʒəˈriːn] n. 人造黄油

prostate [ˈprɔsteit] n. 前列腺

center. "Our message is that the vitamin E form of gamma-tocopherols, the most abundant form of vitamin E in the American diet, and delta-tocopherols, also found in vegetable oils, are beneficial in preventing cancers while the form of vitamin E, alpha-tocopherol, the most commonly used in vitamin E supplements, has no such benefit."

Yang and colleagues, Nanjoo Suh and Ah-Ng Tony Kong, summarized their findings recently in Cancer Prevention Research, a journal of the American Association for Cancer *Prevention Research*. In a Commentary, "Does Vitamin E Prevent or Promote Cancer?"

The Rutgers scientists discuss animal studies done at Rutgers as well as human epidemiological studies that have examined the connection between vitamin E and cancer.

Yang says Rutgers scientists conducting animal studies for colon, lung, breast and prostate cancer found that the forms of vitamin E in vegetable oils, gamma and delta-tocopherols, prevent cancer formation and growth in animal models.

"When animals are exposed to cancer-causing substances, the group that was fed these tocopherols in their diet had fewer and smaller **tumors**," Yang says. "When cancer cells were injected into mice these tocopherols also slowed down the development of tumors."

In researching colon cancer, Yang pointed to another recently published paper in *Cancer Prevention Research* indicating that the delta-tocopherol form of vitamin E was more effective than other forms of vitamin E in **suppressing** the

是伽马形式的维生素E，这是在美国饮食中最常见的；还有德尔塔形式的维生素E，在植物油中也能发现。这两种维生素E都有利于预防癌症。然而，在维生素E补充剂中最常见的是阿尔法形式的维生素E，它并没有抗癌功效。"

杨主任和他的同事们苏南珠、Ah-Ng托尼·孔一起总结了他们的最近的发现，将"维生素E增进或是抑制了癌症？"这一研究结果发表在《癌症预防研究》期刊上，该期刊是美国癌症研究协会的期刊。

罗格斯大学的科学家们讨论了该大学开展的动物研究以及人类流行病研究，这些研究检验了维生素E和癌症之间的联系。

杨主任说，罗格斯大学的科学家用动物进行了结肠癌、肺癌、乳腺癌和前列腺癌的研究，发现植物油中伽马和德尔塔形式的维生素E在动物体内起到了预防癌细胞形成和发展的作用。

"当动物接触到致癌物质的时候，食物中含有维生素E的一组动物的肿瘤比较少，也比较小，"杨主任说，"当癌细胞被注射到老鼠身上之后，维生素E也减缓了肿瘤发展的速度。"

在结肠癌的研究中，杨主任指出了最近在《癌症预防研究》上发表的另一篇论文。该论文表明，德尔塔形式的维生素E比其他形式的维生素E更有效地抑制了结肠癌在老鼠身上的发展。

---

tumor ['tju:mə] n. 肿瘤   suppress [sə'pres] v. 抑制

development of colon cancer in rats.

This is good news for cancer research. Recently, in one of the largest prostate cancer clinical trials in the United States and Canada, scientists found that the most commonly used form of vitamin E supplements, alpha-tocopherol, not only did not prevent prostate cancer, but its use significantly increased the risk of this disease among healthy men.

This is why, Yang says, it is important to distinguish between the different forms of vitamin E and conduct more research on its cancer preventive and other biological effects.

"For people who think that they need to take vitamin E supplements," Yang says, "taking a mixture of vitamin E that resembles what is in our diet would be the most **prudent** supplement to take."

这对于癌症研究来说是个好消息。最近，在美国和加拿大最大的前列腺癌临床实验中心之一，科学家们发现维生素E补充剂中最常用的阿尔法形式的维生素E不仅不能预防前列腺癌，且它的使用大大增加了健康人患上这种疾病的风险。

杨主任说，这就是区分不同形式的维生素E以及进行更多的癌症预防和其他生物效果方面的研究十分重要的原因。

杨主任说，"对于那些认为自己需要补充维生素E的人们来说，与我们的饮食中所含维生素E类似的混合型维生素E才是最精明的选择。"

炫 · 知识

1. vegetable oil 植物油

植物油是脂肪酸和甘油化合而成的化合物，广泛地分布于自然界中。植物油是从植物的果实、种子、胚芽中得到的油脂，如花生油、豆油、亚麻油、菜籽油等。

2. vitamin E supplement 维生素E补充剂

维生素E补充剂是一种营养品。虽然维生素是人类生存不可或缺的元素，但是通常认为，与其通过补充剂来补充维生素，不如直接从合理膳食中得来。

prudent ['pru:dənt] a. 精明的

223

Exercises:

1 According to the passage, which form of vitamin E is not beneficial in preventing cancers?

A. Gamma-tocopherols.

B. Delta-tocopherols.

C. Alpha- tocopherol.

D. They are all not beneficial.

2 Who proved that gamma and delta-tocopherols prevent cancer formation and growth in animal models?

A. Rutgers scientists.

B. Nanjoo Suh.

C. Ah-Ng Tony Kong.

D. Chung S. Yang.

3 Which form of vitamin E is a better choice to people who need to take vitamin E supplements?

A. Gamma-tocopherols.

B. Delta-tocopherols.

C. Alpha-tocopherol.

D. A mixture of vitamin E that resembles what in our meals.

Answers:
1.C 2.A 3.D

Reading Skills

1. 在上下文中找线索 ★★★★★

　　有的时候问题的答案在文章中出现的部分恰好是不容易理解的段落，遇到这种情况的时候，我们可以从上下文中寻找线索，然后再进行判断。

Q1解析： 首先，A、B、C三个答案在文章中都出现过，文章第二段提到了A、B选项中提到的两种维生素E对预防癌症是有帮助的，继续阅读文章第三自然段，可以确定选项C正确

2. 以关键词精确定位出处 ★★★★★

一些细节题是针对文章某个很小的细节出题，对于这样的题目我们必须找到原文中相应的段落。可以通过观察题目中的关键词精确定位，然后在相应的部分就可以找到答案。

Q2解析： 根据问题中animal models这一提示，我们可以发现答案是出现在文章的第六段，排除B和C选项。根据第六段的原文：Yang says Rutgers scientists conducting… 可以排除答案D，因此选A。

Q3解析： a better choice是这道题的关键词，因此要回到文章最后一个自然段找答案。首先，根据上文说的alpha-tocopherol具有适得其反的作用，可以排除C；根据原文提示，taking a mixture of vitamin E that resembles what is in our diet可知答案D是正确的。